# Constitutional Politics
# in Canada after the Charter

**Law and Society Series**
W. Wesley Pue, General Editor

The Law and Society Series explores law as a socially embedded phenomenon. It is premised on the understanding that the conventional division of law from society creates false dichotomies in thinking, scholarship, educational practice, and social life. Books in the series treat law and society as mutually constitutive and seek to bridge scholarship emerging from interdisciplinary engagement of law with disciplines such as politics, social theory, history, political economy, and gender studies.

*A list of the titles in this series appears at the end of this book.*

*Patrick James*

---

Constitutional Politics
in Canada after the Charter:
Liberalism, Communitarianism,
and Systemism

**UBC**Press · Vancouver · Toronto

20 19 18 17 16 15 14 13 12 11 10     5 4 3 2 1

Printed in Canada on ancient-forest-free paper (100% post-consumer recycled) that is processed chlorine- and acid-free.

---

**Library and Archives Canada Cataloguing in Publication**

James, Patrick, 1957-
    Constitutional politics in Canada after the Charter: liberalism, communitarianism, and systemism / Patrick James.

(Law and society, ISSN 1496-4953)
Includes bibliographical references and index.
ISBN 978-0-7748-1786-8

    1. Constitutional history – Canada. 2. Constitutional law – Canada.
3. Canada – Politics and government. 4. Political questions and judicial power – Canada. I. Title. II. Series: Law and society series (Vancouver, B.C.)

KE4199.J36 2010                 342.7102'9                 C2010-900461-2
KF4482.J36 2010

---

Canadä

UBC Press gratefully acknowledges the financial support for our publishing program of the Government of Canada (through the Canada Book Fund), the Canada Council for the Arts, and the British Columbia Arts Council.

This book has been published with the help of a grant from the Canadian Federation for the Humanities and Social Sciences, through the Aid to Scholarly Publications Programme, using funds provided by the Social Sciences and Humanities Research Council of Canada.

UBC Press
The University of British Columbia
2029 West Mall
Vancouver, BC V6T 1Z2
www.ubcpress.ca

*To Carolyn*

# Contents

# Figures

# Acknowledgments

This study has benefitted greatly from the critical commentaries of Kathy Brock, James Kelly, Michael Lusztig, and Ian M. Sirota. I am grateful to Jennifer Barrios, Mai Onda, Indira Persad, Trang Pham, Daniel Smith, and P. Marques Taylor for assistance in the preparation of this book for publication. I also appreciate support from the Center for International Studies at the University of Southern California, which has provided a splendid setting for research on this project and others.

# Constitutional Politics
# in Canada after the Charter

# 1

# Constitutional Politics in Canada: The Charter and Beyond

Our constitutional system was only modified, not overthrown by our recent constitutional renewal ... The limited nature of the change is readily apparent from several perspectives.

– Alan C. Cairns, "The Politics of Constitutional Conservatism"

This book identifies and evaluates theories about the evolution of constitutional politics in Canada that have emerged since the passage of the *Constitution Act, 1982* and the *Charter of Rights and Freedoms*. Given the central role that the *Charter* plays in the story to come, there is a touch of irony in the quote from Alan Cairns. Cairns, who at the time of the *Charter* did not see it as a major departure from what came before, is now perhaps the most distinguished advocate of the view that the *Charter*'s adoption was a transforming event in Canadian history because the *Charter* was the first constitutional document to belong to the Canadian people rather than to their government alone.

Canada's *Charter* is now twenty-eight years old. Distance provides a vantage point that is sufficient to grant perspective but not so far away that it is difficult to sort out the effects of the *Charter* from other events. This assessment of constitutional politics takes the form of an interpretive essay that works toward a synthesis of insights from respective theories to enhance understanding and produce ideas for the future. This review of theorizing steps beyond much of the scholarship in the field, which is nested within the traditions of legal analysis, political theory, or some combination of the two. Its central premise is that the application of concepts derived from the social sciences – system-based theorizing and rational choice – can enhance understanding of constitutional evolution in Canada.

Evaluating constitutional evolution in Canada by necessity demands references to events from Confederation onward, but the focus of this book is the *Charter* and its aftermath. It begins with the questions: What constitutes a theory? How many are there? Do they tend to agree or disagree on the direction of constitutional affairs? It then asks: Is Canada headed toward some form of renewal? Is the end of Confederation in sight? Is the constitutional status quo the most likely future for a still-united Canada? Taken together, answers to these questions reveal where theorizing stands today and offer ideas about future directions for the theory and practice of constitutional politics.

*Constitutional Politics in Canada after the Charter* offers a relatively comprehensive yet brief introduction to the range of issues within Canadian constitutional politics. Any full-fledged theory must confront these issues and account convincingly for dynamics between and among them. The issues appear in no particular order, but those that are more general and government-oriented are addressed before those that are more specific and citizen-related. Discussions of federalism and constitutional uncertainty, along with the courts as a component of especially high interest within the government, are followed by an overview of national unity and the Quebec and western Canadian constitutional agendas. Overviews of major events such as the advent of the *Charter* itself, along with significant efforts to revise it (the Meech Lake and Charlottetown accords in 1987-90 and 1992, respectively) and the second Quebec Referendum on sovereignty association, are then followed by a discussion of political behaviour, economic considerations, and group communications (including citizens in general, women, Aboriginal peoples, and the media).[1] As will become apparent, the number of issues connected to constitutional politics is vast.

Some issues, such as federalism and constitutional uncertainty, are multifaceted, all-encompassing, and omnipresent.[2] Even though discord over the failed Charlottetown Accord occurred more than fifteen years ago, and even though a full decade has passed since the close call with the second Quebec Referendum, it is not certain that stability exists either in federal-provincial relations or the working of the Constitution. The federal government and the provinces continue to spar over jurisdictional issues and financial matters, and some of the conflict has brought into question the viability of the federal system itself. This is true even though the Canadian government of Stephen Harper disavows the centralizing agenda of its Liberal predecessors, particularly during the long reign of Pierre Trudeau. Over just the last few years, for instance, the issues of health care and equalization payments for the provinces have produced intense disagreements between Ottawa and the provinces.

Controversy, for example, surrounded the entry of Ontario into national have-not status because of constitutional rules regarding equalization payments. On 13 April 2009 Ontario received its first-ever equalization payment. The province had always been the economic engine of Canada and normally helped to subsidize provinces with lagging performance. The change in Ontario's status is bound to prompt discussion about the nature of the equalization program itself, because it is "politically unpalatable to have smaller regions subsidize a province that accounts for 40 per cent of the country's economic output" (*Globe and Mail,* 13 April 2009). Indeed, Ottawa had already changed the rules for equalization payments on a previous occasion, in the 1970s, to stave off payments to Ontario. Ontario's status and the reform of existing rules for equalization payments, however, remain unresolved constitutional issues.

Among political institutions, the courts have emerged as the most prominent source of constitutional controversy in the post-*Charter* era (Malcolmson and Myers 1996, 164).[3] Opinion is divided on whether the enhanced power of the judiciary, manifested most visibly in the Supreme Court of Canada, is a good thing for national integration. (As is discussed in Chapter 6, there is even disagreement about whether judicial power truly is enhanced by the *Charter,* at least in relation to the executive.) Pro-*Charter* analysts welcome the opportunity for the courts to take an active role in making restitution to what they perceive to be historically disadvantaged groups. They believe that these actions will make Aboriginal peoples, for instance, more inclined to identify with Canada. Critics emphasize the anti-democratic tendencies that may inhere in legislating from the bench rather than through Parliament. They fear a democratic deficit that could reduce the degree to which citizens identify with the Canadian state. On both sides of the debate, the *Charter* is regarded as a watershed that marks a change in the balance of power among Canadian institutions. In that sense, things have changed a lot since Cairns and others portrayed the *Charter* as something other than a momentous event at the time it came into being. The *Charter* is now regarded as a transformative event that has had a legacy of cooperation and conflict.

Other complex issues, visible at some times more than others, include crises of national unity and the role of Quebec and the West within Confederation.[4] There is no obvious crisis in national unity at present, but the federal electoral map as of 2008 reveals a great deal of regional voting – perhaps more so than at any other time since Confederation. And the Harper government continues to hold minority status. Neither of the two major brokerage parties, the Liberal Party and the Conservative Party, enjoys significant representation in every province and territory. Moreover, that observation can be applied to the last few federal elections. The Bloc Québécois, a party dedicated to Quebec sovereignty, shows great staying power in federal elections. (The term *Québécois* refers to those of francophone descent from the original settler group as opposed to residents of Quebec per se.) None of this bodes well for national integration.

Identity-related problems persist and could easily regain prominence if any large-scale efforts are made toward constitutional renewal. Many observers who lived through the period spanned by the governments of Pierre Trudeau and Brian Mulroney refer to that era (1980 to 1995) of major constitutional reform initiatives and referendums as being one of crisis (see, for example, Owram 1991, 25-26; Schneiderman 1991, 3; Young 1991a, 1991b, 6). Although Quebec separatism remains at a relatively low ebb, its history is cyclical and the nationalist movement is still manifested in the Bloc Québécois' presence in federal politics, the Parti Québécois at the provincial level, and significant support from public opinion.[5] Cairns's (1995, 18) call for efforts to find a middle ground "between realpolitik and abstract moralizing" rings as true now as it did at the time of the second Quebec Referendum. Many Canadians would prefer, but Canada seems unable to obtain, a more civil discourse and a more pragmatic approach, one that recognizes Quebec's special role in Confederation but falls short of the sovereignty association advocated by Quebec nationalists.

Prime Minister Harper's government commands only limited support in Quebec because it is seen as being generally responsive to western interests – but not without sympathy for the decentralizing agenda favoured in Quebec City. Unless his government's position changes in the next general election, it would not be out of bounds to predict a resurgence in sovereigntist thinking within Quebec and a return to confrontation politics with Ottawa. This would be true especially if the Conservative Party obtained a majority in Parliament that did not include significant Quebec representation. This situation, given that province's size, would be unlikely, but it is nevertheless a possibility.

The reaction in Quebec to a possible re-enactment of the Battle of the Plains of Abraham is a recent example of nationalism coming to the surface. Because of the protest generated by the proposed re-enactment, the National Battlefields Commission is still trying to decide on an alternative site for the historic battle, which served as the point of culmination for the British Conquest of the French colony. In addition to various individuals and groups, the Parti Québécois and Bloc Québécois have denounced the plan. The event may even take place outside of Canada itself, possibly in upstate New York, to stem the tide of criticism (*National Post,* 10 February 2009).

Western alienation is yet another on again, off again aspect of constitutional life and politics in Canada.[6] Fuelled by anti-eastern sentiments, waves of populism swept through the western provinces throughout the twentieth century. Western alienation may once again be on the rise because of more than a decade of uninterrupted Liberal majority governments (between 1993 and 2004) that had caucuses dominated by Ontario and, to a lesser degree, Quebec. (Prime Minister Paul Martin headed a brief minority government at the end of the Liberal era.) The new and even transformed Conservative Party under Harper represents the rising power of the West, its wealth, and its expanding population. One example of this shift, currently in progress, is the proposal from Prime Minister Harper to increase the representation of Alberta and British Columbia in the House of Commons to match their share of national population as of the 2011 census (*Hill Times,* 23 July 2007).

Today's Tories do not show the "Red" tinge of years past, when more ideologically liberal sentiments, held primarily by members from central Canada, played a significant balancing role within the party. Instead, the Conservative Party today embodies the West's traditionally "Blue" preference for smaller government and individualism at a national level. Ironically, if the Harper government fails to secure a majority or, at minimum, pass a significant amount of its platform, it may exacerbate Western alienation. This would constitute, in effect, a failed experiment. Westerners, who constitute the majority of support for the Conservative Party, could conclude that no government adopting their philosophy will ever be given a chance by eastern Canada to effect change within the boundaries imposed by Confederation. The next step could be renewed popular support for greater autonomy from Ottawa.

Theories of constitutional evolution must also take into consideration the high-profile events that accompany the politics of package deals. Perhaps the most prominent example is the signing into law of the *Constitution Act, 1982* and the *Canadian Charter of Rights and Freedoms,* which stimulated controversy and strife that reverberate to this day, most notably in Quebec and the West.[7] The *Constitution Act, 1982* and the *Charter* constitute the only major constitutional package deal to pass into law since Confederation. Efforts to complete the founding of Canada, which did not include a domestic formula for constitutional amendment, accelerated in the latter part of the twentieth century.[8] The failure of the Meech Lake (1987-90) and Charlottetown accords (1992), initiatives intended to complete the made-in-Canada process that began with the *Constitution Act, 1982* and *Charter*, also had lasting and significant effects.[9] Those efforts at revision, as described by one observer, "were immensely destructive in terms of creating bitter feelings and harmed their intended goal of national unity" (Franks 2000, 118). Quebec did not sign the *Constitution Act* and *Charter* because its representatives felt they had been deliberately excluded from the decisive negotiations that led to patriation on 1 July of that year. (Prior to patriation, Canada had no domestic procedure for constitutional amendment; ultimate authority still resided with the British Crown.) Thus Meech and Charlottetown, the failed efforts to bring Quebec into the constitution, exacerbated Quebec's sense of isolation from the rest of Canada and heightened interest in sovereignty association and even outright secession. The Quebec Referendum of 1995, whose defeat generated considerable ill will among francophone nationalists, likewise continues to exert an influence on politics in Quebec.[10] The idea of Quebec holding another referendum on sovereignty association seems remote at present, given that the Parti Québécois is out of power, but it never entirely goes away.

The issue of political behaviour – voting and public opinion – and its constitutional implications is more specific but still quite encompassing.[11] Discussions of the issue recognize the potential for bottom-up as well as top-down change in the constitutional order. The geographic distribution of political partisanship, along with the degree of alienation from the system, can have a cumulative effect on national cohesion. The system has been challenged by the decline of nationally competitive, brokerage-style parties on the one hand and the rise of regionally oriented, autonomist parties on the other.

Concrete matters such as economics also can play a role in constitutional affairs.[12] For example, the degree to which a province perceives itself as a financial winner or loser within Confederation can affect its receptiveness to regionally oriented or even separatist political messages. Harsh criticism of the federal system, especially from Quebec, is far from exceptional (see, for example, Fortin 1991, 38-39, 41). The present decade has witnessed a great deal of conflict over federal expansion into previously provincial domains of policy, along with periodic eruptions over equalization payments and fiscal imbalance (Brock 2005, 2006, 2007). Federal-provincial strife over economic issues therefore can generate more fundamental disagreement at the constitutional level vis-à-vis the division of powers, the degree of permissible provincial autonomy, and like matters.

Interest groups and communications technology likewise exert an influence on constitutional affairs. In an era of identity-oriented politics, citizens and interest groups, particularly women and Aboriginal peoples, have emerged as key actors in struggles over constitutional continuity and change.[13] Social movements became prominent in Canadian law and politics even before the *Charter,* but such processes gained momentum in the decades thereafter. Newer movements, with gay rights and environmental activism at the forefront, have joined the constitutional fray, and vocal responses can be expected from those left out of a given constitutional process. Opposition language groups from Meech Lake serve as just one prominent example. The media and commissions and task forces have also influenced the process of constitutional evolution.[14] One prominent example is the way in which television coverage of executive federalism during the Meech Lake ratification crisis of 1990 brought attention to its top-down and exclusive nature. Another instance, from that same era, is the publicity given to former prime minister Trudeau's intervention against the accord.

It is clear that a full-fledged theory of constitutional politics must take multiple issues into consideration. It might emphasize some issues more than others, but in principle it would need to consider cause and effect across the board. It can therefore be expected that only a small number of theories are suitable for comparison. In fact, Chapter 3 reveals that only five theories meet these criteria.

This book extends scholarly discussion and debate in at least three areas. First, by reviewing the first twenty-five years of post-*Charter* scholarship, it serves as a springboard for further study of Canadian constitutional politics. Its verdict on the state of theory should ignite debate, at the level of theory and of observation, about the priorities for the next round of scholarship on federalism, federal-provincial relations, and other matters. Second, its findings enhance understanding of state-society relations in Canada (Pal 1990). By doing so, it facilitates the study of the Canadian case in a comparative context (Landes 1998; Motyl 1999). Third, it links rational choice (that is, self-interest understood in rigorous terms) to an approach, namely, systemism, to increase the latter's range of application to the study of Canada and even other political systems. This book therefore contributes to the applied literature on systemism that assesses and facilitates progress in the social sciences (Bunge 1996, 1998; James 2002). Case studies in the present context are theories about Canadian constitutional politics.

This book should appeal to and resonate with policy makers as well as scholars. The theories identified should generate, at least implicitly, a sense of Canada's future prospects. By specifying the overall configuration of forces – integrative or disintegrative, centripetal or centrifugal – this study may help to identify priorities for policy in the area of constitutional politics. Suppose, for example, that the key events and processes driving Canada in a centrifugal (or, for that matter, centripetal) direction turn out to be at a highly aggregated, macro level and reside within the Supreme Court. (That outcome would strongly confirm one of the theories articulated in Chapter 4.) This result would encourage further thinking about the role of the judiciary, and the nature of proposed changes would depend on the observer's normative point of view. Advocates of either renewed federalism or decentralization could use the findings to formulate policy recommendations as they see fit.

Each of the six subsequent chapters furthers the book's overall goal to employ individual and collective insights from various theories to explain the evolution of constitutional politics in Canada in the post-*Charter* era. Concepts and theories at a general level are explained, specific theories that have liberal and communitarian tendencies are introduced, theories are criticized and compared, and the book ends by answering major questions about the direction of constitutional politics and offering policy-oriented recommendations.

Chapter 2 introduces the concepts of systemism and of self-interest (that is, rational choice) and provides a micro foundation for a review of the field of Canadian constitutional politics in the *Charter* era. Systemism is an organizing principle that stresses theoretical completeness as a key criterion for progress in scientific explanation.[15] The four kinds of linkages found in systemism – macro-macro, macro-micro, micro-macro and micro-micro – are illustrated through an example from Canadian politics, namely, Quebec's use of the notwithstanding clause (section 33 of the *Constitution Act, 1982*) in 1988. The example reveals that a satisfactory explanation of Premier Robert Bourassa's use of the clause, including its causes and consequences, requires reference to each of the four kinds of connection. Substantive matters addressed by theories of

Canadian constitutional politics are then summarized in the context of systemism to demonstrate what a full-fledged theory of the evolution of constitutional politics must entail.

Chapter 3 identifies concepts and the origins of theories, and it defines *constitution* and *constitutional system* from a systemist perspective. Equilibrium analysis, which is borrowed from the discipline of economics, is introduced as a metaphor for political interaction and is applied in later chapters to the empirical and normative assessment of theories about Canadian constitutional evolution. Definitions of partial and general-equilibrium theories of constitutional evolution are accompanied by an example of the former, which is used to help outline the differences between the two approaches. Because they are at the forefront of theorizing about state-society relations and political development, the concepts of social capital and generalized trust are used to assess the normative desirability of the equilibria identified by each type of theory. Explorations of the origins of these five theories – three are associated with the liberal paradigm and two are linked to the communitarian paradigm – set the stage for the chapters that follow.

Chapter 4 provides an exegesis of three theories that are closely associated with liberal understandings of the evolution of constitutional politics in Canada: negative identity, megapolitics, and institutional imbalance. These theories tend to emphasize the role of individual agency and identify equilibria that are conflict-prone and generally unattractive. Diverse in terms of the causal stories they tell, the theories tend to emphasize different variables, including the lack of a sovereign founding event, the pernicious effects of the politics associated with constitutional package deals, and the enhanced power of the judiciary within the system. Given the broadness of the liberal paradigm, this diversity is to be expected.

Chapter 5 presents theories that are closely connected to communitarian understandings of the evolution of constitutional politics: asymmetrical federalism and the citizens' constitution. Both theories emphasize in their explanations of unfolding events the role of collectivities and their struggle for recognition. Both theories seek to resolve basic conflicts between and among governments, energized *Charter* groups, and collectivities that continue to feel marginalized in constitutional terms. The theories do, however, identify different equilibria: asymmetric federalism points in a more favourable direction than the citizens' constitution. As would be expected in an inclusive paradigm, the theories linked with communitarianism stress different causal variables, including tension in symmetrical federal institutions, status-seeking by excluded territorial interests, and the mixed effects of the *Charter* on provincial versus citizen-based interests.

Chapter 6 offers a comparison and critique of the theories associated with these two paradigms. Debate in the literature on theories with a more liberal orientation, for instance, focuses overwhelmingly on institutional imbalance – for example, an imbalance in favour of the judiciary or even an imbalance within the power wielded by various components of the federal government. To reach a bottom-line understanding of constitutional evolution, all of the theories are compared along the following dimensions: primary means of location vis-à-vis origin, key causal variable, equilibrium identified (in terms of existence, stability, and normative desirability), overall position on national (dis)integration, and major challenges to meet.

Chapter 7 provides a tentative answer to the basic questions that motivate this study: When international imperatives and the four kinds of internal connections or linkages are put together, what theories about the Canadian constitutional system can be identified? How well do they account for events in the post-*Charter* era? It also explores the implications of theories for the centripetal or centrifugal movement of Canada's political system and the significance of the country's experience for the rest of the world. It shows that systemism, when used to bring competing theories into bold relief, can help to produce a more compelling response to the question, whither Canada?

# 2
# Systemism and Canadian Constitutional Politics

What does the advent of the *Constitution Act, 1982* and the *Charter of Rights and Freedoms* signify? Even an impressionistic answer to this question demonstrates the need for systematic expression and evaluation of the ideas concerned. Systemism, which emphasizes theoretical completeness, provides a way to organize and visualize diverse theoretical outlooks on the nature of constitutional evolution.

At the time of the *Charter*, observers remarked on a "surprising degree of continuity implicit in the Constitution Act" (Banting and Simeon 1983b, 348). After the passing of more than twenty-five years, that opinion – also expressed by Alan Cairns in the epigraph to Chapter 1 – is virtually never heard. Consensus now begins and ends with the idea that the *Charter* represented a major break point in Canadian history. "The Charter," Janet Hiebert (2002, xi) observes, "introduced a profound change to the nation's governing principles." For some observers it marked the beginning of a new era in which actors beyond government officials began to see the Constitution as their own (Cairns 1991a, 1991b, 1992, 1995, 2000). The views of others are mixed. Put off by the process through which patriation occurred, the most severe critics regard the *Constitution Act* and *Charter* as an ongoing source of resentment for both the government and the people of Quebec (Imbeau 1990, 1991, 1992; Cloutier 1991; Fournier 1991; Laforest 1998a, 1998b). More than twenty-five years after the fact, the province has not signed the document. And other interpretations have been put forward. For example, the *Constitution Act* and *Charter* have been interpreted as a product of Canada's movement, like other societies, in the direction of postmaterial values related to the recognition of social groups. This shift explains an increased willingness among political leaders and the public to recognize collective rights (Brodie and Nevitte 1993a, 1993b; see also Cairns 1993).

The preceding interpretations are defensible and come into play throughout this book. They vary, however, in how they presume cause and effect to operate. One interpretation focuses on Quebec, an entity within the federal system, while the other two – popular sovereignty and postmaterialism – emphasize citizens in general and how they might identify in various ways with a new constitutional document and the order it represents. In other words, ideas about how the constitutional system works and where it is headed can be expressed in either holistic or individualistic terms – at the macro or micro levels. To achieve completeness, any theory must take both levels into account, and external inputs into the system must also be recognized. This reality should be recognized and incorporated into any viable effort to systematically assess the evolution of constitutional politics in Canada during the era of the *Charter*. Systemism accomplishes this task, for it is a frame of reference designed to incorporate all of the logically possible connections between variables expressed in either macro or micro terms (or in both).

**Intellectual Foundation: Systems Analysis and Systemism**
Given its centrality in the discipline of political science at one time, it is appropriate to bring David Easton's systems analysis (1953, 1965a, 1965b) into this discussion.[1] Easton's systems analysis generated considerable discussion for over a decade. In a lengthy review, Peter Leslie (1972, 155) described Easton's work as occupying a leading place in the discipline. Similarly, Oran Young (1968, 37) observed in a prominent review of system-level theorizing that Easton created "one of the few systemic frameworks originally developed by a political scientist rather than adapted for political analysis from some other discipline." (This is not the time or place to review the works concerned, but system-level theorizing in political science to this day tends to favour interdisciplinary borrowing rather than ideas drawn more directly from the discipline itself.) Systemism is therefore by no means the first conceptual framework of its kind. Its similarities with and differences from Easton's conceptual apparatus demonstrate the progress that has been made in thinking about socio-political systems since the 1960s. Since systems analysis fell out of favour in the 1970s, there is no need to focus in any detail on alternative strands of research.

Easton's point of departure is to view politics as a system of behaviour (Easton 1965a, x). He designates his work as part of political behaviour as a movement in academe (Easton 1965a, 4). Four components are identified in systems analysis (Easton 1965, 24-25): a system made up of political behaviour, an environment that can be distinguished from the system at issue, the members' response to stress within the system's operation, and feedback to actors and decision makers that is (or is not) sufficient for the system's persistence. The overall focus of Easton's analysis is the ability of a system to persist in the face of stress. Stress can include change through adaptation to new circumstances (Easton 1965a, 84).

Leslie Green's (1985, 131-32) excellent summary of Easton's exegesis of systems analysis is worth reciting at length:

> The political system is an aspect of the social system. It is an open, transformational system, which functions so as to turn inputs of demands and support into outputs of policies and allocations, the consequences of which then feed back into the inputs. Owing to an inherent scarcity of many valued resources (not least of which is time) there is a propensity to overload or stress, which, if unchecked, could lead to the failure of the system to perform its characteristic function: the allocation of valued goods in an authoritative way. Political systems have the capacity, however, to respond to stress through changes in both system structure and system states; but a system may fail to make such adjustments and may therefore fail to persist through time. Our interest in this empirically determinable consequence flows from the fact that, with the exception of certain small societies, all social systems require some way of authoritatively allocating values, without which they will collapse.

This vision creates a context within which to assess systemism. To what extent is it similar to Easton's formulation? How is it different? And most germane of all, to what extent does it represent an improvement over what Easton proposed?

Offered more than two decades ago, Green's assessment of systems analysis as put forward by Easton rings true today and provides a natural starting point for discussion. Green further observes that systems theory is "nearly friendless among political scientists" (1985, 127). Declining and even vanishing interest can be traced to characteristics that systemism seeks to avoid.

Systems analysis from the high behavioural era focused on regulative responses to stress in the quest for system persistence (Easton 1965a, 124). In that sense it can be interpreted as exhibiting a status quo–oriented or homeostatic bias that overlooked the "personal goals and values of decision-makers" (Leslie 1972, 158; see also Young 1968, 44-48).[2] System-ism, by contrast, does not exhibit that bias. Its agenda is more expansive and does not have a homeostatic element. In addition, systemism gives agency a more central role because it explicitly models micro-level interactions. The objectives and values of leaders and even ordinary citizens are incorporated within systemism – a clear point of difference from Easton's frame of reference.

Systemism does, however, resemble systems analysis in a few significant ways. But the characteristics are not those that stimulated criticism and produced a decline in systems analysis among political scientists. Sys-temism is based on the assumption that a discrete system exists and can be distinguished from its environment. It also conceives of systems as entities nested within one another as subsystems, systems, and super-systems. Some of the conceptual apparatus added to systemism in this study likewise parallels Easton's approach. The concepts of stability and equilibrium form part of this book's framework, but without the holistic tendencies noted above. In addition, systems analysis and systemism both favour diagrammatic expositions to show cause and effect. Feedback is present in systemism in the sense that individual linkages can features such loops; however, that is not the same as Easton's application of feedback as a concept vis-à-vis the quest for system persistence.

Systemism, it would be fair to say, is at least an indirect descendant of Easton's systems analysis. The new approach attempts to move beyond that legacy by avoiding the holistic and homeostatic biases that accom-panied earlier efforts to develop theories about political systems, valuable as they may be in other ways.

Systemism is advocated by Mario Bunge (1996, 264; see also 1998) as a way to think about the world; in principle, it can be applied to any aspect of social life: "The alternative to both individualism and holism is systemism, since it accounts for both individual and system and, in particular, for individual agency and social structure. Indeed, systemism postulates that everything is a system or a component of one. And it models every system as a triple (composition, environment, structure), or CES for short, so it encompasses the valid features of its rivals [indi-vidualism and holism]." From the standpoint of systemism, the choice between unit and system is a flawed dichotomy (Brecher 1999; James 2002). A useful theory must deal with both systems and units – that is, the macro and micro levels – in some way. This point became clear in the brief discussion of ideas about the *Charter*'s consequences that opened this chapter, and it is reinforced by a review and critique of Easton's classic work. The macro and micro levels influence each other; they do not operate in isolation (Archer 1996, xxi). The question, of course, is how best to put together a theory that takes this reality into account.

What about CES (composition, environment, and structure) at a general level and in relation to Canadian politics? *Composition* refers to participants – who may be individuals, social groups, or those speaking for government institutions – and the interactions between and among them that take place because of certain issues. The *environment* is everything beyond the boundaries of the system itself. It may have an influence on the system and vice versa. *Structure* refers to the rules that govern interactions among the participants. For Canada, CES comes through clearly in application. Composition corresponds to the wide range of actors and issues encountered in Chapter 1, while structure corresponds to the rule of law represented by the Constitution. Canada's environment is the international system, which consists of states and transnational actors such as international organizations (for example, the UN) and prominent individuals (for example, Nelson Mandela).

Figure 2.1 presents Bunge's (1996, 149) vision, based on systemism, of functional relations in a social system. The larger box in the figure, for instance, can represent Canada or any other political system, while the smaller box corresponds to the outside world. The figure traces the full

*Figure 2.1*

**Functional relations in a social system: The general case**

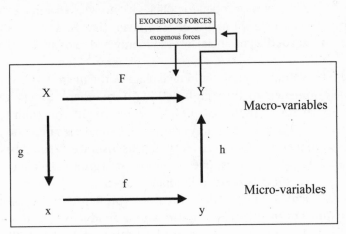

*Source:* Adapted from Bunge (1996, 149).

range of effects that might be encountered in any system that includes both micro and macro variables. (Upper- and lower-case letters represent macro- and micro-level variables, respectively.) Although more rigorous definitions will be provided later, public opinion can be used as an example to bring out the basic difference between micro and macro variables. Opinion in the aggregate, for the country as a whole or a political subunit with national representation such as a province or territory, represents the macro variable. The views of an individual or a few people who do not make up an official political jurisdiction represent the micro variable. Therefore, opinions held in Ontario or Canada as a whole are macro variables. By contrast, political views exchanged among friends at a London Knights hockey game or among people sitting in a car driving around Middlesex County or elsewhere in Ontario are micro variables.

Four logical connections between and among macro and micro variables are possible: micro-micro *(m → m)*, micro-macro *(m → M)*, macro-macro *(M → M)*, and macro-micro $(M → m)$. The goal of systemism is to get away from holism, individualism, and other mindsets that convey only part of the picture of a working system.

Macro variables can influence one another, as in the case of $X$ affecting $Y$. The functional form – linear in some instances and more complex in others – is represented by $F$. Consider Ontario's recent transition (which is perhaps temporary) into recipient status with regard to equalization payments. Opinion in Ontario $(X)$ could cause its provincial government $(Y)$ to engage in major economic reforms as a sense of urgency causes it to be more open to policies it once viewed as too extreme. The functional form $(F)$ might be step level, that is, a major shift in public opinion at the provincial level suddenly had resonance in Queen's Park.

The same causal process would take place at the micro level, as in the case of $x$ influencing $y$ through function $f$. Like others at social gatherings, fans at the hypothetical Knights game might complain to one another about the weak economy $(x → y$, each letter designates individuals or small groups). The functional form in this instance $(f)$ could be incremental, as a gradual increase in economy-related grousing leads to many informal discussions among individual citizens.

Macro-macro and micro-micro linkages represent in theory and reality the limits of theorizing for holism and individualism, in that order. Systemism, by contrast, can account for both of those connections. It recognizes the need to be aware of causal processes that involve social aggregates, such as governments and mass opinion, and those that operate beneath that level. Just as important, systemism recognizes that effects can also move *across* levels. Consequently, the macro-micro linkage $X$ to $x$ through function $g$ also appears in the figure, as does the micro-macro connection $y$ to $Y$ through function $h$. The former could take the form of macroeconomic problems at the national or provincial levels *(X)* that cause a local business to go bankrupt *(x)*, with the process unfolding incrementally (that is, with $g$ operating as a linear function). The latter could involve the crestfallen business owner *(y)* writing a letter to his or her member of Parliament *(Y)* excoriating the government for its poor performance, with the function $h$ being step level because of the rapid occurrence of the event.

Finally, systemism takes into consideration that the system could be subjected either to continuous influence or shocks from the external environment. In the figure, the box outside the system feeds into it. Either whole systems or micro entities within them could have an impact on the social system in question. In recognition of this, the box is divided into two halves that have upper- and lower-case characters, respectively. The upper half of the box could represent US macroeconomic policies that impinge on the Canadian system as a whole. The lower half of the box could represent decisions made by immigrants who have targeted Canada as their destination – decisions that, if followed through on in sufficient numbers, could alter the political landscape. In a like manner, the system may also influence its environment, as is acknowledged by the arrow that points outward from $Y$. It could be argued, for instance, that Canada's multiculturalism policies have influenced debates on that subject in varying places around the world.

Consider the relatively incomplete pictures of social life that individualism and holism offer. Individualism focuses on $y = f(x)$ ($y$ equals a function of $x$) or micro-level processes. This specification is incomplete because a causal chain can be traced farther back and at a different level altogether. Put differently, the whole of a political system is more than the sum of interactions between and among its subgroups or individuals. What about $x = g(X)$, the prior effect of $X$ on $x$, expressed in terms of function $g$? This connection is left out of individualism, which cannot incorporate macro-level processes into its unit-centred vision of the system.

Holism, by contrast, begins at the macro level and stays there. It focuses on system properties alone and treats all else as a black box. The other processes, which transmit effects from $X$ to $Y$ indirectly, are not incorporated into the theoretical approach. Consequently, $Y = F(X)$, a relationship based only on macro variables, becomes the whole story.

Systemism demands that an explanation tell the full tale of units and systems. An account that simply holds one type of linkage constant is inherently incomplete and unconvincing. All four linkages, along with exogenous forces, must be considered. A telltale sign of weak theorizing is silence or an aside that explains that one type of linkage is being held constant. Constants play a time-honoured and well-supported role in the natural sciences, but not in the social sciences. Human beings, whether alone or in groups, insist on doing new and different things that challenge attempts to develop theories about their behaviour.

A model must be built on micro foundations; in other words, how are actors envisaged within the system? In particular, are they goal-directed or subject to other motivations? Theorizing begins with these questions; once answers are derived, environmental forces and the four types of linkages can be assessed to complete the picture.

One of the initial challenges in the application of systemism is identifying a micro foundation: what are actors expected to do? Politics at the two levels of interaction, macro and micro, can be studied more effectively, at least in principle, through the consistent application of one theoretical perspective. Models based on self-interest (that is, rational choice) are well suited to such an enterprise.[3] These models are based on the assumption of self-interest and focus directly on how and why policies are made. The more specific characteristics that link this economic vision of human behaviour to political processes may be summarized as follows: (1) methodological individualism as a point of departure, (2) the assumption that individuals strive after their own interests in a rational way and try to maximize utility (this assumption may be called the fundamental behavioural hypothesis of rational choice), and (3) the methods and techniques of economic analysis (Booth, James, and Meadwell 1993). Rational choice also operates independently of ideological commitments. It is possible, for instance, to be either a rational Marxist-Leninist or a capitalist. Rational choice is about means rather than ends; self-interest can be pursued by people who prefer vastly different end states. This vision of agency can be used to explain strategic interaction among rivals over any number of issues and, thus, by definition, is devoid of the ideological leanings associated with a left-right spectrum. Rational choice is therefore a theoretical perspective that can be applied to both micro- and macro-level processes as put forward in diverse theories.[4]

As an illustration of rational choice within a collective setting, consider the legal mobilization of Canadian feminists in the *Charter* era (Manfredi 2005, 15, 18, 20). The Women's Legal Education and Action Fund (LEAF), the principal organization of its kind active in Canadian politics, participated in thirty-six Supreme Court of Canada cases between 1988 and 2000. It had an 84 percent success rate for outcomes and a 70 percent success rate for substantive arguments. These numbers are not accidental. With limited resources and popular support for its various causes, LEAF acted rationally when it (1) pursued a legal rather than a legislative strategy and (2) adopted a strategy of targeting cases with a relatively high probability of success. As a result LEAF effected considerable change in the direction it had intended, namely, legal acceptance of the doctrine of substantive equality. Thus, even individuals and groups who appear to be, sometimes in their own words, rather distant from the rationality and efficiency concerns of economists can act in ways that support the postulate of self-interest.

Two further qualifications should be offered regarding the presence of rational choice in this exposition. It is applied in a qualitative sense; no effort to include game theory or other technical components is made in the presentation of theories. These developments would change the character of the theories themselves and present them in an alternative disciplinary matrix. Instead, the purpose of what follows is to convey the theories as accurately as possible through narrative and non-mathematical diagrammatic exposition. Another qualification is that self-interest is not selfishness. Rational choice does not impute any particular value system. Actors in the Canadian political drama are therefore free to be selfish or altruistic or anything they wish to be in the pursuit of their goals. Rational choice is about how objectives are pursued, it is not a designation of the ends themselves. Thus, the basic assumption in the reconstruction of theories in Chapters 4 and 5 is that the actors within them will maximize their interests, however they are defined.

To sum up, systemism offers several advantages as an organizing principle for the comparative assessment of theories about the evolution of Canadian constitutional politics. It can articulate any given theory in terms of CES, thereby providing the basis for comparative evaluation. Systemism's diagrammatic exposition is well suited to conveying the kind of multicausal, complex explanations that are expected in this context. Self-interest serves as its flexible and inclusive micro foundation. Systemism, most importantly, promotes awareness of theoretical completeness as a criterion. A compelling theory should have a story to tell about each type of linkage within a social system and the exogenous forces that have an impact on it.

### Systemism in Action: Quebec's Use of the Notwithstanding Clause

Although it is beyond the scope of this chapter to apply systemism to the Canadian constitutional system in detail, an example is offered to show how the language of systemism can be used, in principle, to locate any given event in a network of causes and effects that operate within and across the macro and micro levels (and include relevant environmental factors). The example also offers a rigorous demonstration of how an entity can operate at the macro and micro levels, respectively.

Quebec's use of the notwithstanding clause in December 1988 stands as one of the most prominent events in the post-*Charter* era of constitutional politics (Cohen 1990; Breton 1992; Monahan 1993). The notwithstanding clause, or section 33, applies to only certain parts of the *Charter of Rights and Freedoms;* it was a concession to reluctant provincial governments (especially those of Manitoba and Saskatchewan) that feared they would be unable to protect their respective domains under the new constitutional arrangement. Section 33 applies to section 2 (fundamental freedoms), sections 7 through 14 (legal rights), and section 15 (equality rights) for a renewable five-year override of a judicial decision.

The Supreme Court of Canada's judgment of 15 December 1988 against Bill 178, which pertained to the preeminence of the French language on commercial signs in Quebec, produced an immediate and dramatically negative reaction in that province. It is estimated that ten thousand people rallied at the Paul Sauvé Arena in Montreal and demanded that the Premier of Quebec, Robert Bourassa, invoke the notwithstanding clause. Bourassa responded quickly and invoked section 33 on December 21. The Quebec government thereby brought back Bill 178, which required the French language to be featured more prominently on commercial signs.

This event is cited frequently in explanations of the demise of the Meech Lake Accord, which would have recognized Quebec as a distinct society, in June 1990. The standard story is that the public and many within the elite outside of Quebec saw Bourassa's action as evidence that the province could not be trusted within a revamped constitutional system that included its special recognition as a distinct society. How

Figure 2.2

**The Canadian constitutional system: The notwithstanding clause and its aftermath**

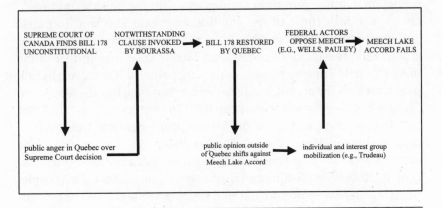

would Quebec's use of the notwithstanding clause and its aftermath be interpreted in terms of systemism?

Figure 2.2 offers a systematic treatment of cause and effect with regard to Quebec's action in December 1989.[5] The chain of events begins with the Supreme Court of Canada's decision against the constitutionality of Bill 178. A powerful macro-micro *(M → m)* effect ensues as the court decision translates into massive public anger in Quebec. This produces a micro-macro *(m → M)* effect as public outrage leads to a sense of urgency on the part of Premier Bourassa. As an actor in the federal system, speaking for the government of Quebec, Bourassa creates a macro-macro *(M → M)* effect when he invokes the notwithstanding clause, which protects Quebec's legislation from the Court's ruling and restores Bill 178. (Macro and micro levels are designated in this figure by the use of upper- and lower-case characters.)[6]

A macro-micro *(M → m)* linkage follows the province's action: public opinion outside of Quebec moves against the Meech Lake Accord (McRoberts 1997, 202; Mulroney 2007, 742). The accord is increasingly seen as a document that favours Quebec, a province that is perceived as being willing to use the notwithstanding clause to override anything, constitutionally speaking, that it might find distasteful. Hearings produce opposition that cites the distinct society clause and concerns about spending power. In particular, Quebec's use of the notwithstanding clause heightens hostility toward that province, which is expressed most directly against inclusion of the distinct society clause in the accord. (Critics of Quebec also expressed concerns that the province might not cooperate in future government programs with nationwide implementation, although this had less emotional appeal.) This shift in public opinion, in turn, produces a micro-micro *(m → m)* effect: individuals and groups mobilize to speak out against Meech Lake, and former prime minister Pierre Trudeau provides a rallying point for resistance. His full-page attack on the accord, published in *La Presse and* the *Toronto Star* on 27 May 1987, over a year before the Bill 178 controversy, had included scalding language and made the former prime minister "the spiritual guru of the anti-Meech forces" (Russell 2004, 139). Opponents of the accord saw a potential threat to rights enumerated in the *Charter,* particularly from a Meech-equipped Quebec government. Aboriginal peoples stood out in that sense and played a key role at the end of the process.

As citizens stimulated and encouraged one another's opposition to the accord, a micro-macro *(m → M)* effect occurred: actors at the federal (or macro) level – such as the governments of Newfoundland and Manitoba (represented, respectively, by Premiers Clyde Wells and Howard Pauley [who was later replaced by Gary Filmon]) – respond by stiffening their resistance to the accord as the deadline for ratification approaches. For example, although Manitoba had introduced the accord into its legislature just before the Supreme Court's decision on Bill 178, the premier withdrew it after Quebec invoked the notwithstanding clause. These events occurred against the backdrop of Manitoba's own language controversy, which from 1984 onward had produced lingering resentment on the part of many and made the actions of the francophone-dominated province of Quebec seem especially provocative. Manitoba's reversal on the Meech Lake Accord strengthened the resolve of Wells and others.

The final linkage *(M → M)* represents the accord's failure on 23 June 1990, following the Manitoba and Newfoundland legislatures failure to ratify it. Elijah Harper, an Aboriginal member of the Manitoba legislature, took actions that ultimately prevented a vote on the accord.[7] More than a lone actor in this case, Harper became a symbol of resistance to the accord, most notably among Aboriginal peoples.

One response to the preceding analysis of Quebec's use of the notwithstanding clause and its aftermath might be – so what? Each of the linkages outlined in Figure 2.2 appears in older narratives of constitutional politics in general and the Meech Lake Accord in particular. The advantage offered by systemism, however, is that it allows events and processes to be disaggregated and assessed in terms of direct *and* indirect effects within *and* across levels of the Canadian constitutional system. It guards against overlooking steps in the causal process by raising awareness of what goes on at both the macro and micro levels and in between them. Systemism provides a means to manage complexity – and what could be more intricate than the last several decades of constitutional evolution in Canada?

Although it is important to the study of politics in Quebec and Canada in and of itself, Quebec's use of the notwithstanding clause is just one of many events (and processes made up of sets of events) that must be evaluated to assess their impact at the system and unit levels. Systemism allows for a rigorous assessment of the causes and effects of any given process. A theory can therefore be appraised to determine whether it deals completely with a sequence of events. Whether it meets this criterion will weigh heavily on the theory's credibility when it comes to assessing the overall impact of integration or disintegration of the Canadian political system.

Applying systemism to a specific context, such as constitutional politics in Canada, requires an operational rendering of entities at the macro and micro levels. Because the potential for confusion is considerable, formal definitions and illustrations are particularly useful for sorting out where things belong.[8] Macro entities are individuals or social aggregates at the national (i.e., system) level. Examples include institutions such as the federal government, components of it (e.g., the Supreme Court), and provincial governments. Micro entities are individuals or social aggregates at the subnational level: an individual voter or members of a city council or interest group. One way to help separate which actors belong where is to work though some examples.

Robert Bourassa and Clyde Wells, for example, both served as formally sanctioned representatives for federal entities during the conflict over the notwithstanding clause; in other words, each acted as a provincial premier. Consequently, Wells and Bourassa appear at the macro level in Figure 2.2 because each acted on behalf of a social aggregate at the national level, namely, Newfoundland and Quebec, respectively. Because Pierre Trudeau spoke out against Meech Lake as a private citizen, he counts as a micro-level entity. By contrast, when Trudeau acted as prime minister during the negotiation of the *Constitution Act, 1982*, he acted as a macro-level entity, that is, on behalf of the government of Canada.[9]

Public opinion offers another useful test case because it takes both individual and aggregate forms. The individual voter or holder of an opinion on a forthcoming issue, such as the Quebec Referendum (1980 or 1995) or the Charlottetown Accord (1992), exists as a micro-level entity. Public opinion as a bottom line, however, is a social aggregate at the national level. For example, to say that a little over 50 percent of voters in the Quebec Referendum of 1995 cast a "no" ballot is to describe a reality that exists in national terms; the percentage expresses the overall profile of opinion among, in this case, millions of individuals.

One way to look at the preceding demarcation of the macro and micro levels is through the lens of either the liberal (which emphasizes individual interests) or communitarian (which emphasizes collective identities) paradigm. Because they are the prominent and competing approaches in the study of Canadian politics (as is noted by Cairns 1991a, 1991b, 1992, 2000, and Kymlicka 1993, 1998), any theory will readily fall into one or the other paradigm. It could be said, probably without much controversy, that both interests and identities feed into the motives and actions of macro- and micro-level actors, as is the case in any theory. To focus exclusively on interests and identities would be to miss certain critical elements – and it is all too easy to buy into the simplicity offered by single-cause explanations. Alan Cairns, Will Kymlicka, and other sophisticated theorists, however, go beyond single-cause explanations to combine effects. Their emphasis on either individuals or collectivities is more in the tradition of Aristotle's concept of the prime mover than anything else – you have to start somewhere.

Systemism provides a way to connect theories about Canadian constitutional politics to one another *and* to the pursuit of self-interest, that is, rational choice. Communitarian theories can be expected to stress efforts among groups to have their status recognized in the constitutional system – self-interest among members is defined in that way. By contrast, liberal theories emphasize what individuals per se are trying to achieve. Actors, therefore, can be rational within both theories; they simply differ in the degree to which they identify with one another and one another's goals.

Systemism also provides a way to interpolate and extrapolate steps in a given theory. A theory may leave out steps that are implied by its causal story, for example, $m \rightarrow m$ and $M \rightarrow M$ linkages may occur without an intervening connection between the macro and micro levels. Interpolation then becomes necessary. Likewise, if theory tells an incomplete causal story, the stages it does not include must be extrapolated.

One final qualification should be offered about systemism. Systemism is not being put forward here as a theory of constitutional politics in Canada. Rather, it is offered as a conceptual framework that facilitates the analysis and synthesis of a range of fully integrated theories and more isolated propositions about how the constitutional system works.

### Substantive Illustrations

Systemism as a framework for analysis begins with exogenous (environmental) inputs, that is, international imperatives. It requires the identification of environmental effects, and in the case of the Canadian polity, the reference is to the international system. Analysis naturally begins with the founding of Canada. Confederation in 1867, based on the *British North America Act,* upgraded colonial status by means of negotiations encouraged by the British government. The story of external inputs continued because the new nation bordered what would become, only a few decades after Confederation, the world's leading power. Major developments such as the Canada-US Free Trade Agreement (CUFTA) and the North American Free Trade Agreement (NAFTA) might factor as effects in one or more explanations. More subtle, but perhaps no less important in recent decades, are the forces of globalization. Shifts in the characteristics of citizenry around the world, most notably in the direction of greater competence and activism, are summed up by Rosenau (1990, 1997) with the term *micro revolution.* Therefore, the direct and easily visualized impact of the United States on Canadian constitutional affairs must be assessed along with the more elusive effects of globalization at the citizen level.

Macro-macro *(M → M)* linkages focus on collectivities (and their representatives) that operate at the national level – in most cases, executive federalism as manifested through negotiations between and among the First Ministers (Cairns 1988a, 1988b; Courchene 1988; Gibbins 1988; Caplan 1989; Simeon and Robinson 1990; LaSelva 1993; Russell 1993a). Negotiations over the Meech Lake Accord among the First Ministers in 1987 and 1990 serve as one example of macro-macro processes. Interactions between and among the judiciary (represented principally by members of the Supreme Court) and the federal and provincial governments must also be addressed. Court rulings, both on an individual basis and in the aggregate, are important because of their influence on ongoing and future legal proceedings and constitutional evolution (Breton 1988; Manfredi 1993, 2001; Morton 1994; Knopff 2001).

Macro-micro *(M → m)* connections are actions taken at the system level that filter down to individuals and groups. Regardless of whether or not they are successful, major initiatives ranging from the *Constitution Act, 1982* to the Charlottetown Accord elicit reactions from citizens as individuals and as collectivities (Pal 1993a, 1993b). The setting of referendums such as the one on the Charlottetown Accord and those on Quebec sovereignty are also relevant (Simpson 1993); campaigning and voting are simply the immediate micro-level responses to such initiatives. Judicial decisions that affect subnational political actors likewise fall into the macro-micro category. Take, for example, the Supreme Court's ruling on Bill C-68, the *Firearms Act* (1995). The *Act* required all gun owners to register their firearms with the federal government. Alberta appealed the legislation, claiming that it went beyond Ottawa's authority, and the Court ultimately ruled in favour of the federal government. This ruling applied to all governments and individuals throughout the land. Thus, the decision constitutes a macro-micro linkage because it emanated from a federal institution and influenced all political actors, individually and collectively, in at least an indirect way. Finally, the impact of the national media on the public must also be factored into any analysis (Meisel 1991; Raboy 1991; Taras 1991).

Micro-macro *(m → M)* linkages involve the activities of interest groups, court litigants, intelligentsia, other social groupings, and individual voters that affect national politics. Interest groups, most notably those recognized by the *Charter,* are forces with which to be reckoned (Flanagan 1992, 2000; Kymlicka 1993; Landry 1993; Pal 1993a, 1993b; Vickers 1993; McRoberts 1998; Smith 1998). In particular, both individual and collective action in relation to the court system is worth noting. The court actions of collectivities such as women's groups and Aboriginal peoples in the post-*Charter* era have stimulated significant theorizing about the cumulative effect of litigation on the constitutional order (Knopff and Morton 1992; Morton and Knopff 2000; Brodie 2001). Another important connection is created by voting in elections and referendums, which can have a direct and decisive influence on the direction of constitutional affairs (Clarke and Kornberg 1994; Levine 1994; Kornberg and Clarke 1994; LeDuc and Pammett 1995). Finally, think tanks and academics can affect constitutional politics in both direct and indirect ways through the formulation of ideas that find their way into various bargaining processes (Abelson 2002).

Micro-micro *(m → m)* connections trace attitude formation and intergroup competition. How individuals and subnational groups come to hold beliefs that affect their behaviour in constitutional affairs is a challenging question to answer, but some understanding of these processes already exists (Cloutier 1991; Howe and Fletcher 2000). Competition for status between and among groups, most notably in relation to *Charter* recognition, is also included in these connections (Brodie 1993, 1996).

## Conclusion

Systemism is a valuable framework for dealing with the complexity of constitutional evolution. It sets reasonable standards for theoretical completeness through the exploration of linkages within and between the macro and micro levels in a system. A viable theory must take into account inputs from the environment and, if it is sufficiently advanced, should include a functional form for each linkage. Effective theorizing also requires a unit-level foundation. Thus, in conjunction with systemism, rational choice is a basis for micro-level interaction. All theories can be articulated in a way that incorporates self-interest as it is described in this study. The case of Quebec's use of the notwithstanding clause in December 1988 illustrates systemism's potential for articulating theories. Systemism involves a visual representation of events that fosters understanding of how cause and effect are presumed to unfold, and systemism's diagrammatic expositions can also be used to more effectively compare theories.

# 3
# Identifying Concepts and Theories

What is meant by the term *constitutional system*? What is the nature of a theory? And what does it mean to say that a theory exists about the evolution of constitutional politics in Canada? This chapter offers answers to these questions as it fulfills three interrelated objectives. The first, defining key concepts, leads naturally into the second, a discussion of the nature of theory. Theory is defined as a generic concept, with two basic types – general equilibrium and partial equilibrium. An example of a partial-equilibrium theory is offered to highlight the differences between the two and to aid in the identification of full equilibrium theories. Finally, liberal and communitarian theories of constitutional politics that satisfy the conditions of full equilibrium – and which are designated on the basis of tendencies rather than through a rigid dichotomy – are identified.

## Concept Formation

### The Constitution and Its Functions
Although the question, what is a constitution? can be answered in a great many ways, the context here is Canadian. The discussion that follows focuses on Canadian sources, but the literature represents a wide range of perspectives.[1] The first part of Figure 3.1 lists in chronological order definitions located in studies of Canadian constitutional politics. The presence of just eight definitions in the table is in itself revealing – it suggests that studies of constitutional politics are generally not self-consciously theoretical in approach and have an overall tendency to assume that the meaning of central concepts is understood implicitly. Note also that only one of the definitions, from Hogg (1977), antedates the 1990s, the phase of would-be major constitutional reform following the patriation of 1982.

*Figure 3.1*

## The Constitution as a concept and its functions

| Source | Definition |
|---|---|
| *The Constitution as a concept* | |
| Hogg (1977, 2) | All the important rules, whatever their source, which allocate government power within a nation ... [I]t also encompasses rules which are not contained in the basic constitutional document, and even some rules which are not enforceable in the courts. |
| Reesor (1992, xii) | Fundamental rules, written and unwritten, legal and extralegal, that determine how a government operates. |
| Gairdner (1994, 59) | A set of conventional rules and general principles by which the people and their various levels of government are allowed to make their deals; but it must never, in itself, be a deal. |
| Peacock (1996b, vii-viii) | Has authority and provides for government. It establishes the structure of government, the powers government possesses, how these are to be allocated among the various branches and institutions, how the balance between power and liberty, government and individual rights, is to be maintained, and how the constitutional design may be amended through means other than violent revolution. |
| Malcolmson and Myers (1996, 31) | A set of rules that authoritatively establishes both the structure and the fundamental principles of the political regime. |
| Guy (1998, 267-68) | A body of formal and effective rules and practices, written and unwritten, according to which the people and the political institutions of a society are governed. |
| Archer et al. (2002, 20) | Supreme law that defines the scope of state power and divides it among the various institutions that make up the state ... [I]ncorporates both the unwritten principles that guide the execution of public activities ... and the sources of political legitimacy in a particular territory (i.e., myths, symbols and rituals). |
| Russell (2004, 248) | The formal constitution and amendments to it ... [are] organic statutes that are not formal amendments ... political practices that have become hardened into constitutional conventions and political agreements about the proper use of government powers ... [and] judicial decisions interpreting the formal Constitution and the principles underlying the constitutional system as a whole. |

▶

◄   *Figure 3.1*

| Source | Definition |
| --- | --- |
| *Functions of a Constitution* | |
| Hogg (1977, 2) | Establish, empower and regulate the principal institutions of government. |
| Malcolmson and Myers (1996, 31-33) | Establish political authority among actors; assign legislative, executive and judicial powers; divide regional and national powers in federal states. |
| Landes (1998, 50) | Constitutions structure the polity by establishing the boundaries of political action; that is, they outline the basic rules of the political game. |
| Brooks (2000, 85-86) | Representation; power limits and divisions; rights. |
| Archer et al. (2002, 12) | Powerful influences on the ways in which citizens perceive themselves and their relationship to the state. |
| Russell (2004, 248) | Create or alter major institutions of government; regulate use of constitutional rules and government powers. |

Despite some differences in wording, the definitions agree on a few basic points. All agree that a constitution is about how a government works, either in term of operations, deals, powers, or principles. Seven of the eight definitions mention rules or laws explicitly, and the other (from Peacock) notes that a constitution will mandate how powers are to be allocated. Six of the eight definitions (Hogg, Reesor, Gairdner, Guy, Archer et al., and Russell) mention that a constitution includes both formal and informal rules and practices. Three of the eight definitions (Peacock, Malcolmson and Myers, and Archer et al.) refer to the establishment of the structure of government. Other aspects of a constitution mentioned in at least one definition include the following: (1) it must not in and of itself be a deal; (2) it must describe how balances are maintained between power and liberty and between government and individual rights; (3) it must have a means for amendment; and (4) it must have legitimacy. Aside from the second point, which concerns both macro-micro $(M \to m)$ and micro-Macro $(m \to M)$ connections, the definitions focus on observed and implied macro-macro $(M \to M)$ linkages. This is not surprising given the long tradition of executive federalism – meetings between the prime minister and provincial premiers – being paramount in the Canadian context.

The second part of Figure 3.1 displays the functions of a constitution as defined in studies that get explicitly into that issue. Rules of the game, along with limits and divisions of power, are prominent ideas in the definitions. Perhaps the most interesting observation is the one from Archer et al. (2002), which emphasizes the impact of a constitution on how citizens see themselves. This takes the form of an explicit macro-micro $(M \rightarrow m)$ linkage. Taken together, the functions of the Constitution are a set of macro-micro connections that extend from the government to the people.

What is Canada's place, constitutionally speaking, among states in general? Canada's entry in the handbook *Nations of the World* includes the following description for its Constitution: "Although Canada is formally a constitutional monarchy with the British monarch as the nominal head of state, for all practical purposes the country is a sovereign state. The governor general is the Queen's representative in Canada." The form of state is listed in this same source as a constitutional monarchy (Grey House Publishing 2000, 238). The persistence of the governor general as Canada's head of state is what defines this status. Real power, however, resides in Canada itself, especially since the patriation of the Constitution in 1982. As is summed up in Figure 3.1, the Canadian Constitution as a concept encompasses a democratic governmental structure and functions, along with formal and informal rules of law.[2] Its functions include rules of the game for the practice of politics and limits and divisions for the exercise of power. This suggests that Canada will be more prone to be influenced by, and exert influence on, other democratic states.

**A Constitutional System**
Systemism is the organizing principle for this study, and the point of departure for that approach is identifying what *system* means within a given field. Mario Bunge (1996, 270) defines a system in general terms as follows: "A *system* is a complex object, every part or component of which is related to some other component(s) of the same object (e.g., families, schools, firms and informal networks). An object is a *subsystem* if it is both a system and a part of another system (e.g., universities and governments). And an object is a *supersystem* if it is composed of systems (e.g., a chain of supermarkets or an entire society)." As a political system, Canada fits into the preceding series of definitions in a relatively straight-forward manner. Canada is a complex object – one of the few points no one seems to dispute! – that includes components that are related to

one another and that can be described in terms of various points of division. State and society, for instance, is one such dichotomy. Within the democratic state, components such as the legislature, executive, and judiciary can be identified. The Canadian federation also constitutes a supersystem. Provinces and territories are systems within the Canadian supersystem. Canada also is part of a supersystem; it experiences exogenous inputs from the exterior world of states, international organizations, and prominent individuals.

## What Is a Theory?

### Theories and Paradigms

Theories within a paradigm represent a belief in common parametric settings but differ in terms of the presumed network of effects observed in the empirical world. A paradigm designates parameters, and the characteristics and goals of actors are regarded as falling within boundaries set by the theories in a given paradigm (James 2002, 69). Parametric boundaries are axiomatic and not subject to falsification. However, theories within a paradigm, which generate propositions, are subject to testing and can be falsified. The fate of a paradigm, therefore, depends on how well its theories account for what is observed. The communitarian paradigm emphasizes the group rather than the individual as the basic unit of analysis. By contrast, the liberal paradigm emphasizes individual agency over group identification. Theories in these two paradigms stress group identification and individual action, respectively.

Within each paradigm, theories are differentiated in more nuanced ways that relate to how they see relationships among variables. Their visions of cause and effect vis-à-vis exogenous inputs and macro and micro levels will vary within the parametric boundaries. For example, communitarian theories could differ on the likely effects that a change in the balance of power among branches of government will have on group identity. One theory might see the shift as a threat to the welfare of one or more collectivities, while the other might not. The difference of opinion would be based on beliefs about causation in an empirical sense. Disagreement might also emerge over the direction of cause and effect between variables and so on. But no communitarian theory would fail to privilege collective identity in its account of constitutional evolution. The same is true for the role of the individual vis-à-vis liberal theories. This difference comes out in the use of language: communitarians refer to collective identity as a fundamental reality, while liberals describe interest groups in terms of instrumental membership.

The difference between the communitarian and liberal paradigms is one of degree more than kind. No reasonable person would say that a viable social theory could focus exclusively on either individuals or communities to the exclusion of the other. Weberian ideal types are not at issue here. Instead, differences between the paradigms are nuanced and normative. In addition, different theories can coexist within the same paradigm. But what really distinguishes paradigms at the most fundamental level is whether they place greater normative value on individual rights or a sense of collectivism. Just as there is plenty of room between Adam Smith and Karl Marx for theorists of political economy to occupy, so also there is a continuum rather than a dichotomy between communitarian and individualistic values.

A theory, more formally, designates a hypothetico-deductive system that produces an interrelated set of propositions (i.e., hypotheses) (Bunge 1996, 114).[3] Propositions should be falsifiable in empirical terms. The designation of key variables is what distinguishes one theory from another. Theories, as so defined, therefore, are highly suited to direct competition with one another on the basis of historical evidence (Bunge 1996, 118). Each theory consists of a set of assumptions from which a logically consistent class of hypotheses that pertain to the empirical world are derived. As assumptions are combined to produce hypotheses that may be either wholly or partially inconsistent with one another, competing theories emerge. This variation is not only possible but certain because no set of axioms will be sufficient to provide the basis for an exhaustive set of propositions (see Gödel's theorem, cited in James 2002). The introduction of new assumptions accounts for the divergence between theories and ultimately defines the boundary between intraparadigmatic competition and the shift to a new paradigm. A theory remains within a given paradigm as long as its system of variables does not entail assumptions that contradict those that are granted parametric status. A communitarian theory, for example, could not draw upon classical liberal principles to develop explanations for constitutional developments. Identification with collective interests is prior and fundamental to agency. Self-interest is defined that way in the communitarian paradigm. Collective identity is genuine rather than adopted for purely instrumental reasons. Diverse ideas, however, could still coexist among communitarian theories without crossing that line. Communitarian theories can and will differ in their expectations about how one or more collectivities would respond to a given stimulus.

Theories within a paradigm can vary in important ways. Even in a system with only a few variables, a vast range of specific and potentially important differences can produce many theories. Consider the following possibilities, which are restricted to abstract relations within a single network of variables: (1) exogenous versus endogenous roles, (2) direct versus indirect effects, (3) direction of anticipated substantive impact, and (4) uni-directional versus bi-directional effects (James 2002, 78-80). Each of these differences will be illustrated in Chapters 4 and 5, using the theories from Canadian constitutional politics that are introduced later in the chapter.

Efforts to resolve differences between and among theories within a given paradigm naturally converge on empirically oriented issues related to research design and the interpretation of evidence. Aggregate data versus comparative case studies, preferred data sources, specification of monotonic versus non-monotonic relationships, lags and leads between variables, and a host of other interrelated issues are meaningful only when there is consensus about parameters. When there is no consensus, debate focuses on more basic definitional issues and tends to move in a normative direction. Although evidence can still be interpreted in different ways, the ability to assess competing hypotheses in a common context exists in principle and can be improved through incremental efforts in a given paradigm (Kuhn 1962, 1970).

## General and Partial Equilibrium

### Concept Formation

Although theories can differ along many dimensions, the most salient aspect at this point is scope. Theories can be divided into two basic kinds: general and partial equilibrium. Economists developed the concepts of general equilibrium and partial equilibrium to assess the properties of markets.[4] These concepts can be put to good use in a metaphorical sense to develop a standard to identify full-fledged theories of constitutional politics. Todd Sandler (2001) provides a clear explanation of what each concept represents: "The study of an isolated market is known as a *partial-equilibrium* analysis, where the market's own price is the focus of attention. For *general equilibrium*, the interrelationship of all markets is investigated and all commodities' prices are relevant." General equilibrium occurs when a set of prices, one for each market, allows all markets to clear. In other words, everything is connected to prices (Sandler 2001). By contrast, in a partial-equilibrium analysis, all markets save one are held constant. The dynamics of supply and demand, of price and consumption, are isolated for one market. A model of this kind, as might be expected, is a starting point for analysis. The ultimate goal is to build up to a general equilibrium, that is, "a set of market prices that simultaneously makes every excess demand zero" (Sandler 2001, 133). Three issues emerge with respect to general equilibrium: existence, stability, and desirability (Sandler 2001, 138-41).[5] In other words, does equilibrium exist? If so, is it stable? Finally, how desirable (or, for an economist, efficient) is the equilibrium?

Obviously, a constitutional system is not an economic system. So how, then, does the metaphor apply? Why are the concepts of general and partial equilibrium useful for identifying and evaluating theories about the evolution of constitutional politics in Canada? Part of the answer lies in the fact that a basic concern in the identification of theories is completeness. Comparison, criticism, and synthesis are most rewarding if they are focused on relatively complete theories. This raises the question, what constitutes a full-fledged theory as opposed to some lesser entity? And herein lies the link to the concepts of general and partial equilibrium. Issue areas in politics may be compared to markets – this is the essence of the metaphor. A general-equilibrium theory of constitutional politics must cover the full range of issues, just as an economic analysis must investigate the interrelationship of all markets.

Although it might be easier to identify a set of markets as opposed to issues, the difference is one of degree rather than kind. To some extent, each exercise is inductive and time specific. For example, on the economic side of the fence, consider the travel industry. In antiquity, to the extent that markets could be identified, the sectors would have included travel by land and sea. Modes of movement would have been simple to enumerate – a caravan of horses and wagons on land and wind- or human-powered ships by sea. Today, however, the travel market is quantitatively and qualitatively different: there are new means for moving over both land and sea, and an entirely new sector – air and space travel – has emerged.

On the political side of the fence, describing a full set of issue areas is a daunting task, but drawing boundaries between and among issues is aided by received wisdom. Chapter 1 describes a series of issues in constitutional politics, including federalism, amendment, national unity, the roles of Quebec and the West, Aboriginal peoples, and so on. Although it is obvious that these issues overlap – they cannot be listed as a set of mutually exclusive and exhaustive categories – it is also clear that a theory that cannot take into consideration one or more important aspects of constitutional affairs falls short of general equilibrium. It is also easy to determine whether a theory claims to bear on one issue or a discrete subset among the totality that makes up constitutional politics.

For these reasons, it is feasible to use the concepts of general equilibrium and partial equilibrium from economics in a metaphorical sense to classify theories about constitutional politics. It is, at the very least, a starting point. An extensive review of the literature produces no other taxonomy of theories regarding Canadian constitutional politics. The equilibrium concepts also provide a rigorous context for the evaluation and potential synthesis of theories. A general-equilibrium theory of constitutional politics will have the following two characteristics: (1) it can be applied in principle to the results of political processes across the full range of issues, past or present, within the evolving constitutional system; and (2) it contains at least one connection from each of the kinds of linkages delineated in systemism, including exogenous input, macro-macro, macro-micro, micro-micro, and micro-macro. The second condition follows from the first. Any theory that purports to span the full range of issues cannot, *a priori*, be either holistic or reductionistic in nature. By definition it would be unable to contend with the complete set of political processes. Its incompleteness in that sense would render the theory incapable of addressing some significant issues. A partial-equilibrium theory, by contrast, possesses only the second of these two properties. For these reasons the three criteria related to general equilibrium – existence, stability, and desirability – can be raised in combination only with respect to the more inclusive kind of theory.

The existence of a general equilibrium in the economic realm means that markets clear. Prices adjust with supply and demand across all markets in ways that include significant indirect and even unobservable connections. In the domain of constitutional politics, equilibrium refers to a distribution of capabilities among actors that keeps the existing system in operation. To convey the meaning of *equilibrium,* the idea of (in)stability must enter the discussion. One example of instability that has the potential to produce disequilibrium is the rise of regional political parties such as the Reform Party or the Bloc Québécois. An extreme case of instability in a democratic system such as Canada would be a successful unilateral declaration of or referendum on independence by one of the provinces. A civil war that produces separation for one or more political subunits would be the ultimate case of a high level of instability producing disequilibrium in a system. Thus, capability takes the place of price within this extended metaphor. As long as political power is distributed and exercised in a way that permits the constitutional system to function within its current boundaries, stability exists. Once actors forsake voting and other constitutionally regularized means of political participation to effect incremental change, the system is unstable and can end up in a state of disequilibrium.

Stability is the second consideration. When they are in equilibrium, political processes can be either relatively cooperative or conflict prone. Constitutional strife in equilibrium could include litigation by social movements, executive federalism, and other actions within the boundaries of Confederation. Extra-constitutional strife, including violence, would represent extreme instability. Stability is measured by the relative absence of efforts to alter the fundamental nature of the system that, if sufficiently intense, could cumulatively lead in the direction of disequilibrium.

Compare, for instance, labour movement politicization in Canada and Poland in the 1980s and 1990s. Canadian unions generally backed the New Democratic Party (NDP) and fought, in particular, against trade liberalization via CUFTA and NAFTA as envisaged by Brian Mulroney's Conservative government. Although rhetoric became intense, labour participated in the political process in conventional ways, such as campaigning in elections for anti–free trade candidates. These actions sublimated conflict and permitted the system, although undergoing instability, to remain in equilibrium. By contrast, the Solidarity movement in Poland objected strenuously to the Soviet-imposed distribution and exercise of political power – the very system itself. Over time, the labour movement in Poland successfully dismantled the political system. After a period of high instability and disequilibrium, a new system based on a democratic constitution came into being and remains in equilibrium to this day.

The third consideration – the normative desirability of an equilibrium – is assessed on the basis of social capital and generalized trust. Social capital is a standard concept in evaluations of political well-being (Coleman 1990; Putnam 2000). Social capital can build in the same way as financial capital and is measured by group formation and solidarity. It refers to the total value of all social networks and the inclination to do things for one another that are their result (Putnam 2000). Social capital is important for the development of a democratic society because it is connected to generalized trust. This second concept is even more fundamental to a normatively desirable socio-political system (Uslaner 2002).

There are two kinds of social capital – bonding and bridging (Putnam 2000). Bonding and bridging refer, respectively, to the extent of solidarity among groups composed of people who are like or unlike one another. From a normative standpoint, the accumulation of bridging is preferable to bonding when it comes to social capital. Bridging and bonding can be thought of as positive and negative social capital, respectively, although when both are accumulated at the same time they can interact to make the overall contribution favourable. The formation and enhanced solidarity of exclusive groups is unlikely to facilitate cooperation and trust in society. Social networks that anyone can join, by contrast, are anticipated to have positive effects (Putnam 2000). An equilibrium's normative desirability can be appraised in terms of its relative encouragement of each of these kinds of social capital. The accumulation of bridging is welcomed, even if it might entail some bonding, but the latter in isolation should be avoided if possible.

The connections enumerated by social capital, interestingly enough, do not produce generalized trust (Uslaner 2002).[6] There is no significant empirical evidence that shows that the kinds of specialized associations emphasized by Putnam – clubs based on common interests such as stamp collecting, boating, movies, and the like – are sufficient to affect society as a whole. Instead, the causal connection runs in the opposite direction – from generalized trust to civic engagement. Social capital can therefore be used as an indicator of the level of generalized trust within society. However, there is a precautionary point to keep in mind: research on generalized trust reveals that membership in an exclusive group will make a person less trusting. This serves as a warning about the potential consequences of bonding without bridging in regard to social capital.

### The Aboriginal Orthodoxy as a Partial-Equilibrium Theory

One of the most controversial aspects of constitutional politics in Canada is the role of Aboriginal peoples. In *First Nations? Second Thoughts*, Tom Flanagan (2000) provides an exegesis and critique of, in the language used here, a partial-equilibrium theory: Aboriginal orthodoxy. It is worth noting that Flanagan's views on the theory rest at the negative pole of academic opinion on this issue, whereas the majority of scholars' views are closer to the positive pole. Consequently, Flanagan seeks to show that systemism can be used to convey theories about even the most contentious issues in a way that maximizes clarity and facilitates debate. The Aboriginal orthodoxy can be summed up as follows (Flanagan 2000, 4): "[T]he aboriginal orthodoxy is an emergent consensus on fundamental issues. It is widely shared among aboriginal leaders, government officials, and academic experts. It weaves together threads from historical revisionism, critical legal studies, and the aboriginal activism of the last thirty years." The orthodoxy begins with the assertion that Aboriginal peoples are distinguished by their presence in North America long before other settlers. This assertion has given rise to the concept of Aboriginal peoples as First Nations, which is used to justify land claims, preferential policies for hiring, and a range of other privileges (Flanagan 2000, 17, 22). Because Aboriginal peoples, as Canada's first residents, were evicted by force from their lands, the Aboriginal orthodoxy entails self-government. Given that the lands held as reserves by Aboriginal peoples lack economic viability, the next step is economic support, which is justified by the sense of loss felt by Aboriginal peoples, who need public support in order to enjoy a way of life that is theirs by entitlement.

Figure 3.2 shows the basic connections within the Aboriginal orthodoxy when it is transplanted into the frame of reference of systemism. The first connection is an exogenous input to the system, with two components, one micro and the other macro, which are represented by upper- and lower-case characters. Primacy in territorial control, which was invested in Aboriginal peoples as social groupings, and forced eviction, an action of governments both before and after Confederation, combined to produce exclusionary federalism. Aboriginal peoples, in other words, occupied the land that now makes up modern Canada but hardly played an equal role in the founding of the Canadian state at Confederation. Federalism, from the beginning, took an exclusionary form.[7] The next linkage, a macro-macro one, extends logically from exclusionary federalism to the treaty system and the *Indian Act*, which were a means to manage Aboriginal peoples. They had no input into the creation of the *Act*, and it did not recognize their latent sense of nationhood. Given the treaty system and lack of input at the federal level, Aboriginal peoples faced a situation in which their identity, to be preserved, had to develop outside of the system imposed by Confederation. This is represented by a macro-micro linkage from the treaty system and the *Indian Act* to Aboriginal identity formation and the rejection of assimilation. This, in turn, produced a micro-micro connection

*Figure 3.2*

**The Aboriginal orthodoxy**

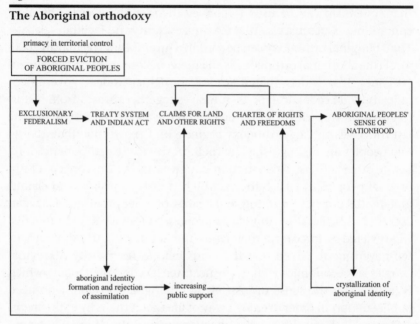

in society as a whole as identity formation among Aboriginal peoples found increasing support among the public. Activists, academics, and members of the legal community who promote Aboriginal interests stand out in this capacity.

The mobilization of Aboriginal peoples and their supporters produced a micro-macro effect as increasing public support led to Aboriginal claims for land and other rights. Disputes over these issues with both the federal and provincial governments increased dramatically over time: "Specific claims number in the hundreds and are increasing all the time. It is probably no exaggeration to assert that every band in Canada has made, is making, or is preparing to make at least one such claim" (Flanagan 2000, 150). Although not all claims are successful, and some even produce intra-Aboriginal conflict,[8] many court cases have enhanced the status of Aboriginal peoples in terms of both rights and territory. The next connection, which is macro-macro in nature, occurred as claims for land and other rights led to a sense of nationhood among Aboriginal peoples. This sense of nationhood is reflected in the federal courts, where Aboriginal peoples increasingly base their claims on the argument that they constitute a separate, founding nation within Canada.

Another connection, also micro-macro, paralleled the one just described and created reinforcing effects. Increasing public support for Aboriginal issues led to the *Constitution Act, 1982* and the *Charter*. Although it is obvious that these documents came into being in response to many other factors, the inclusion of section 35, which affirms the status of Aboriginal peoples, in the *Constitution Act* can be traced to a rising level of public support. This linkage, in turn, feeds back at the macro-macro level from the *Charter* to further claims for land and other rights. The *Charter* accelerated organized political activity by Aboriginal peoples at the federal level, which reinforced the macro-macro connection from claims for land and other rights to an Aboriginal sense of nationhood. The final pair of connections, which are macro-micro and micro-macro, create feedback within the system. A sense of nationhood at the macro level leads to the crystallization of Aboriginal identity at the micro level. This process culminated in the early 1980s when the National Indian Brotherhood, which hoped to become a truly representative organization, decided to change its name to the Assembly of First Nations. This effect, in turn, feeds back through micro-macro connections as Aboriginal nationhood becomes more in evidence at the federal level. For example, the shift in use from the word *band* to *nation* among both Aboriginal peoples and the public is approximately twenty-five years old (Flanagan 2000, 67).[9]

Given its emphasis on Aboriginal peoples as collective actors, it is clear that the Aboriginal orthodoxy reflects primarily communitarian thinking. The inclusion of all four types of causation (macro-micro, micro-micro, and so on) qualifies the Aboriginal orthodoxy as a partial-equilibrium theory, but because it focuses on just one issue area, it does not qualify for status as a full equilibrium theory. However, it does play a role within more encompassing full equilibrium theories that reside within the communitarian paradigm. It almost goes without saying that Aboriginal collectivism is conveyed more favourably within the communitarian paradigm than it is in the liberal.

### Locating Theories

One of the most striking characteristics of studies of constitutional issues in Canada is their tendency to avoid theory. The discipline of Canadian studies, most notably in relation to politics, is generally historical and descriptive in nature.[10] Theory appears implicitly in a wide range of studies, but advocates of one position or another usually do not describe what they put forward as theories, probably because much of this literature seeks to influence policy and therefore eschews language that might be more technical and potentially off-putting to a general audience. Therefore, a method for identifying theories within the vast literature on Canadian politics must be developed. Three means are available: (1) designation of a magnum opus, (2) sociological or school-based recognition, and (3) rational reconstruction. All three come into play in this study.

One way of locating theories is to rely on works that have achieved landmark status. This approach is inductive and requires the identification of a magnum opus. In some instances a work stands out in an obvious way, usually as a result of abundant citations or even real-world impact over a long period. One example is Marx's three-volume *Das Kapital,* which is viewed without question as the foundation for Marxism in its many variants. Other examples, restricted more or less to academia, include William Riker's (1962) theory of political coalitions and James Coleman's (1990) exegesis of social exchange theory. The former initiated a program of research on rational choice and political behaviour, while the latter synthesized existing work into a greater whole and stimulated interest in the use of social capital as a concept in the study of political sociology. As in the case of Marx's trilogy, the key to magnum opus status is subsequent recognition.[11]

Another, more common, way to locate theories is sociological or school-based. This is naturally the case because so few works meet the preceding standard. Examples of school-based identification abound, in and out of the study of politics. The Frankfurt School of philosophy (Adorno, Habermas, and the like) stands out as an example that has reach throughout the social sciences and even the humanities. The English School of international relations (reviewed by Devlen, James, and Özdamar 2005), the Calgary School of Canadian political thought,[12] and a host of other examples could be provided from political science. A school is a collection of scholars who are working, either implicitly or explicitly together, on a set of interrelated intellectual problems within a common paradigmatic frame of reference. Members of a school might self-identify and cross-reference in some way, but it is more common, at least at an early point of development, for the designation to be external. A school therefore could be identified with some form of paradigmatic normal science – cumulative research within the boundaries of a single paradigm – as defined by Kuhn (1962), in which adherents are united by subject matter, theoretical perspective, and (for the most part) research methods. In the field of Canadian politics, the Calgary School is a good example. It is defined by a mixture of western regionalism, libertarianism, and social conservatism. Members of the school, who work primarily but not exclusively at the University of Calgary, have identified themselves explicitly with it, and members of the field in general do so as well.[13] Scholarship identified with the Calgary School includes studies of the court system, federalism, interest groups, and other topics related to the constitutional system in general and specific issue areas.

As a way to identify theories, rational reconstruction differs qualitatively from the other two means. It is deductive rather than inductive in nature. The act of rational reconstruction involves taking works that appear to be complementary and combining their logically interconnected statements into a network of cause and effect that satisfies the conditions for status as a partial- or general-equilibrium theory. In other words, propositions are fused together into a theory that (1) can be applied, at least in principle, to generate further propositions about any issue area within the system of constitutional politics and (2) includes at least one linkage from each of the basic types identified by systemism. Flanagan's presentation of the Aboriginal orthodoxy stands as an example of rational reconstruction.

Rational reconstruction is essential to the task of identifying a complete set of entities that are candidates for status as general-equilibrium theories. Even if a magnum opus or school is identified, the need for theoretical completeness will still require some degree of rational reconstruction. Most disciplines in the social sciences have struggled to agree upon a well-identified set of theories that can provide the basis for normal science. Therefore, some amount of reconstructive work will be needed to add pattern and meaning to theorizing as identified through major works, school-based identification, or both. Consider this observation by Stuart Shanker (1988, 197-98):

> Axioms are constantly being invented or revised in order to ... address problems which would defy the reach – i.e. the intelligibility – of the pre-existing axioms. The evolution of a ... field typically consists, therefore, in the gradual development of such system-families. But the further this process advances the greater become the pressures for rationalization if the subject is to remain manageable. Like the unplanned development of a medieval city these systems soon become too cumbersome

for efficient communication, and interest shifts accordingly to refashioning the axiom set without diminishing the scope of the system (by introducing alternative – possibly more abstract – axioms).

What makes this admonition about unwieldy theorizing especially interesting is that it is aimed at mathematics, presumably the most rigorous of all disciplines, not Canadian studies or any of the social sciences. It almost goes without saying, then, that using a combination of means to identify theories is appropriate for the field of Canadian constitutional politics.[14]

Liberal and communitarian paradigms represent the great divide in the study of Canadian constitutional politics. These paradigms are by definition in conflict with each other (Whyte 1991, 241) because, in micro terms, communitarians emphasize collectivities and liberals stress individuals. Among the many academic treatments of constitutional politics in Canada, five meet the criteria for a general-equilibrium theory, and three – negative identity, megapolitics, and institutional imbalance – fall within the liberal paradigm. The communitarian paradigm encompasses the other two theories: asymmetric federalism and the citizens' constitution.

Negative identity theory emerged primarily as a result of rational reconstruction as ideas about the history and political sociology of Canada centred on the negative roots of Canada's national character. Proponents of the theory argue that Canadian identity has been defined in opposition to that of the United States (Lipset 1990; Pal 1993a, 1993b; Cooper 1996a, 1996b; Bissoondath 2000; Granatstein 2000a, 2000b). Identity formation goes back to the founding of Canada, when its neighbour was armed to the teeth and potentially in search of new conquests following the Civil War – even back to the American Revolution and the migration of Loyalists to Canada. Confederation produced political integration, but this achievement was more a reaction against the perceived revolutionary and violent tendencies of the United States than an action in favour of any particular vision. In a sense, Canada's response to America's manifest destiny was simply not to have one. Proponents of negative identity theory offer a lack of positive self-definition as an explanation for Canada's constitutional struggles and disappointments. This national shortcoming is manifested and reinforced through a series of processes that operate at the micro and macro levels. In sum, the key causal factor in negative identity theory is an exogenous input – a fragmentary foundation or birth that was imposed, to a large degree, by the outside authority of the British Empire – that, in turn, makes Canada vulnerable to centrifugal forces that are the result of belated and even pernicious efforts to self-define.[15]

Megapolitics theory (which also includes a modest amount of rational reconstruction) emanated from a magnum opus or, perhaps, several interlocking studies by the same author – Peter H. Russell's *Constitutional Odyssey: Can Canadians Become a Sovereign People?* (1992, 2004; see also 1991a, 1991b, 1991d, 1991e, 1993a, 1993b). The key concept, constitutional megapolitics, refers to major package deals such as the Meech Lake and Charlottetown accords. From Russell's point of view, these attempts to solve many problems at once only make the situation worse. The causal story is straightforward. Intense politics associated with major constitutional initiatives damage the social fabric and are bound to create perceptions of irreversible victory and defeat regardless of the outcome. The net result is less national unity and a reduced spirit of cooperation. Thus, the argument that follows from megapolitics favours the pursuit of incremental change rather than, in Prime Minister Brian Mulroney's colourful expression at the time of Meech Lake, rolling the dice. Since Russell introduced megapolitics, it is fair to say that virtually every treatment of Canadian constitutional evolution references his work. These subsequent studies help in the process of rational reconstruction and get megapolitics across the goal line as a general-equilibrium theory. Russell's theory also includes a complex series of linkages that span the required complement from systemism.

Institutional imbalance is a theory identified with a particular school of thought, but it also includes a magnum opus and some elements of rational reconstruction. The scholarship on institutional imbalance is produced primarily by members of the Calgary School. Two members of the School, F.L. Morton and Rainer Knopff, combined to publish *The Charter Revolution and the Court Party* (2000; see also Knopff and Morton 1992) as a major critique of the *Charter's* consequences for constitutional evolution. This study, along with others by the same team, is pervasive in subsequent debates. The basic idea is that a constitutional system cannot maintain a stable and desirable equilibrium if any one of the branches of government becomes too powerful. Criticism from Morton and Knopff, joined by others, focuses on the *Charter* as a document that unleashed the judicial branch at the expense of Parliament and even democracy itself. Minoritarian interests that normally would lose through voting processes end up winning in court instead. The result increasingly is instability that stems from a process in which the system itself encourages further efforts toward identity seeking. Moreover, a mindset that favours the redistribution rather than the creation of resources becomes the norm, to the detriment of society as a whole. The causal story here focuses on the *Charter* as a crucial, transforming, and ultimately pernicious event. Its net effect is anti-democratic and pervasive throughout the constitutional system.

Asymmetrical federalism is a theory built primarily through rational reconstruction. Arguments in favour of it follow from community-oriented thinking in both provincial and non-geographic terms (Greschner 1991; Taylor 1993, 1994; Kymlicka 1989, 1993, 1995, 1998; McRoberts 1997; Laforest 1998a, 1998b). One strand of the theory focuses, not surprisingly, on Quebec. The case is made that Quebec's exclusion from the *Constitution Act, 1982* and the *Charter of Rights and Freedoms* can only be rectified through a process of renewal that grants the province special recognition. The people of Quebec, if given constitutional status (for example) as a distinct society, will be able to reconcile their dual identity in a way that does not reject Canada as a whole. Failure to do this is likely to result in the gradual alienation of Quebec from Confederation. The complementary, non-geographic strand of thinking in asymmetrical federalism pertains to the recognition of multicultural identities. In this case, the achievement of a stable and desirable equilibrium depends upon finding a place for the collective as well as the individual identity of Canadians. A highly visible instance of this would be Aboriginal peoples. Thus, the two strands of asymmetrical federalism entail the same logic but with different featured players: special accommodation, which can be achieved by relaxing symmetrical federalism, is needed to create an appropriate place for Quebec and multicultural groups that span provincial boundaries.

Citizens' constitution is a theory that emerged from a magnum opus and related writings by Alan C. Cairns with some rational reconstruction. *Charter versus Federalism: The Dilemmas of Constitutional Reform* (Cairns 1992; see also 1991a, 1991b, 1991c, 1993, 1995) spells out a vision of Canadian constitutional politics that is primarily collectivist and micro-oriented. (It also passes the same test as do major works by Russell and Morton and Knopff vis-à-vis pervasive influence.) Over time, Canadians who belonged to various subgroups became more conscious of their dual identities and began to seek status. Micro-level change took the form of a secular trend toward increasing public suspicion of constitutional reform from above as manifested through executive federalism. The key part of the causal story concerns the making of the

*Constitution Act, 1982* and the *Charter,* which started out in an elite format but eventually included, given the standards and traditions of the time, an astonishing degree of public input, most notably from increasingly organized and visible collectivities. The latter even managed to alter the wording of proposed constitutional clauses and ultimately helped to create a document with much more authority than any of those at the elite level had imagined at the outset. In turn, as is suggested by the theory's name itself, the *Charter* transformed Canadian politics in a positive way, with citizens in general – not just those in groups granted explicit status – becoming conscious of their status as rights bearers and more empowered than before to compete with governments for control over the direction of the country.

## Conclusion

As the above analysis shows, a constitution is an exegesis of the structure and function of government, with a place for the rule of law and a sense of (in)formal rules of the game. In some instances, such as Canada, these designations appear in the absence of a preamble or overall statement of purpose. Constitutional systems, which include macro and micro components, are amenable to analysis from a systemist perspective. In the case of Canada, a system may form part of a supersystem, that is, the international community, which can and sometimes does provide exogenous inputs that influence constitutional evolution. Equilibrium analysis is an appropriate frame of reference for evaluating Canada's system. This book applies the concept in a metaphorical way by using the properties of existence, stability, and normative desirability to assess the visions offered by various theories of constitutional evolution that can be classified as either general- or partial-equilibrium theories. While the former apply to the constitutional system as a whole, the latter, such as the Aboriginal orthodoxy, focus on a given issue area. By employing a combination of three methods – the identification of a magnum opus, sociological or school-based identification, and rational reconstruction – this study identifies five theories of general equilibrium, three (negative identity, megapolitics, and institutional imbalance) from within the liberal paradigm and two (asymmetrical federalism and the citizens' constitution) from within the communitarian paradigm.

This identification of five candidate theories, however, must be qualified. First, it is possible, perhaps even virtually certain, that further efforts toward rational reconstruction will reveal additional latent theories. Such work, if it builds on what appears here, would be welcome. However, resources are limited, and this study identifies a diverse set of theories from which much can be learned through rigorous diagrammatic exposition, comparison, criticism, and synthesis. Put differently, the work carried out in Chapters 4 and 5 is regarded as a higher priority than the creation of a presumably "new" theory. Second, some might quarrel with the placement of a theory in one paradigm or another. They should consider the following question. Prior to this book's publication, to what extent have scholars in the field self-consciously reflected on a scheme of organization for its theories? What appears here should be regarded as an initial effort to develop a taxonomy. Work that refines it will be more than welcome.

# 4
# Liberal Theories: Negative Identity, Megapolitics, and Institutional Imbalance

This chapter uses diagrammatic forms and equilibrium-related criteria to describe and evaluate the three theories of Canadian constitutional politics – negative identity, megapolitics and institutional imbalance – in the liberal paradigm. The existence and degree of stability of each theory is appraised, as is its normative desirability. And the analysis concludes with an overview of the theories' collective vision.

## Negative Identity

Negative identity theory begins with the insight that lack of an affirmative identity, from Confederation onward, is the foremost cause of Canada's constitutional problems. Barry Cooper (1996b, 28) observes that "Canadians, never having undergone the experience of revolution, have never had the experience of making a sharp break with an imperial power and have never known the difficulties of founding a regime, either." As a result, Canada lacked the integrating effects of a vision at the national level: "[T]here are no common myths, no widespread agreement to sustain a common 'vision' of the nation or even of citizenship" (Cooper 1996b, 28). Consider, for example, the competing interpretations and internalized myths, inside and outside of Quebec, about the Riel Rebellion and Canada's participation in the two world wars.

Canada, to continue the story, ends up without a national identity because it is a product of counter-revolution. It is a residual country (Lipset 1990, 42). Confederation in 1867 was an incomplete process that had an air of administrative convenience rather than a higher national purpose based on shared values and visions. Note that Canada's annual national holiday was labelled Dominion Day and was initiated in 1868 to celebrate the union of the *British* colonies in North America.

This measure came about, moreover, as a proclamation from the governor general, that is, the head of state designated by the British Crown – not the Prime Minister of Canada. The name of the holiday did not change to Canada Day until 27 October 1982, after patriation of the Constitution.

To the extent that an overarching identity existed at the time of Confederation or exists even now, it is defined largely in negative terms, that is, in opposition to that of the United States. In particular, Canada rejects traits regarded as pernicious Americanisms such as extremism in either capitalism or other forms of competition (Lipset 1990, 53; see also Smith 1994). Neil Bissoondath (2000, 29) observes that "Canada's public identity continues to be built on opposition ('We aren't like them'), on institutions (medical and employment insurance, welfare, old-age pensions) and on theatrical display (mainly ethnic celebrations)." Identity built through the negation of ideas and miscellaneous manifestations of difference produces incoherence and uncertainty. The search for an alternative creation story, one that rejects revolution and the sudden and violent break from British rule that marked the founding of the United States, provides the basis for this way of thinking. In sum, given the proximity and power of the United States, Canadians must seek to avoid a mindset that could move their country into the position of being a miniature replica of its more powerful neighbour. Instead, from Confederation onward, cultural development in Canada has followed a cautious, Tory-inspired script, with the central state playing a major role (Lipset 1990, 110; Laforest 1995, 131).

Transmission of Canada's negative identity takes place at the macro level and is manifested at the micro or citizen level. Jack Granatstein (2000b, 14), in an assessment of the teaching of history in the Canadian school system, describes the mainstream approach as a "type of anti-patriotism." "Only in Canada," he observes, "would anyone suggest that a national perspective on the past be left out" (Granatstein 2000b, 15). Bissoondath (2000, 28) offers an even harsher judgment: "Our ignorance of ourselves has led us to make a fetish of the foreign heritages and identities that now populate our social landscape." In more recent times, this could be explained as a by-product of the federal multiculturalism policy developed in the Trudeau era, but the roots go deeper. The *Constitution Act, 1867* (formerly the *BNA Act*) contained no preamble or statement of national purpose. Although far from unique, Canada is the exception among states represented in an authoritative compilation of constitutional data (Maddex 1995). The lack of a preamble or statement opened the door to incremental and, in all likelihood, incoherent identification of national purpose.

Among Canadian federal governments, that of Prime Minister Pierre Elliott Trudeau stands out as being the most persistent in its efforts toward identity formation. Trudeau, through the concept of a just society, attempted to nurture and promote various group identities to oppose the gravitational effect of the colossus to the south and an especially menacing form of collectivism from within, namely, Quebec nationalism and separatism. Ironically, Trudeau – who was most at home on the political center-left – took hold of Tory collectivism in a dramatic fashion and applied it to new domains. (Trudeau's use of the *War Measures Act* and commitment to individual rights identify him as a liberal more than a social democrat.) The components of Trudeau's would-be Canadian identity included official bilingualism, multiculturalism, provincial equality, reinforcement of national institutions, and eventually the *Charter* (McRoberts 1993, 93). The *Charter* constitutionalized the collective rights favoured by Ottawa – those of cultural and language-based minorities – while it simultaneously excluded any *territorial* notions of asymmetry and enhanced federal power. All of this occurred, in terms of the distribution of power, at the expense of the provinces. Agendas put forward by the West and Quebec, in particular, found no place in the new regime.

Support for collectivities that span provincial borders, logically speaking, should undermine regional threats to national unity. This idea served as the foundation for the Trudeau government's strategy and tactics in the face of rival, decentralizing visions from the West and Quebec. The Canadian state began to fund interest groups quite well and for a very long time. As Pal (1993b, 243) observes, the "identity that underlies group solidarity is not given; it has to be formed and created and maintained." This certainly happened with official languages, minority, multicultural, and women's groups that obtained explicit recognition in the *Charter*.[1] *Charter* advocates hoped that trans-provincial solidarities would provide the glue that Confederation had always seemed to lack in sufficient quantity.

Unfortunately, from the standpoint of proponents of negative identity theory, these federal policies have institutionalized rather than resolved Canada's identity crisis. Funding *Charter* groups "fragments rather than unifies national identity" (Pal 1993b, 255-56; see also Flanagan 2007,

264, for its effect on partisan politics). Aspiring *Charter* groups proliferated as a natural and rational response to the incentives provided by
government. By the early 1990s, the federal government and provinces
had recognized over thirty groups as "worthy of special treatment" (Lipset
1990, 181). It is a well-established property of social interaction that as
the number of actors increases, the possibility of obtaining agreement
decreases (Olson 1965; Sandler 1992). Thus, further efforts to placate
unsatisfied groups can be expected; indeed, after the close call of the
Quebec Referendum on 30 October 1995, the federal government established a Canada Information Office, which had a $20 million budget,
to promote multiculturalism in opposition to "the 'lies' propagated by
separatists" (McRoberts 1997, 239). Contemporary Canada is therefore
special "because of the role played by governments in constructing
identities" (McRoberts 1993, 93). In the language of systemism and in
terms of the prime mover, the process of identity formation in Canada
is macro-micro.

From the standpoint of negative identity, however, Canada as a whole
ends up being less than the sum of its parts. Rival nation-building projects continue to produce conflict in a country that lacks a primary,
overarching identity, with the result that both time and energy continue
to be expended by governments that are competing for the allegiance
of citizens. Nationalism is certainly far from dead in Quebec. Although
it suffered an agonizingly close defeat in the referendum over a decade
ago, the events of that era have come back to haunt federalists. At the
time of writing, there has been no legal resolution to the sponsorship
scandal, in which the federal government engaged in enormous politically motivated payoffs to firms in Quebec, all in the name of defending
national unity during the referendum campaign of 1995. The details
came out during the Gomery Commission, after Jean Chrétien had
stepped down as Prime Minister, but it did not help matters that Chrétien had been replaced by Paul Martin, who had been finance minister
at the time of the scandal. (Although Martin was found to be clear of
wrongdoing, guilt by association came into play.) The unintended consequence for Ottawa has been the credibility the misconduct has given
to Quebec sovereigntists who accused the federal government of cor-
ruption and waste. Suspicion increases, even if it remains latent for a
time, and the separatist parties at both the provincial and federal levels
can be counted on to take advantage of long memories regarding the
misconduct of the Chrétien government. This is true even though the
Liberals have been replaced in Ottawa by the Harper Conservatives.

From the standpoint of negative identity theory, the road ahead for Canada is problematic. A high degree of path dependence exists because of accumulated decisions about the allocation of constitutional status. Barry Cooper's (1996b, 222) theoretical overview of polity evolution offers some insight: "[A]rticulation and integration are both required for the formation of a single body politic. Articulation, that is, the growth of communal consciousness to the point where action becomes possible without the institutional integration of the now articulate communes, is a recipe for fracture. On the other hand, integration without articulation may create the external formalities of a body politic, but it would be one without substantive meaning." It is clear from this passage that neither articulation nor integration is of much use without the other. Canada appears to have followed the former path, namely, articulation without integration. Collectivities are recognized, even created, yet they lack an overarching sense of purpose aside from denying that Canadians are Americans. From the perspective of negative identity theory, this lack of purpose stems from the polity's origins and efforts to improve upon the lack of an integrated foundation. As more groups develop communal consciousness and as collective identity intensifies among those already in existence the result will be repeated attempts at integration that end in failure. Groups will not subordinate themselves to a higher purpose because that could entail lower status under a revised constitutional order. Self-interest rears its ugly head.

The likelihood that a constitutional proposal will pass declines as articulation continues. As more groups become articulated, further vested interests emerge in opposition to efforts toward integration. In addition to fusion, fission must also be considered. Group boundaries are inherently unstable in any redistributive (i.e., constant sum) game. A subset of any particular group, motivated by either the redistribution of political rents to a smaller collectivity or non-material considerations, may redefine its identity in a way that no longer includes all members. One example is conflict between and among Aboriginal peoples and women's groups that have potentially overlapping membership.

Why does negative identity classify as a liberal theory? Liberalism is an atomistic worldview. It privileges universalism only insofar as it provides a standard set of protections against violations of basic human rights. Negative identity theory fits under the liberal banner because it identifies the lack of a sovereign founding event based on individual liberty as being the basic challenge to Canadian viability. Whether manifested in Quebec nationalism, the mobilization of Aboriginal peoples, Trudeau's ardent nationalism, or other social forces, various forms of collectivism seek to fill the identity gap but merely complicate matters because they add up to nothing coherent.

Systemism can be used to translate the preceding arguments into a causal map of constitutional evolution that can, in turn, be used to evaluate the degree of completeness and logical consistency of negative identity theory. But a few qualifications are in order. The figures in this chapter and the one that follows depart significantly from the relative simplicity of Figure 2.1. As a generic example, that figure includes precisely one instance of each type of linkage. By contrast, multiple linkages of each kind, along with feedback loops, are the norm in the diagrams that follow. Complexity is a natural property of anything that can qualify as theory in this domain; it is inherent in Canadian constitutional evolution, particularly during the period leading up to and from the *Charter*. Each figure begins with Confederation in 1867 and culminates in the *Constitution Act, 1982*, the *Charter*, and their aftermath. Solid lines in the figures represent linkages articulated by the theory in question. Broken lines stand for connections that, from the standpoint of rational reconstruction, are logically entailed by the theory. Although Figure 2.1 includes functional forms for each linkage, incorporating them in the figures that follow is beyond the scope of this exercise in the identification and assessment of theories about constitutional evolution because the field is not sufficiently advanced. Finally, none of the figures that follow will show how the Canadian system has influenced the international supersystem of which it is a part because that question, although interesting, is also beyond the scope of this study.

Figure 4.1 illustrates how cause and effect operate in the Canadian constitutional system according to negative identity theory. The story begins with an exogenous input from an external definition of political order that produces negative identity and a disposition toward collectivism. With the British Empire as the overseeing power, Confederation took place via the Charlottetown Conference and the *British North America Act* in 1867. These events occurred without the burst of energy that accompanies an internally generated founding event based on a separate sense of identity. (The United States is just one example of such a process, within which violence is not a necessary condition.) Although Confederation occurred peacefully – a point to be celebrated – Canada's origins took on a negative character by definition. The United States was born out of a revolution with an anti-statist and individualistic character; Canada came about as a negative response to these properties.

*Figure 4.1*

**Negative identity**

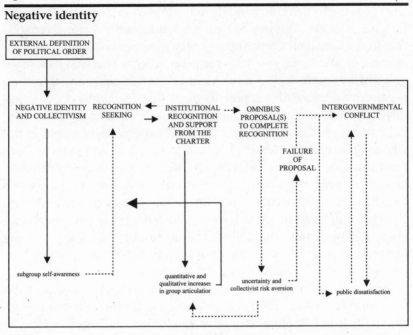

More than a simple fear of a US military invasion following the Civil War lay beneath this reality: Confederation was also an attempt to repel an invasion of ideas – in particular, uninhibited popular sovereignty (Lipset 1990, 1). The phrase "peace, order, and good government of Canada," from section 91 of the *Constitution Act, 1867*, sums up that mindset quite effectively. A definition of self in opposition to American values, along with a Tory-influenced collectivism, came into being. As Charlotte Gray (2000, 85) observes, "individualism has never been celebrated in Canada" and accolades are reserved for "collective virtues" such as peacekeeping, compassion for disaster victims, and the like.

Figure 4.1 continues with a macro-micro connection from negative identity and collectivism to subgroup self-awareness. This process takes place either instantly or gradually, depending on the group in question. For those of French descent in Quebec, the process can be traced back to before Confederation to the Conquest of New France in 1760. It would be more accurate to say that the process reinforced a pre-existing disposition among francophones toward collective consciousness. An understanding of Confederation as a pact between two peoples, with Quebec as the French entity and the other provinces standing for English Canada, persists to this day. For groups that have since gained recognition in the Canadian Constitution – such as minority-language groups, women, or Aboriginal peoples – the process began later and took place in a discontinuous way. Naomi Klein (2000, 32) offers an interesting perspective on these developments by casting Aboriginal peoples, immigrants, and women as the "refuseniks" of Canadian political history. Long stretches of neglect are punctuated by moments of refusal in the face of government attempts to exercise authority. Examples include Innu and Cree resistance to Hydro-Québec, the Mohawks and the Quebec government, and women from the National Action Committee and the Charlottetown Accord. From the perspective of negative identity theory, Confederation created and reinforced a tendency toward subgroup self-awareness. These processes unfolded more rapidly in some instances than in others, but they all resulted in more self-awareness among subnational collectivities over time.

Group self-awareness leads to recognition seeking (a micro-macro linkage) at the federal level. The broken line in Figure 4.1 acknowledges the implicit but essential nature of this linkage in negative identity theory. This process unfolded throughout the twentieth century and included struggles such as the Manitoba school question and women's suffrage. Collectivities of various kinds appealed to the federal and provincial governments for recognition in various forms. The means pursued included both electoral politics and action through the courts.

Accumulated effects of recognition seeking produced higher levels of political complexity in Canada. Consider, for example, the following assessment of federal programs, most notably in the Trudeau era and beyond, directed toward the promotion of minorities and women (Pal 1993b, 276): "[I]n many respects this mobilization went against the grain of 'normal' government, ran the risk of mobilizing too many groups to make too many demands, and was prone to so many administrative weaknesses that the programs were virtually impossible to wield effectively as clean instruments of state power." From the standpoint of negative identity theory, the net result of government encouragement of recognition seeking is a trend toward incoherence and divisive interactions. In sum, national identity is not a Lego-style structure that keeps on expanding. What, exactly, is supposed to hold the whole thing together?

These processes continue in the system until the next stage is reached: a macro-macro connection from recognition seeking at the federal level to institutional recognition and support from the *Charter*. This linkage occurred approximately during the Trudeau era in Canadian politics, up to and including patriation of the Constitution. The Trudeau government not only recognized various collectivities, it also provided them with financial assistance. The effects of this policy are represented in the figure as a macro-level feedback effect. The emphasis on ethnic and racial minorities, women, and language-based minorities in the *Charter* can be traced to Ottawa's ongoing effort to counter Quebec separatism and build an overarching national identity. Ottawa, in other words, helped these groups create infrastructure (Epp 1998).

The recognition of subgroups had a bifurcated effect. The first is represented by a macro-micro connection from institutional recognition and support to quantitative and qualitative increases in group articulation. Existing groups became more visible as a result of the government's encouragement, which might be called quantitative articulation, and new groups formed, which can be called qualitative articulation. Women's groups, to give an example of quantitative articulation, became active across a wider range of policy domains: "Action committees were structured to represent the constituencies of Native women, women with disabilities, and visible minority women and were allocated budgets [by the National Action Committee on the Status of Women] so that they might work more effectively" (Pal 1993b, 230). As for the qualitative articulation of new groups, a summary of those seeking section 15 recognition speaks volumes (Manfredi 2001, 115): "Among the groups involved in this process have been the Aboriginal Women's Council, the Canadian Association of Sexual Assault Centres, the Canadian Civil Liberties Association (CCLA), the Canadian Disability Rights Council (CDRC), the Canadian Jewish Congress (CJC), the Charter Committee on Poverty Issues, the Coalition of Provincial Organizations of the Handicapped (COPOH), the DisAbled Women's Network Canada, Equality for Gays and Lesbians Everywhere (EGALE), the National Action Committee on the Status of Women (NAC) and the Native Women's Association of Canada (NWAC)." The list shows a clear proliferation of interests far and beyond those designated during the federal government's initial forays into granting status. Some, such as the NWAC, combine pre-existing categories, while others, such as EGALE, introduce new social groupings altogether.

Given these developments, a micro-macro linkage emerged from the quantitative and qualitative increases in group articulation to additional recognition seeking. This connection, as the figure reveals, took the form of a feedback loop that ultimately reinforced, at the macro level, institutional recognition seeking and support. As the political system became more penetrated by interests and bargaining increased in complexity, the result was another macro-macro linkage – this time from institutional recognition and support to an omnibus proposal to complete recognition. The broken line in the figure indicates that this macro-macro connection is implicit in negative identity theory. The omnibus proposal was the natural outcome of pressure from status-seeking collectivities, some of whom were and are in competition with one another and the state for influence. Most notably, the theory implies that we should expect powerful but still excluded collectivities with a territorial base to get tough and demand renewed federal efforts to achieve recognition. The anticipated response might be a one-time affair or a series of major initiatives. As a theory, negative identity does not preclude the emergence of various federal tactics in response to ongoing and possibly time-sensitive pressures. The federal strategy, however, is dictated by the overall situation: some change is needed to complete a process that can be expected to become more conflict-prone and expensive with time and that, because of the subjective self-designation of groups, has no natural point of termination. Thus, a proposal or series of them, at the constitutional level, is to be expected.

Once the proposal is developed, a macro-micro linkage from the proposal to uncertainty and collectivist risk aversion will take place. This reaction among the public should be expected because of the very nature of the system itself. Socio-political conservativism – manifested in uncertainty and a tendency toward self-criticism (Lipset 1990, 67) – and concerns about unbridled popular sovereignty combine to dispose the polity against accepting any major proposal. Adding to this difficulty is a micro-level property that by now is well in place, namely, a micro-micro feedback loop toward quantitative and qualitative increases in group articulation, which in turn leads to recognition seeking at the system level from still more groups. Each of these connections is represented by a broken line that traces its essential but implicit role in the theory. The same is true of the remaining linkages, which complete the story of attempted constitutional revision.

Accumulated uncertainty and collectivist risk aversion at the micro level led to failure of the proposal at the macro level. Consider where some of the most prominent complaints against the ill-fated Charlotte-town Accord came from. The National Organization of Immigrant and Visible Minority Women expressed concerns about racial equality, the Coalition of Provincial Organizations of the Handicapped and Canadian Disability Rights Council wanted explicit recognition, and the Canadian Ethnocultural Council claimed that the accord ignored ethnic and racial minorities (Lusztig 1994, 768). As these groups and others criticized the Charlottetown Accord, the results of the long-term process of expanding group self-awareness and institutional recognition became clear: a polity made up of a dense network of collectivities with no overarching identity and a disposition to reject movement in any direction that might threaten their interests.

Consider, in that sense, the following summary of what happened to the Charlottetown Accord (Dobrowolsky 2000, 131-32):

> This document was a mishmash with, if not something for everyone to condone, certainly something for everyone to condemn. Reaction was swift and mostly negative. For example, Aboriginal leaders were vehemently opposed to the proposals, especially the one that called for Native self-government only in ten years.[2] They demanded recognition of their inherent right to self-government and less delay. Labour organizations and environmental groups denounced the property rights proposals and demanded a social charter. Gay and lesbian organizations criticized the Canada Clause. Most progressive social movements feared that the recommendations would negatively alter social programs and many pointed to parallels with the Accord on this issue.

Reactions such as these would likely hold true not only for the Charlottetown Accord but also for *any* proposal, abstract or real, that might develop in the future. Key *Charter* and aspiring *Charter* groups can be expected to scrutinize and find fault with details. In turn, the mass public, confronted with increasingly complex proposals for integration and inundated with infighting from recipients of recognition and would-be members of the constitutional club, will likely refrain from supporting whatever process of adjudication – referendum or otherwise – is in place. This happened with the Charlottetown Accord even though it had the unanimous support of the federal and provincial governments and many political elites.

The proposal's failure leads naturally, as a macro-micro linkage, to public dissatisfaction with the process as a whole. Charlottetown, for instance, looked more like "constitutional horse trading" among elites than an attempt to defend individuals against the state (Gairdner 1994, 23). But a macro-macro link also connects the proposal's failure to intergovernmental conflict. The basis of the conflict is competing attempts to define the nation's direction, which the proposal, negotiations over it, and its failure represented.

Micro-macro and macro-micro feedback loops that link public dissatisfaction to intergovernmental conflict are the final connections in the figure. The aftermath of the Charlottetown Accord, for example, included a self-proclaimed victory for pro-*Charter* interest groups and helped to build momentum toward a Quebec referendum. It is difficult not to interpret the *Charter* as a document that embraces some collective rights as it implicitly excludes others. These excluded groups will likely lobby for change, those already in the driver's seat will likely fiercely defend the status quo, and federal and provincial governments will continue to fight over constitutional powers.

How does negative identity fare when it is held up to the criteria of equilibrium analysis? According to Todd Sandler (2001), existence is the first criterion, and as the "big picture" in Figure 4.1 shows, negative identity theory satisfies it. The equilibrium is one of conflict within the boundaries of Confederation, although not without the risk of matters getting out of control. In other words, instability in the system is not sufficient to overthrow the existing constitutional order. The equilibrium is a product of accumulating social capital via subgroup formation in the absence of an affirmative founding event. In the terms made popular by Robert Putnam (2000) and discussed in Chapter 3, bonding groups have accumulated in number and density, that is, they have acquired a degree of cohesion over time. This micro process is in line with the macro imperatives offered by the *Charter*. The activated collectivities put into motion a process that culminates in a stalemate between and among a dissatisfied public and the provincial and federal governments. In a sense, the *Charter* can be seen as the exclamation point on the sentence that tells the story of increasing negative social capital through incremental and increasingly constitutionalized political conflict.

The second criterion is stability. Does the system return to equilibrium after a disturbance? There is strong evidence that the answer is yes. Consider the fate of the Meech Lake and Charlottetown accords, along with the Quebec Referendum of 1995 – three intense events that occurred in close proximity. All three of these efforts to bring about large-scale change failed to overturn the status quo of the constitutional Cold War.

The political processes that led to the *Charter* and the major constitutional initiatives that followed are true to the Canadian traditions of collectivism and incrementalism. Although the *Charter* itself may look like a major departure from the status quo, negative identity theory makes the case that it is really a reinforcement of political trends that go back a long way. A constitutional system in which collectivities accumulate and exert pressure for recognition within the framework institutionalized by the *Constitution Act, 1982* and the *Charter* already seems to have proven staying power. Although it is persistent in that sense, the equilibrium is pervaded by conflict and, therefore, unstable, but within existing system bounds.

Normative desirability, the third and final criterion, is the most difficult to assess. Tendencies in the Canadian political system toward accumulating social capital received reinforcement from the *Charter*. However, in an effort to promote the interests of women and minorities – which were not labelled social capital at the time but clearly fell within that description – the Trudeau government and its allies missed the mark. The *Charter*'s explicit recognition of some groups but not others – the latter including geographic entities such as Quebec – encouraged one form of social capital as it impeded another. Bonding is enhanced, but there is no accompanying increase in bridging.

Theories about the effects of social capital, which are summarized in Chapter 3, offer a straightforward account of what to expect. The *Charter* offers recognition to groups that by definition are exclusive: a person can change his or her gender or ethnicity or language identification only through gradual and difficult processes. (Whether they would ever want to, or are compelled to do so, is an obvious complication worth noting.) Consequently, we can expect a decline in generalized trust as interest groups attempt to protect or expand their turf at the expense of others. The intense conflicts over the Meech Lake and Charlottetown accords played out in just this way, particularly in the case of the latter. Rejection of the Charlottetown Accord was so overwhelming that it was as if people were casting their ballot in support of an anti-referendum. More than anything else, a lack of trust toward elites and interest groups permeated the pattern of negative voting throughout the country.

Sandler (2001, 134) provides an example from the economic realm that helps to explain, from the standpoint of negative identity theory, what went wrong with the Canadian process of constitutional revision. The explanation takes into account the role played by unintended consequences. In 1991 the US Congress passed a yacht tax, that is, a special tax on expensive pleasure boats. Redistribution of wealth from the rich to the poor was the intended goal, but things worked out differently. Although proponents of a general-equilibrium outlook would have advised those who supported the tax to consider the full range of potential effects in a complex, multi-market economy, those advocating the tax failed to do so. The new measure ended up causing a significant drop in demand for pleasure boats and a steep decline in sales. Workers building the boats, who tended not to be highly paid, absorbed the brunt of the damage. The rich simply bought other luxury goods instead.

This example helps to illustrate the unintended consequences of the *Charter's* conferment of constitutional status on exclusionary groups. Although policy makers hoped to build national identity in an incremental way and undermine centrifugal forces at the provincial level, enhanced social capital, in the absence of bridging social capital, resulted in (1) competition for constitutional status, (2) reduced trust in the political system, and (3) higher levels of dissatisfaction among those shut out of the new club. In sum, negative identity theory points to a normatively undesirable constitutional equilibrium. The equilibrium is relatively predictable but also inherently unstable, and it will likely reinforce tendencies toward a Tower of Babel with regard to the subject of national purpose.[3]

## Megapolitics

Megapolitics is a theory that emphasizes the destructive effects of major constitutional initiatives. Attempts to reform the Canadian system writ large are labelled mega-constitutional politics (Russell 1991a, 1991d) and include events such as the negotiations leading up to constitutional packages such as the Meech Lake Accord and ongoing discussions among politicians, interest-group representatives, media spokespeople, and other participants about how national identity should be constitutionalized. The basic insight of megapolitics theory is that the act of seeking constitutional revision itself, when carried on publicly and through omnibus proposals, contributes to the very result it is intended to avert – further national unravelling.[4] Even before the overwhelming failure of the Charlottetown Accord, Peter Russell (1991a, 709; 1991d, 75) asserted that megapolitics had "frustrated, demoralized and yes, even bored our people" (see also Mulroney 2007, 914). By the time of Charlottetown, he summed things up as follows (Russell 2004, 177; see also Russell 1993b, 36, and Gibbins and Laforest 1998a, 1998b, 2): "Canada certainly owned the record for the sheer volume of constitutional talk."

If national behaviour since 1993 is any indication, Russell had a good sense of what many Canadians, especially those outside of Quebec, wanted, namely, a break from megapolitics over the Constitution. However, the pernicious dynamic introduced by megapolitics ensures that the appetite for destruction merely goes into abeyance. It does not disappear.

Megapolitics theory predicts that higher levels of conflict will evolve within the system. Whatever may happen, be it Confederation continuing in some form or one or more secessions, the legacy of megapolitics will be one of conflict and a reduced level of trust among the parties involved. The dialogue concerning concessions to either territorial interests (i.e., provinces) or non-territorial subgroups (e.g., Aboriginal peoples) will encourage more of the same. This will continue even in the case of groups that do receive most or even all of what they are asking for at a given time.

The constitutional process of 1982 alone was enough to establish that expectation within the system. For example, in the lead up to the referendum on the Charlottetown Accord, complaints proliferated. The Canadian Ethnocultural Council, which represented thirty-seven ethnic groups, objected to being left off the list. Ottawa responded by adding multiculturalism to the list of constitutionally protected entities, but the disabled then complained – and so on. The exasperation that Russell (1992, 204) felt after telling this story is clear: "If the disabled had been included, homosexuals, seniors, juniors, and Lord knows who else would complain about their exclusion."[5] Peter Meekison (1992, 78) sums up the problematic nature of this dynamic: "Everything cannot be discussed at once and everything cannot, and should not, be in the constitution. We are better off leaving things out and leaving them to the political process than inserting them into the constitution. The constitution cannot solve all of our problems." From the standpoint of adherents of megapolitics, constitutional packaging is addictive. It is also dangerous. There is a built-in temptation to bundle together excluded interests and recognize them in some way. Issues related to Quebec's status, self-government for Aboriginal peoples, and Senate reform (i.e., the western agenda) will not go away: "Sooner or later we will have to start down the path of constitutional reform again" (Beatty 1993, 53). Megapolitics can be expected to take a cyclical form for these reasons. But the side effects, which include resistance to change by those already recognized and generation of new demands for status, render the process highly unlikely to succeed.

One final point in this overview of megapolitics concerns its classification. It is easy to see group-related concerns in Russell's major expositions. He is not without sympathy when it comes to recognizing Aboriginal peoples or accommodating Quebec (Russell 2004). However, the key consideration in classifying a theory within a paradigm is central tendency. Russell's theory, which is a by-product of his critique of large-scale constitutional initiatives, is fundamentally liberal. It focuses primarily on how Canadians as individual citizens are harmed by the confrontation politics embedded in megapolitics. Megapolitics, for this reason in particular, falls within the liberal paradigm.

How, then, does the constitutional system function – or, rather, malfunction – according to the theory of megapolitics? Figure 4.2 shows the cycle of megapolitics in generic terms. The process begins with an exogenous force. Canadians, according to the theory, are not a self-governing people. As Russell (1991e, 94) observes, "We never *made* our constitution in any way." Canadians therefore are not sovereign in the same sense as Americans or others with a true founding event based on a micro-level process, that is, a process that begins with the people and then influences the government. Instead, the origins of Canada are in the *British North America Act* and macro-level, elite bargaining. Thus, the first connection in the figure extends from the external definition of the political order to the absence of a sovereign founding event at the macro level. Within megapolitics theory, absence of a sovereign founding event helps to explain the pernicious and ultimately self-defeating process of constitutional revision.

Absence of a sovereign founding event compels the federal government to develop a proposal to bring home the Constitution (macro-macro). The result is the *Constitution Act, 1982* and the *Charter of Rights and Freedoms*.[6] The existence of a "made in Canada" Constitution, however, creates another macro-macro linkage to one or more omnibus proposals to improve or complete the founding event of the country. Within megapolitics theory the lack of a founding act or myth is an ever-present factor, but it is understood that other, more immediate variables will also motivate proposals for the revision of the constitutional order that come about in episodic ways. The omnibus proposal produces both macro-macro and macro-micro effects. At the macro-macro level, consideration of the proposal results in a lack of focus on more fundamental problems, most notably those of an economic nature. This could be said of both the lead up to and aftermath of the proposal. As Russell (1991b, 67; see also 2004, 164) observes, "our absorption in

*Figure 4.2*

**Megapolitics**

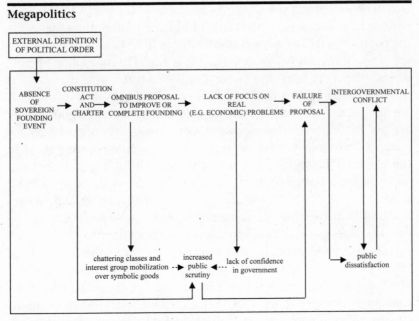

constitutional politics will prevent us from tackling the serious economic and environmental problems that now confront Canada." This oversight is a product of the system's focus on redistribution rather than the creation of wealth. The nature of constitution making as a vocation guarantees this emphasis. Constitutional status is indivisible and inherently competitive. In sum, it is a zero-sum game.

At the macro-micro level, the omnibus proposal produces extensive and intense reaction from the chattering classes, that is, intellectuals, politicians, opinion-group leaders. Discussion intensifies over symbolic goods – constitutional recognition in some form or another (Russell 1991e, 90). The public can naturally be expected to react with increasing scrutiny. This is as true of the successful initiative that brought home the Constitution in 1982 as it is of the failed packages that followed. Moreover, note in the figure the indirect, long-range macro-micro effect of the *Charter* itself on increased public attention to the process of constitutional change.

Public attention to constitutional revision is reinforced through two further stages of effects: one macro-micro and one micro-micro. The first is produced by the relative neglect of economic issues. This leads to a lack of confidence in government – why should the public trust leaders who seem absorbed with basic issues of identity rather than managing the country well? The second effect extends from lack of confidence to greater public scrutiny (Pocklington 1991, 42): "The inscription of one's rights – the more often the better – in the constitutional document is the indispensable sign that one is taken seriously. Even if one's rights are not *violated*, it is still an unacceptable affront to one's dignity if they are not *publically re-acknowledged* at every reasonable opportunity." A parallel micro-micro effect is produced by infighting among those in the know – if they cannot agree, why should the public put its stamp of approval on a possibly transforming constitutional initiative? Russell (1991a, 1991d, 1991e, 1993b) does not include these micro-micro connections in his analysis of megapolitics. Each, however, is implied by the other linkages and thus appears as a broken line.

From increased public attention comes failure of the proposal – a micro-macro connection. The difference between the *Constitution Act, 1982* and the *Charter,* on the one hand, and later failed proposals, on the other, comes into bold relief. Established interests represented in the *Charter* are strong enough to fend off further efforts toward revision. Feminist groups, for example, played a key role in defeating both the Meech Lake and Charlottetown accords. This behaviour suggests that interest groups are "risk averse when assessing the value of future gains against the possibility of losing what has already been achieved" (Manfredi 2001, 47). Most notably, any representation of the main excluded territorial interest – Quebec – is virtually a sufficient condition for failure.

The process continues when the proposal's failure leads (in a macro-macro linkage) to intergovernmental conflict. There is no reason to expect the excluded territorial interests simply to pack up and go home. Although Quebec might be the most prominent interest in this context, the lack of institutional reform can be expected to lead to conflict between the federal and western provinces while other provinces may be drawn into conflict over the distribution of rents from natural resources and similar matters. All of this is encouraged by the redistributive mindset that accompanies increasingly constitutionalized politics. The theory anticipates a similar macro-micro effect as the losers of the proposal stage are reminded of their exclusion and the public is frustrated by yet another round of talks with no end in sight. The final connections displayed are micro-macro and macro-micro. Intergovernmental conflict and public dissatisfaction reinforce each other, as would be expected from a redistributive political discourse.

Consider the federal government's effort to placate Quebec, the most obvious loser after the defeat of the Charlottetown Accord in 1992. Quebec responded with the referendum of 1995, which resulted in a very close call indeed (50.6 no and 49.4 yes, if uncounted ballots, which amounted to about 2 percent of the votes cast, are apportioned to the two sides). Opinion data for that difficult time bears out the intensity of dissatisfaction in Quebec (Denis 1996, 43): "A post-referendum Sondagem poll found that Quebecers expect a lot from Ottawa if they are to remain in the federation: 63 percent want Québec to control all tax collection, 85 percent want a transfer of such powers as communications and labour-force training, 78 percent want recognition of the distinct society status, and 73 percent want a constitutional veto." The Chrétien government almost immediately passed a motion in the House of Commons to recognize Quebec as a distinct society, and a year later it gave Quebec a veto on constitutional amendments via the *Constitutional Veto Act* (Archer et al. 2002, 117). Attempts to conciliate Quebec, however, did not dissipate conflict at its most basic level. If anything, federal actions made the West feel more ignored than ever.

And, as is predicted by megapolitics theory, these conciliatory measures did not close the books on constitutional demands from Quebec. The special recognition of Quebec did not translate into constitutional status, as it did for women, Aboriginal peoples, minority language groups, and others who had obtained either section 15 or other status. In 1999 conflict between Ottawa and Quebec City once again escalated and resulted in dueling bills on the legalities of separation from Canada. This strife followed the Supreme Court of Canada's judgment in *Reference re Secession of Quebec* in 1998 – a ruling that pleased neither side in the struggle over Quebec's place in Confederation. Although Quebec could not make a unilateral declaration of independence, the Court ruled that Canada would have to engage in good faith negotiations regarding separation if a referendum with an unambiguously worded question produced a vote in favour of secession – a qualification triggered by the vaguely worded questions posed to the Quebec electorate in 1980 and 1995.

Ottawa's Clarity Bill, passed soon after the Supreme Court's ruling, required a clear majority and an unambiguous question for any future referendum. Quebec, in response, passed Bill 99, which repudiated Ottawa's authority on such matters and reaffirmed "the right of the Québec people to self-determination" (quoted in Archer et al. 2002, 121). Thus, intergovernmental conflict continued as Quebec and the other provinces continued to have opposing views on the main issues.

Another aspect of intergovernmental conflict, also anticipated by megapolitics theory, was revealed following the Calgary Declaration of 1997, by which the First Ministers stated that if the power to amend the Constitution is granted to one or more provinces, it must be extended to all. The provinces hoped to push Ottawa off the path to special recognition for Quebec. They responded to Ottawa's concessions to Quebec by asking for matching status. It is interesting to note that Keith Archer and colleagues (2002, 119) expressed the opinion that the Calgary Declaration's prospect as a constitutional initiative was not good at all. Public opinion outside of Quebec still tends to oppose special status for the province. Even the brief Calgary Declaration ran into immediate criticism from Aboriginal groups (Young 1999, 121). In sum, support for the *Charter* virtually guarantees a high level of scrutiny and even suspicion concerning future constitutional package deals that might alter its effect. And intergovernmental conflict has occurred in the last decade over equalization, health care, and fiscal imbalance. Lack of financial ability to cover costs of programs normally under provincial control has generated increasingly loud complaints from the premiers. Ottawa responded in 2004 with an accord on health care, for instance, which effectively moved into provincial jurisdiction in a more notable way than in the past. Conflict within executive federalism over these issues persists to this day. All of this lends support to megapolitics as a theory of constitutional evolution.

How does megapolitics fare when held up to the criteria of equilibrium analysis? Existence is the first aspect to consider. Megapolitics theory identifies an equilibrium that consists of constitutional conflict in cycles of varying amplitude and periodicity – but within boundaries set by the constitutional order. Once a Canadian-derived founding event of some kind is in place, waves of constitutional strife can be anticipated at varying intervals and with different degrees of intensity. The era of the *Constitution Act, 1982* and the *Charter*, along with the Meech Lake and Charlottetown accords, stands out as one with short cycles and high levels of conflict. The period since then has been characterized by more elongated and lower intensity conflicts and can be expected to do so according to the logic of megapolitics. Constitutional packages, successful or not, create an appetite for further reform that never entirely goes away. Negative bonding rather than positive bridging social capital accumulates, which, in turn, ensures a new cycle of conflict.

What about stability? Megapolitics theory predicts that the equilibrium will have a minimal level of stability. Pressure for constitutional reform resumed soon after the decline and fall of the Charlottetown Accord. Aboriginal peoples demanded self-governance (i.e., governance beyond administrative control with imposed orders), the West called for institutional changes that would enhance regional representation, and Quebec nationalists held a referendum on sovereignty (Archer et al. 2002, 115; see also Russell 2004, 272). Recognized interests joined those still excluded and made new demands for constitutional renewal. Normatively speaking, what is the anticipated result of this ongoing pressure?

The equilibrium that megapolitics identifies is less than appealing. Cyclical pressure from both non-territorial, status-seeking groups and provinces does not bode well for either social capital or generalized trust. Instead, the quest for package deals to revise the *Constitution Act, 1982* will merely aggravate underlying perceptions of exclusion. These enterprises, no matter how carefully conceived, are unlikely to meet with success in the face of opposition from established interests. The cleavages that exist are between bonding rather than bridging groups. Rounds of intense competition between them reinforce cohesion within the bonding groups that seek to obtain, protect, or enhance constitutional status. The process, as outlined by megapolitics theory, also increases social distance between these groups. Even worse, there is nothing to suggest that this competition encourages the emergence of bridging groups.

Levels of public trust are likely to be lowered each and every time that constitutional megapolitics ensues. Tupper (1991, 27) poses interesting questions in that regard: "[W]ho is to say that a better informed citizenry will necessarily be more tolerant? More importantly, is it not possible that Canadians, armed with greater understanding of each other's demands, will become more stubborn and less willing to compromise?" Unfortunately, the answers to both of these questions seem to be other than those hoped for by advocates of constitutional reform. Constitutional packages, successful or not, eat away at the fabric of society by setting the stage for defeats that feel permanent to those who perceive themselves in a losing role. Negative rather than positive social capital will accumulate and, in turn, lower levels of trust. Peter Russell (1991d, 75; see also Blakeney 1991, 66) issued a dramatic warning even before the Charlottetown Accord had come and gone: "Constitutional politics are extraordinarily dangerous, and they are likely to pull this country apart." The warning has roots that perhaps go back as far as Machiavelli, who made similar warnings regarding the Italian city-states of centuries ago.

## Institutional Imbalance

Institutional imbalance theory puts forward the idea that the Canadian system of government went in the wrong direction with the advent of the *Charter*. Its proponents argue that subsequent decades of seemingly endless conflict over the Constitution are a direct product of the contents of the *Charter* itself. Popular as it may be with the general public, the *Charter* created an imbalance between the legislative and judicial branches of government: "With this [pro-*Charter*] image in mind, it was natural that people trusted judges to protect their freedoms and came to see the charter as a democratic weapon against arbitrary government. Unfortunately, the inspiring image was fanciful; it had about as convincing a likeness to real life as a child's book of fairytales" (Milne 1991, 301). In particular, the Supreme Court of Canada no longer plays a restrained role in interpreting laws: the power of the Court overawes that of Parliament and exacerbates the very problems it claims to ameliorate or solve with its rulings.

This unfortunate situation can be explained by the specific contents of the *Charter*: "The existence of liberal standing rules under the Charter makes litigation easier and multiplies whatever anti-democratic tendencies the document might contain" (Manfredi 1993, 35; see also Martin 1991, 122, 123). Since the *Charter* is entrenched in the Constitution, "attention must be paid to the manner in which judges interpret and apply this document of open-ended rights subject to broad judicial construction" (Manfredi 1993, 370). The key question asked in institutional imbalance theory is whether it is in the national interest to have judges legislating from the bench, that is, striking down laws in large numbers and even reading provisions into existing law. The answer, from the standpoint of institutional imbalance theory, is no.

Judicial activism as a by-product of the *Charter* is seen as a destructive force within Confederation. Consider the following: between 1867 to 1982 there were fifteen hundred constitutional cases that came before the courts; in the eight years that followed the *Charter*, that figure rose to ten thousand (Milne 1991, 301). Even if the vast majority of these cases went nowhere, the escalation in court activity represents a major and even anti-democratic shift in political culture. The pernicious side effects of the *Charter* are summed up by F.L. Morton and Rainer Knopff (2000, 15): the *Charter*'s equality rights "have been read to prohibit not just clearly discriminatory laws, but also laws that, precisely because they treat everyone the same, have a disparate impact on some groups, an interpretation whose breadth again surpasses that of its American counterpart ... Policymaking is judicialized, legalized, and conducted in the vernacular of rights talk to a greater extent than ever before. Therein lies the Charter revolution." The revolution's basic nature is antidemocratic: power over policy is redistributed from democratically elected officials to unelected judges. Consider the remarks of former prime minister Brian Mulroney (2007, 510): "The 1982 Trudeau amendment was to Americanize the country as never before, transferring to the judiciary from Parliament the ultimate decision-making power in sensitive questions of public policy." The description offered by Allan Hutchinson (1995, 15) is even more colourful: "[T]he enactment of the Charter of Rights and Freedoms in 1982 was a unilateral Canadian confirmation of a free-trade agreement in constitutional arrangements and liberal aspirations."

Anthony Peacock (2002, 19) observes that judicial rationalism, in which the *Charter*-empowered Supreme Court engages in social engineering from the bench, is not a promising path to follow. The Court assumes "a knowledge of moral, social, and political phenomena that [it] cannot, with its limited resources and capacities, possess" (Peacock 2002, 19). This level of judicial activism in a constitutional order can bring nothing but instability and conflict – legal precedents accumulate and make it increasingly difficult for legislators to know what is feasible.

The public can be expected to become alienated from a political system that is constrained so frequently from implementing its wishes. Consider the conclusion reached from a comparative analysis of Canada, Israel, New Zealand, and South Africa (Hirschl 2004, 187): "[A]n excessive reliance on courts to determine contentious issues such as a polity's *raison d'etre* may undermine the very essence of democratic politics as an enterprise involving a relatively open, at times controversial, but arguably informed and accountable deliberation by elected representatives" (see also Toews 2003, 350). In particular, elected politicians may become wary of legislating in potentially sensitive areas. This creates an even greater imbalance in favour of the courts via self-censorship among elected officials.

Canada's institutional revolution, as just described, brings together several political actors in an ongoing assault on democratic processes.

Thus a key concept in the theory of institutional imbalance is the Court Party, a faction that includes judges, interest groups, and members of the knowledge class who favour social engineering consistent with further entrenchment of the collective rights found in the *Charter* (Knopff and Morton 1996, 63, 70; Morton and Knopff 2000; see also Brodie 2001). The Court Party's unconstrained sense of what can be achieved by a well-placed vanguard of leaders in society is a product of its elitism and lack of identification with Canadians as a whole. Academics, in particular, should be chastised "for their complicity in the misguided efforts to justify and encourage the increasing tendency to litigate lasting and effective social change" (Hutchinson 1995, 25).

If the argument is taken a step further, it can be asserted that the political system is distorted because even *inaction* by elected officials or bureaucrats can be taken as a sign of hostility to favoured – that is, *Charter*-based – groups (Knopff and Morton 1996, 76). Evidence suggests that the Court cultivated interest groups as supporters for its activism; for example, almost all applications for leave to intervene began to be granted in the *Charter* era (Brodie 2001). The result of these and other forms of distortion created by the court system in the post-*Charter* era is institutional imbalance.

How, then, does the constitutional system operate from the standpoint of institutional imbalance theory? Figure 4.3 begins with an exogenous input. The *BNA Act* of 1867 provides external definition for the political order. The result is legislative supremacy from the time of Confederation onward. A macro-macro linkage occurs: legislative supremacy produces collectivist – in this context, regional – mobilization. Over the course of decades, western alienation and especially Quebec nationalism emerge in response to the perceived excess power of the federal government. When the Liberal Party achieves near-hegemonic status as the governing party in federal politics throughout the twentieth century, western leaders at the provincial level play the anti-Ottawa card to combat what they see as central Canadian dominance and a lack of responsiveness to their concerns. Meanwhile, the Quiet Revolution and the rise to power of the separatist Parti Québécois put pressure on succeeding governments in Ottawa to consider constitutional reform as the path to national unity. These political processes culminate in the macro-macro connection from collectivist mobilization to adoption of the *Charter of Rights and Freedoms*.

The adoption of the *Charter* leads to the redistribution of power to the judicial branch (also a macro-macro linkage). This linkage is easy to trace

*Figure 4.3*

**Institutional imbalance**

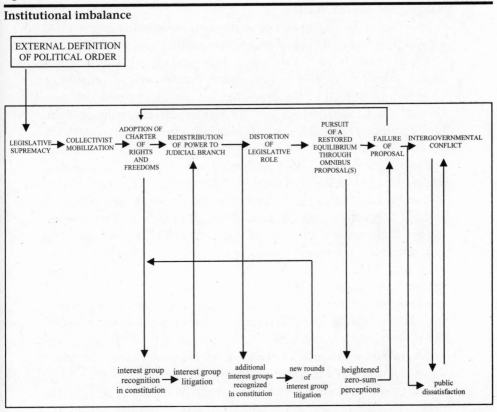

because the *Charter* contains open-ended clauses about both individual and collective rights, none of which can be followed without clarification from the judiciary. While it is true that Canada had a *Bill of Rights* prior to the *Charter*, it applied only to the federal government and lacked the politically charged content of the later document. Thus, a greater role for the court system is the necessary result of a document such as the *Charter*. The fact that governments had a grace period of a full three years to revoke or rewrite legislation to achieve compliance with section 15 of the *Charter* is revealing in and of itself. (The remainder of the *Charter* applied immediately upon promulgation in April 1982.) The federal government also knew that the provinces needed time to fix laws that were outdated for reasons other than the *Charter*. From Ottawa's point of view, the *Charter* would refashion politics and even national culture in ways that would undermine rival regionally oriented, decentralizing visions of Canada.

Adoption of the *Charter* also generates a macro-micro linkage to interest group recognition in the Constitution. Collective rights are granted an explicit place in the Constitution when women, minority language groups, ethnic minorities, and Aboriginal peoples receive recognition. Litigation from each of the preceding interest groups followed soon thereafter and had a clear effect: "[T]he first 16 years of Charter-of-Rights Jurisprudence (1982-1998) saw the Court ruling in favour of rights claimants in 125 of 373 Charter cases and striking down 58 statutes (31 federal and 27 provincial)."[7] Although only a minority of claims succeeded, a ratchet effect is at work: victories by rights claimants are institutionalized while defeats are not. Nothing prevents further appeals, which are perhaps timed strategically to take advantage of the changing composition of the Court or shifts in public opinion that enhance prospects for a more favourable outcome. Statistics from Christopher Manfredi's (2005) work on feminist court activity, which are discussed in Chapter 3, reveal the tactical element in rights claims.

Interest group litigation also leads to the redistribution of power to the judicial branch. This micro-macro linkage reinforces the institutional power shift created by the *Charter* per se, that is, it favours a more active and efficacious judiciary. Court decisions, which frequently favour rights claimants, add to the momentum.

A macro-micro linkage then follows, from the enhanced power of the judiciary to the recognition of additional groups in the Constitution. Not all groups seeking recognition via section 15 succeeded during the framing of the *Charter*, and "this failure only moved the quest for constitutional recognition into the micro-level arena of litigation" (Manfredi 2001, 115). Consider the list of groups (provided earlier in this chapter, i.e., from Manfredi 2001, 115) that pursued recognition through the courts in later waves of cases based on the quest for equality. These groups met with enough success to ensure future efforts. Thus, another micro-micro linkage is created that extends from the recognition of additional collectivities in the Constitution to new rounds of interest group litigation.

Even if all potential groups achieve recognition in the Constitution some day, previous winners can still come back for even higher levels of status. Litigation expands qualitatively and quantitatively and has a micro-macro feedback effect as new rounds of interest group litigation lead to the further redistribution of power to the judicial branch.

Depending on the point of view adopted, this feedback could be labelled either a vicious circle or virtuous cycle. From the perspective of institutional imbalance theory, the choice is obvious.

Advocates of institutional imbalance theory draw attention to a disturbing macro-macro connection between enhanced judicial power and the distortion of the legislative role. One problem is that, unlike the legislature, which has extensive staff and related resources that can be devoted to research, the courts cannot engage in the social and political inquiry that is required to assess status accurately. Judges have to sift through considerable amounts of evidence about the geneaological, sociological, political, economic, and even psychological interactions among diverse groups (Peacock 2002). The natural result of the need to cope with such an intimidating mountain of data is to develop a shorthand of some kind – one that satisfies rather than optimizes the requirement of the process (Simon 1978). Efficiency, in particular, becomes a concern: remedies are mandated by the courts without any concern for the financial burdens imposed on governments that are forced to comply. Governments, in turn, may produce benefits for members of a given interest group but comparatively high costs for citizens in general (Manfredi 2001, 154). It is therefore hard to imagine that the long-term implications of the Supreme Court usurping a role that is more appropriate for legislatures will be positive.

Another distortion concerns the "reading in" of clauses by the Supreme Court, particularly through its rulings. The members of the Court are either impatient with or simply opposed to legislative incrementalism and iterated bargaining (Rush 2002). Affirmative remedies are not at all unusual in *Charter*-related decisions (Morton and Knopff 2000, 15; Manfredi 2001, 107). As a result, legislatures are not able to experiment with the gradual recognition of some groups and not others (especially if the latter happen to be favoured by the Court). As Mark Rush (2002) points out, because the legislatures do not know whether a particular group will obtain the Court's favour, the process of passing laws is distorted from the outset by so-called *Charter*-proofing.

Legalized politics, as described above, produce a macro-macro connection from distortion of the legislative role to pursuit of a restored equilibrium through an omnibus proposal. When the legislative system is rendered subordinate to the judiciary, the federal government can no longer provide the country with an overall direction. Pressure builds on the federal government to propose a comprehensive settlement to reduce the instability and conflict caused by the actions of the Court Party.[8]

Consider, for example, Robert Martin's (2003) assessment of the Charlottetown Accord. It represented an effort to address the wide range of grievances expressed during the Meech debate but without resolving – and perhaps even aggravating – the underlying causes. In other words, omnibus proposals should be expected in the post-*Charter* era because legislation will not work – groups seeking status cannot all be satisfied, or even known, at once or at any given time – and the demands from various directions continue to build pressure on the system. Moreover, some claims may be in direct or at least potential conflict with one another. The most obvious example is Quebec versus a host of non-territorial interests.

Although an omnibus proposal can be put forward, its prospects for success are not good and lead to (through a macro-micro linkage) heightened zero-sum perceptions. Groups can be expected, because of the inherently redistributive nature of status as a commodity, to end up in conflict with one another over (1) perceptions of a hierarchy among the groups recognized and (2) the addition of new groups (Brodie 1993, 1996, 263, 267). These problems became apparent, to give but one example, during debates about the Charlottetown Accord. Feminist groups expressed concerns about whether inclusion of Quebec as a distinct society within the so-called Canada Clause would compete with recognition of women in sections 15 and 28. It is possible that the accord, in an overall sense, was regarded as an attempt to develop a hierarchy of status in which women would lose hard-fought gains. Russell (2004, 181) views the articulation of instruments such as the Canada Clause as an "impossible task of symbolic engineering."

Micro-level strife feeds back into the macro level when zero-sum conflict leads to failure of the proposal. Russell (2004, 226) expresses the problem vividly: "The Charlottetown Accord was defeated because, outside Quebec, it was perceived as giving Quebec too much, while inside Quebec it was perceived as not giving Quebec enough." Sovereignty, in other words, reared its ugly head as a zero-sum issue.

Game theorists have demonstrated formally that no zero-sum game has a stable solution – it is always possible to reallocate resources to upset the existing agreement about their distribution. Omnibus proposals in the *Charter* era seem to reflect the truth of this claim, as institutional imbalance theory predicts. Consider the prospects for the Charlottetown Accord's success in light of the following summary statistics on public consultation (Mandel 1994, 106-7; see also Brock 1993, 29): "'Idea Line' phone number, with 75,069 calls; guided group discussions – more than

13,000 involving 315,000 participants; solicited letters and briefs (7,056), special age-specific discussion kits handed out in schools (13,000 with 300,000 participants) and 7,681 discussions with 180,667 people." Although at one level it was encouraging, this degree of participation did not bode well for the achievement of consensus. One observer described the prevailing mood in response to the extensive consultation as one of crankiness (Russell 2004, 222). In addition, Canadians outside of Quebec had reached a make or break point regarding the place of Quebec in Canada and would not tolerate any further protracted negotiations (Russell 2004, 230). Consequently, the process of consultation, which looked remarkably open-ended, was more suitable for the beginning of a long-term discussion than the lead-up to a referendum on a single document among a population suffering from constitutional fatigue.

Failure of the proposal, at the macro level, leads to intergovernmental conflict. Governments will continue to compete for power in an increasingly judicialized battleground. Conflict between Canada and Quebec over the legalities of referendums, secession, and like matters again comes to mind, as does the Calgary Declaration and more recent intergovernmental quarrels about equalization and fiscal imbalance. The proposal's failure also produces public dissatisfaction at the micro level. The identity politics initiated by the *Charter* "make ordinary democratic politics more difficult" (Morton and Knopff 2000, 151). Those enfranchised by the *Charter* and those excluded will likely ask for more from the constitutional system, and their demands will, in turn, produce rival demands and more public impatience with the process as a whole. Consider, for example, the public reaction to complaints made during the Charlottetown campaign by the National Action Committee on the Status of Women, Mohawks, Treaty Chiefs, and Manitoba Chiefs: "Canadians could not help but feel confused and angry since they believed that they had responded in good faith to the needs of these communities" (Brock 1993, 31). The figure ends with a feedback loop that links intergovernmental conflict to public dissatisfaction.

Institutional imbalance, as the name implies, is a theory that views the equilibrium emerging in the aftermath of the *Charter* as one that favours one branch of government over the others. To be more precise, judicial dominance at the macro level comes about through a series of reinforcing processes aided and abetted by the *Charter*. The document's minoritarian character created a political culture in which interest groups competing for constitutional status effectively bypassed democratic politics altogether. The new equilibrium is one of persistent conflict in which governments are in conflict with one another in a more legalistic way than in the past. This is not to the liking of the public, which has been tired by the process and periodically lets its fatigue be known, as when it rejected the elite accommodation manifested in the Charlottetown Accord.

Now that the *Charter* is in place and interest groups with a vested interest in it have grown in number, the likelihood of fundamental change coming about through normal political processes has been reduced. "Contrary to democratic expectations and liberal assumptions," observes Hutchinson (1995, 28), "rights-talk is more debilitating than therapeutic." The territorially oriented claims of Quebec and the West, for instance, appear to be more marginalized than ever but do not go away. Ongoing conflict is the norm and will lead to disequilibrium if regional alienation reaches sufficiently high levels in one or both instances or if public fatigue produces a major backlash. Judicial dominance gives the system predictability, but its stability is low.

The state of equilibrium identified by institutional instability theory is also low. The *Charter* created a new order in which the consequences of losing and the payoffs from winning are far higher than those of political competition in the electoral process. The legitimacy of the system itself may come under question as a result of how decisions are made. Consider Robert Martin's (2003) observation that unelected judges and lawyers are superseding the authority of elected, accountable officials. Pro-*Charter* advocates might point out the need to rectify injustices through extraordinary means, but proponents of institutional imbalance theory would argue that the net effect is harmful. Instead of allowing reform to take place through more natural, albeit protracted, electoral processes, the new judicially centred system exacerbates conflict by creating categories of self-identified permanent losers. It does not respond to persistent regional agendas, which are in direct competition with status-seeking non-territorial groups already "in" the Constitution.

Christopher Manfredi (2001, 103) makes the following observations regarding equality rights and high levels of citizen involvement: "While this development injects a new degree of openness and citizen participation into constitutional politics, it also carries with it the danger of constitutional and social disintegration. Competing rights claims are more difficult to reconcile than competing interest claims precisely because constitutional claims are indivisible." One implication is that constitutional reform is more akin to brain surgery or air traffic control than to things that people in general are qualified to do. Although it is wise to be on the lookout for the possibly harmful effects of elitism, Manfredi's analysis points out the problems inherent in the pendulum swinging too far in the opposite direction.

Ironically, despite all of the increased citizen participation involved, negative rather than positive social capital will likely accumulate as a result of the new era of constitutionalized politics. Bonding rather than bridging is imperative at the group level under conditions of increasingly judicialized competition. Unenlightened self-interest is the norm. After all, what incentive do social groupings have to engage in bridging under such conditions? Virtually none. And the behaviour of interest groups since the *Charter* has borne this out. Public trust can be expected to decline as a result.

**Conclusion**

Liberal theories about the evolution of constitutional politics in Canada have several points of convergence. All three theories, explicitly or implicitly, point to intergovernmental conflict and public dissatisfaction being the net result of the process of reform. And each theory identifies a conflict-prone, unstable equilibrium that promotes bonding at the expense of bridging with regard to social capital. The implications for generalized public trust are universally negative. The *Charter* and the processes it set in motion have only increased centrifugal forces.

Although they do not contradict one another, the theories do emphasize different variables in their causal stories. As was observed in Chapter 3, this type of diversity is to be expected within a paradigm such as liberalism. Negative identity theory stresses Canada's lack of a positive founding event, which has induced attempts to rectify the situation through the *Charter* and subsequent reform. Collectivism and negative self-definition (rejection of American visions and values), however, have ultimately undermined attempts to achieve a genuinely positive foundation. For proponents of megapolitics theory, the lack of a sovereign founding event or process – as opposed to the specific contents of the Constitution itself – is at issue. Regardless of their nature, omnibus proposals that are put forward to achieve a new constitutional arrangement will instead increase divisions in society and make the system more dysfunctional. The message of institutional imbalance theory is that the *Charter* created synergy among collectivist groups and produced a new regime in which the judiciary obtained excessive power. This imbalance has produced initiatives to reconcile persistent conflicts that inhere within the new system. Given the inherent contradictions in these attempts, however, efforts to achieve constitutional harmony will not succeed.

All things considered, the equilibria identified by liberal theories are not appealing. The next chapter reveals whether communitarian theories have anything more positive to say about the *Charter* era.

# 5
# Communitarian Theories: Asymmetrical Federalism and the Citizens' Constitution

Communitarian theories of Canadian constitutional politics – asymmetrical federalism and the citizens' constitution – are united by the communitarian paradigm's primary emphasis on the essential role of collectivities in political life. Such theories reject the idea of the political person as an isolated monad. Instead, in one way or another, communitarian theories emphasize identity experienced in a collective form. Group identity most obviously can take a spatial form, such as the connection made by Québécois between their etho-linguistic heritage and "home base" in Quebec. However, and this is where the *Charter* comes most directly into play, it also can be non-spatial (i.e., not involving occupation of contiguous territory), as with Aboriginal peoples or ethnocultural groups.

## Asymmetrical Federalism

Asymmetrical federalism is an idea that has origins in the pre-*Charter* era, but as a theory, it has come into greater prominence over the last two decades.[1] The key insight of asymmetrical federalism is that the system's best and perhaps only chance to remain intact depends on the Canadian people and their governments realizing that differences in subnational political entities should be not only recognized but also accepted and promoted. A process of accommodation, one that involves multiple asymmetries, is the way out of the present constitutional predicament. For example, groups that demand self-government should receive guaranteed representation to reconnect them to the larger federation (Kymlicka 1993, 82).

Asymmetrical federalism's adherents are in a position to point out that the federal system already includes noteworthy differences among the provinces. Some of these features of Confederation have been in place for a very long time. Prince Edward Island, for instance, is guaranteed a minimum number of seats in the House of Commons because of its very small population (Gibson 1992, 54) and Newfoundland received special status – for example, a distinct regime for fisheries, subsidies and tax rentals, and federal transitional grants – when it entered Confederation in 1949 (Mulroney 2007, 768). Creation of the Territory of Nunavut in response to the Aboriginal quest for self-government is a more recent example of special asymmetrical constitutional recognition.

Perhaps the most prominent asymmetry in Confederation is Quebec's guaranteed representation on the Supreme Court. At least three justices must be from Quebec to represent that province's Civil Code (in contrast to Anglo-American common law). Consider, in addition, the list of Quebec-related asymmetries compiled by Milne (1994, 112-13): "language provisions, civil law, denominational education, provision of uniformity of laws in all provinces but Quebec, rights to representation, provincial paramountcy in relation to pensions, minority language education rights exempted, compensation on transfers of provincial powers in matters of education and culture, immigration, tax collection, opting out/tax abatement and variations in program delivery." It is interesting to note, in reference to immigration in particular, that asymmetry dates from the Trudeau era in the late 1970s, when Ottawa and Quebec City signed the Cullen-Couture Accord, which granted the province extensive powers over immigration (McRoberts 1997, 152-53, 175). More recent asymmetries include accords on health and equalization signed in 2004. The Health Accord includes special recognition of Aboriginal peoples and a separate deal for Quebec to interpret and implement the agreement. Asymmetries followed the signing of the equalization agreement and included, for instance, an agreement between the federal government and Newfoundland and Labrador on offshore resource revenues and equalization payments.

Some argue that because asymmetry already exists, it would not break with established principle to create more differences to solve important problems. Former Saskatchewan premier Allan Blakeney (1991, 63), for instance, claimed that symmetric federalism would not be able to accommodate provincial equality, a flexible amending formula, and a Quebec veto. The implication, given the centrality of such issues, is that asymmetry is not only feasible but may even be essential to the survival of Confederation. In this context, it is interesting to note former prime minister Brian Mulroney's (2007, 233) observation that "Ontarians are the only voters in Canada who always place their country, not their province, first when they consider public affairs and policy." (From the standpoint of rational choice, Ontario's exceptionalism makes sense – it is the only province large enough to equate its welfare with that of the country as a whole.) Asymmetries might therefore be expected to accumulate as all of the provinces, with the likely exception of Ontario, demand further decentralization of power in a variety of areas.

Whether asymmetry could work if adopted openly in principle is another question. Opinions vary. Jane Jenson (1998, 232) describes the essence of the issue: "For asymmetry to work, it must be possible to imagine that a single country may host a variety of collective projects without threatening either the country's existence or the well-being of its members. One can protect and advance individual rights *and a projet de société* simultaneously." Implicit in Jenson's commentary is that asymmetrical federalism could work – it just needs the right environment in which to flourish.

The theory of asymmetrical federalism begins with the observation that Canada, like many other states, is composed of multiple nationalities. Because "Canada contains these internal minority nationalisms," observes Will Kymlicka (1998, 15), "it is not usefully seen as a traditional 'nation-state' but rather as a multination state." One obvious example is the Assembly of First Nations: "These groups have defined themselves as 'nations' and, as such, they claim the same inherent rights of self-determination as other colonized or conquered nations around the world" (Kymlicka 1998, 15). For Kymlicka (1995, 37), who is a persistent exponent of asymmetrical federalism,[2] group-based recognition is consistent with a liberal point of view: "[L]iberals can and should endorse certain external protections, where they promote fairness between groups, but should reject internal restrictions which limit the right of group members to question and revise traditional authorities and practices." In other words, collective rights can be recognized, but they must also exist within the larger framework of individual rights established by the Constitution.

Kymlicka (1998, 24) describes the foundation of asymmetrical federalism within the Canadian context: "In a federal system that contains both regional-based and nationality-based units, therefore, it seems likely that demands will arise for some form of *asymmetrical federalism* – i.e., for a system in which some federal units have greater self-governing powers than others. We see this not only in Quebec's demands, but also in the demands of Aboriginal peoples. Their 'third order of government' will necessarily be a very asymmetrical one." The idea behind asymmetrical federalism, then, is to preserve the Canadian political system while improving its operation. But why would these arrangements be necessary? Is the federal system, with its *Charter of Rights and Freedoms*, unable to guarantee that collectivities will survive and prosper?

Proponents of asymmetrical federalism answer these questions by pointing out that pressures toward assimilation can be overwhelming, even in a society that is committed to individual liberty. Minority rights "help ensure that members of minority cultures have access to a secure cultural structure from which to make such choices [i.e., about maintaining group identity] for themselves, and therefore promote liberal equality" (Kymlicka 1989, 192). It cannot be assumed that the existence of a level playing field, political speaking, will ensure the viability of groups that have suffered in the past.

Put simply, justice requires "a conscientious recognition of cultural diversity" (Wolf 1994, 85). Donna Greschner (1991, 224; see also Young 1990, 72), for example, argues that disparaging references to women and Aboriginal peoples as interest groups that subvert the democratic process display "a blindness to the histories of exclusion and the imperfections of the so-called democratic process." Social justice is about more than the distribution of material resources (Young 1990, 15). Members of these groups need recognition, which has been held back for many generations, to reach their potential.

Charles Taylor (1993, 183) takes this argument regarding asymmetry a step further by offering the idea that diversity can be recognized on more than one level. Advocates of the *Charter* are supporters of first-level diversity – the principle that multiculturalism is the point of unification for all Canadian citizens. Differences are recognized but within the overarching environment of a uniquely Canadian identity, which includes a commitment to social programs and the equalization of regional development (Taylor 1993, 159, 160). Deep diversity, by contrast, refers to identification with Canada itself: "To build a country for everyone, Canada would have to allow for second-level or 'deep' diversity, in which a plurality of ways of belonging would also be acknowledged and accepted" (Taylor 1993, 183). Members of collectivities such as Aboriginal peoples or Québécois identify with Canada, but they also have a complementary membership in another community.[3]

This observation leads into the politics of recognition (Taylor 1994, 26; see also Young 1990, 20): "Due recognition is not just a courtesy we owe people. It is a vital human need."[4] Recognition is important, even essential, because human life is inherently dialogical (Taylor 1994, 32).

People are defined in relation to one another. From a communitarian standpoint, this is a point that the liberal perspective misses entirely. The example of Quebec's reaction to the failure of the Meech Lake Accord is most relevant here (Taylor 1993, 196; see also 1994, 58, 61): "Seen from inside Quebec, it is not so clear that we want to go. But we broadcast very effectively the impression that we do, or else that we can only be kept inside by certain economic advantages. We somehow manage to obscure the fact that recognition matters to us, even while we make demands (such as the 'distinct society' clause) which aim at precisely this." Recognition constitutes an especially difficult issue for symmetric federalism because it is holistic and indivisible. A group cannot be 60 percent or 20 percent recognized – recognition is all or nothing. As Kenneth McRoberts (1997, 223) observes, support for sovereignty "does not seem to be much influenced by calculations of the costs and benefits of federalism; collective identity is far more important." This makes for a difficult but, from the standpoint of proponents of asymmetric federalism, worthwhile politics indeed.

Efforts to keep the system together naturally focus on counteracting the centrifugal forces created by unrecognized collective identities. Self-government, through guaranteed federal representation, is the recommended solution, because it will reconnect each relevant community to the larger federation (Kymlicka 1993, 82). Special recognition for non-territorial groups – such as ethnic minorities, women, and the disabled – rather than threatening national unity, can be viewed as "promoting civic participation and political legitimacy" (Kymlicka 1995, 176). Recognition of communities can therefore build, rather than weaken, national unity. Joseph Eliot Magnet (2003, 293) argues that the loyalty even of interior nations (Quebec is an obvious example) can be obtained in just this way.

Asymmetries already exist within Confederation to some extent. From the standpoint of proponents of asymmetrical federalism, however, these positive steps are more of a beginning than an ending to the process. Additional reform is required to maintain Canada as a just and stable political community. It is, however, ironic that asymmetrical federalism, at least in Canada's constitutional evolution, has proven easier to implement in practice than in principle.

Given that Kymlicka has identified a liberal element in asymmetrical federalism – and there is no denying that it has a presence in his writings in particular – can it be classified as communitarian? As in other instances, the criterion for classification is the overall character of a theory.

*Figure 5.1*

**Asymmetrical federalism**

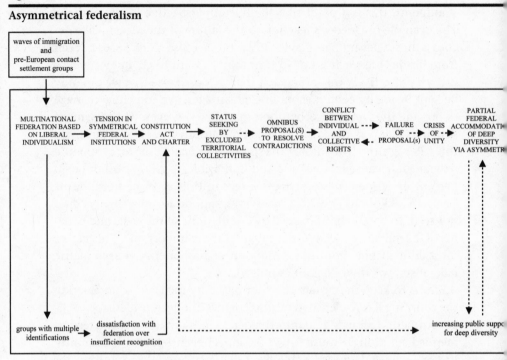

Asymmetrical federalism emphasizes group rights, while the potential costs to either individual liberty or rights measured in other ways receive only secondary attention. Its relative emphasis therefore justifies its placement within the communitarian paradigm.

How does the constitutional system operate according to the theory of asymmetrical federalism? Figure 5.1 begins with long-term micro processes that are exogenous to the system. Waves of immigration, combined with pre-European contact settlement groups (i.e., Aboriginal peoples), create the basis for a multinational polity. In other words, Canada began as an ethnically diverse society and became more so over time. This process continues and reinforces a basic macro property: a multinational federation based on liberal individualism. The latter component is a product of the dominant groups in place at the time of Confederation. Britain and France, which provided the overwhelming majority of the initial waves of immigrants who displaced Aboriginal peoples from power over the territory that became Canada, had well-established but incomplete democratic traditions by the mid-nineteenth century.

The political system that developed from Confederation onward, therefore, had a bifurcated nature: it contained multiple collectivities and even nations within a liberal constitutional order that recognized individuals as political agents. At the macro level, the multinational federation based on liberal individualism leads to tension in symmetrical federal institutions. Although some accommodation takes place – notably special status for Quebec in areas such as income tax, immigration, and pensions (Taylor 1993, 164) – the process remains far from complete. The fundamental inconsistency is the equal status of political subunits within the federal system, namely, the provinces. Tension builds because multinational entities do not run smoothly within a system of equal provinces. Subunits that seek recognition for collective rights of some kind, such as Quebec, run into persistent problems with a federal government committed to preserving the principles of liberal individualism and, more cynically, its own power.

The tension in symmetrical federal institutions culminates in the *Constitution Act, 1982* and the *Charter*. Executive federalism proved to be a disappointing path to constitutional reform in the era preceding the *Charter*. By the 1970s mounting western alienation and the election of a sovereigntist government in Quebec had required a swift response by the federal government. Given its experience with the first Quebec Referendum and confrontation with Alberta over the National Energy Program in 1980-81, Ottawa introduced the *Charter* and passed it after an intense period of conflict with virtually all of the provinces.

Meanwhile, developments at the micro level also lead to the *Constitution Act* and the *Charter*. The existence of a multinational federation based on liberal individualism leads to the existence of groups with multiple identifications. The presence of these groups is crucial to asymmetrical federalism as a theory. If they were fully assimilated to the majority culture, these collectivities would cease to be relevant, at least in political terms. Deep diversity, however, sets the conditions for the struggle to survive, which in turn produces a micro-micro connection from the presence of groups with multiple identifications to dissatisfaction with the federation over insufficient recognition. *Insufficient* is the key word because the system does offer cumulative, if limited, steps toward the recognition of minority rights. For example, the Royal Commission on Electoral Reform and Party Financing allowed non-territorial groups to have special representation in the creation of geographic constituencies (Kymlicka 1995, 176). Furthermore, in the late 1960s and early 1970s, the federal government's adoption of official policies on language minority groups (1969), multiculturalism (1971), and women (1974) led to an especially high level of activity in the recognition of minority and other disadvantaged groups. Each of the departments dedicated to these issues in the Secretary of State's Citizenship Branch included funding for advocacy (Pal 1993a, 1993b, 4).

Despite these changes, the conflicted nature of identity for the groups in question continues to be a key driver of change. Cumulative reforms beneath the constitutional level are no substitute for explicit recognition of a collectivity as an entity within Canada. Efforts at accommodation therefore lead to dissatisfaction among groups and perhaps emphasize their lack of constitutional status, even as employment and financial compensation in other forms are provided by governments at various levels. From this dissatisfaction comes a micro-macro linkage: the federal government offers the *Constitution Act* and the *Charter of Rights and Freedoms* as a means to resolve building confrontations within the system.

The *Charter* ultimately represented two opposing decisions on status-seeking groups: the Trudeau government said *no* to territorial groups and *yes* to several of their non-territorial counterparts. Quebec's desire for constitutional recognition ran into a brick wall, and the province did not sign, and still has not signed, the document. The *Charter* therefore may be regarded as a partial recognition of collective rights, namely, those of groups designated as acceptable – or perhaps helpful – to the federal government: Aboriginal peoples, women, minority language groups, and ethnic minorities. The *Charter* also opened the door for recognition of unnamed groups via litigation based on section 27. (Section 27 directs that the *Charter* be interpreted in a manner that will preserve and enhance the multicultural heritage of Canada.) A more complete vision of group status – including the general right of self-designation, even among those with a territorial basis – had not yet penetrated either state or society to a sufficient degree for Quebec to receive recognition. Consequently, the *Charter* leads, at the macro level, to status seeking from excluded territorial entities. Although Quebec is the featured player, western Canada, with its desire for a Triple-E Senate (i.e., elected, equal, and effective) and other changes, also plays a role. Both Quebec and the western provinces, the provincial "have nots," called for decentralization, albeit in different ways. The two also collide with each other in their demands for recognition in a new constitutional order: Quebec's calls for asymmetry are countered by the West's demands for symmetry with decentralization.

Status seeking by excluded territorial entities leads, in another macro-macro linkage, to an omnibus federal proposal intended to relieve pressure on the system. (This connection, which is only implied by the theory, appears as a broken line.) But should all would-be nations be included as co-equals, or are there reasonable limits to any process of recognition? Would a hierarchy rather than an across-the-board listing make more sense? Perhaps Quebec should receive pride of place, with the western agenda of Senate reform receiving some recognition as well. Or should a series of initiatives be put forward, with Quebec, presumably the most disgruntled collectivity, being first on the list? The theory of asymmetrical federalism naturally produces the expectation, especially among historically disadvantaged groups that only recently obtained recognition, that identity must be reaffirmed. Therefore, the prospects of a proposed agreement will likely increase with the initiative's degree of inclusiveness.

One example of this kind of proposal is the Meech Lake Accord, in which Quebec as a province received special recognition through the distinct society clause. Adoption of the accord (or any other constitutional proposal that contained such a provision) would have legitimized actions on the part of the Quebec government to protect and even promote the French language and culture in that province. Inherent contradictions within the multilateral federation can therefore be expected to stimulate efforts by the federal government to preserve national unity through one or more proposals that go at least part of the way toward self-government for at-risk collectivities.

Supporters of asymmetrical federalism, however, predict that conflict will occur, regardless of the nature of the proposal put forward at the federal level. At the macro level, omnibus proposals to resolve contradictions lead to conflict between advocates of individual and collective rights. This certainly was the case with the Quebec-oriented Meech Lake Accord and even the later and more inclusive Charlottetown Accord. Will Kymlicka (1998, 30) sums up the basic problem for any proposal that is inherently asymmetrical and has a Quebec-related agenda. English-speaking Canadians tend to reject ethnocultural nationalism because of strongly held beliefs: "Their conception of Canada as a single national community includes the idea of unrestricted mobility rights, common national standards in social services, portability in social entitlements, as well as the right to use the English language in courts, schools and government functions from sea to sea." Each of the points listed can be traced to liberal individualism in the founding political cultures. Charles Taylor (1993, 172) is more harsh than Kymlicka in his judgment of the reactions of Canadians outside of Quebec to the latter's demands for recognition: "Charter patriotism" causes a rejection of "the legitimacy of collective goals."

Under these conditions, it is hard to be optimistic about the likely success of any omnibus proposal. Inclusive or scaled-down proposals would likely suffer from different sets of problems. The former type of proposal would be too much of a departure from liberal individualism for English Canada to accept, while the latter – whether it recognized Quebec alone or a limited number of other groups instead – would forfeit the support of excluded groups. Conflict between individual and collective rights therefore leads, at the macro level, to failure of the proposal. This connection is implicit in the theory of asymmetrical federalism, as is the feedback from failure to another proposal.

The failure of one or more constitutional package deals, which represents a sustained rejection of territorially based identity, has an immediate and negative effect: a crisis of unity. This crisis takes the form of extreme alienation in one of the disgruntled provinces. Although it was ultimately defeated, the Quebec Referendum of 1995 achieved a clear majority among francophone voters. Perhaps more than any previous event in Quebec, the referendum conveyed the seriousness of Quebec's quest for recognition. The referendum reflected a crisis of confidence about Confederation that resulted from the cycle of failed proposals for recognition of Quebec in the Meech Lake and Charlottetown accords. The depth of Quebec's quest for recognition clearly transcended more ephemeral demands for specific powers or economic rents and became increasingly clear to the federal government.

The connection, at the macro level, between the crisis of unity and partial federal accommodation of deep diversity via asymmetry reflects the federal government's evolving mindset. The Chrétien government recognized Quebec as a distinct society in the House of Commons and also loaned the province its veto power over constitutional amendments. At least one observer noted the irony of the Calgary Declaration, which came out a short time later, being signed in a location that had been "the hotbed of the symmetry rhetoric" (Courchene 2004, 6).

A few years later, however, in response to a Supreme Court ruling on potential secession from Canada, the federal government also showed an awareness of the need to limit collective rights to preserve, as Kymlicka (1995, 173-74) describes it, "a stable liberal democracy." Any future provincial referendum would have to be worded in a clear way and pass by a significant margin to hold sway over the rest of the country. As the theory of asymmetrical federalism predicts, the series of measures just described produced mixed reactions in Quebec because of ongoing insecurities that derive from constitutional marginalization. Consequently, the figure displays no further linkages to Quebec as a macro-level entity. It is too soon to say what the result of the sum of the forces just described will be.

Constitutional evolution, as represented in Figure 5.1, ends with a feedback loop of micro-macro and macro-micro linkages and a long-range macro-micro connection. Federal accommodation of deep diversity via asymmetry leads to increased public support for deep diversity and vice versa. Public support for deep diversity reflects the long-range influence of the *Charter* on national character. Data suggests that public opinion has shifted substantially in favour of groups that couch claims in the language of equal rights (Howe and Fletcher 2000, 5). This link is implied in asymmetrical federalism's positive verdict on the *Charter* as the event that institutionalized the first level of diversity. The first level of diversity can be expected to permeate the general public and, if opinion polls are any indication – they show overwhelming and consistent support for the *Charter* – that is just what has happened. As a result, the feedback loop comes into operation. The federal government is scared straight by its brush with a nearly successful referendum and begins to accommodate the aspirations of Quebec in at least an incremental way. The public, in a departure from the past that is influenced by years of living under the *Charter*, is either positively disposed toward, or at least open to, that process getting underway. This shift in opinion has been reflected, for example, in the generally uncontroversial creation of the Territory of Nunavut, along with a Senate seat, in recognition of Aboriginal aspirations, and the Calgary Declaration, which recognizes asymmetry within a general framework of equality.

Does asymmetrical federalism meet the criteria of equilibrium analysis? From the point of view of communitarianism, equilibrium depends on the existence of shared values. Writing a decade ago, Kymlicka (1995, 188) observed that shared values had reached an all-time high, even if social unity had yet to be achieved. Equilibrium could be stabilized through a gradual accommodation of the Quebec agenda on recognition at both the micro and macro levels. Although it emphasized individual rights, the *Charter* also entrenched the principle of group rights. It did not include Quebec but set in motion a long-term process by which deeper levels of self-designated status, including those with a territorial basis, could enter the constitutional system. Thus, from the standpoint of asymmetrical federalism theory, the equilibrium in place is dynamic but convergent. The principle of asymmetry is increasingly becoming the norm as political problems are worked out.

Obtaining a stable equilibrium will be difficult but not impossible. Kenneth McRobert's (1997, 245) declaration that "the Trudeau strategy has failed" sums up the attitude of advocates of asymmetrical federalism. An alternative approach – one that treats Quebec's quest for recognition favourably – is needed. But Guy Laforest (1998b, 71), in a proposal for a set of partnerships between governments and collectivities within Canada, urges caution, even if such a regime should come into being: "Maintaining the equilibrium between the partners and partnerships in the Union is a formidable challenge. It calls for a subtle architecture that is feasible and sensible." The triangle of partnerships proposed by Laforest (1998b, 69) would include (1) a federal partnership between the central government of the union and the provinces, (2) a Canada-Quebec partnership between two distinct societies, and (3) sharing America – Aboriginal peoples and their cultures, i.e., a mutual cultural exchange between Aboriginal and non-Aboriginal peoples. Thus, even advocates of asymmetrical federalism intuitively understand that a more complex system, one that includes recognition of collectivities, will at the very least have the same problems as a high-performance sports car – it will be impressive when it performs well in capable hands but will need repairs often, regardless of ownership. At its worst, the system could be a house of falling cards.

Yet, the gradual process of recognition – which has been completed for *Charter* groups and is in progress for others, including Quebec – points toward stability. Consider the following statement by Charles Taylor (1993, 188), which was made when he reflected on the generally successful but troubled nature of Canada around the time of the Charlottetown Accord's repudiation: "Why are we under threat of breakup? Part of the answer lies in that very peace and prosperity. We are so used to it that we have trouble imagining real adversity, the kind that other countries live with all the time. But this is only part of the story. The root cause of our impending fracture can be put in one word: recognition." The positive inference from this critical-sounding assessment of Canada is that healthy doses of recognition will put the country on the right track. In the case of Quebec, half measures have taken place, and the public, under the influence of the *Charter* for over two decades, may accept more steps in that direction. The equilibrium in place therefore looks relatively stable for the foreseeable future.

Adherents of asymmetrical federalism view the constitutional equilibrium of Canada in relatively favourable terms. Although it occurred only in the House of Commons and not in the Constitution itself, recognition of Quebec as a distinct society – coming as it did from a Liberal government headed by Prime Minister Jean Chrétien, who had been directly involved in the creation of the *Charter* and was regarded as a villain by Québécois nationalists – is a positive development. So, too, is the creation of Nunavut. These territorially oriented shifts in federal policy reflect significant and cumulative asymmetries initiated by the *Charter* itself. Canada, in other words, seems to be moving in the direction of a true multi-nation state. This development may not prevent secession – it is impossible to know (Kymlicka 1998, 43) – but it certainly points in the right direction.

What, then, are the implications for social capital and generalized trust? Asymmetries, as they accumulate, will likely have both direct and indirect effects. Bonding capital should increase as each additional collectivity is recognized, and the anticipated indirect effect on bridging capital should be positive. As bonding capital increases, social norms will change. The public itself will be transformed and will begin to see minorities, territorial and otherwise, as highly valued components of an overarching national identity. This goes beyond traditional efforts on the part of governments and interest groups to decentralize the Canadian political order. As social diversity becomes a unifying value, bridging capital will increase. Deep diversity will also have another positive effect: those who belong simultaneously to multiple collectivities will create bridging capital from the bottom up. In sum, from the standpoint of asymmetrical federalism theory, constitutional evolution will result in enhanced levels of generalized trust and cooperation among citizens.

**Citizens' Constitution**

Citizen's constitution theory focuses on the *Charter* as a transforming document in the history of Canadian politics. Alan Cairns developed the theory in a series of publications during the *Charter* era (1983, 1988a, 1988b, 1991a, 1991b, 1991c, 1992, 1993, 1995, 1996, 1998, 2000). The issues covered in these writings range from substantive events such as the Meech Lake and Charlottetown accords to more theoretical matters such as the nature of federalism and the place of collectivities within the system. Among the theories considered here, the citizens' constitution is the one that puts the most explicit emphasis on the *Charter* as a point of culmination in a process that leads to a new system. As Cairns (1988a, 259) observes, the "conjunction of a growing rights consciousness, the linking to the Constitution of groups who previously had little or no constitutional recognition, and the symbolic power of the *Charter* have modified the Canadian constitutional order in ways that will take decades to work out." The *Charter* is thus seen as a product of both citizens and governments: "Not only did the precise wording of the *Charter* derive from interest group suggestions, but the very existence of the *Charter* would have been problematic in the absence of strong public support" (Cairns 1991a, 23).

The key insight of citizens' constitution theory is that the *Charter* permanently altered the constitutional discourse in Canada (Cairns 1991a, 1991b, 1991c). Consider the words of a critic of the patriated Constitution and multiculturalism: "[A]n event such as Pierre Trudeau's patriation of the Constitution in 1982 can be important not only in political terms but also psychological ones: even with all its flaws, the social contract to which we adhere is one designed by us for us; it is a declaration of faith in ourselves, a vital political step – however contentious it may be – towards full nationhood, a symbol of ourselves and the vision that shapes us" (Bissoondath 2002, 69). The Constitution is no longer a matter for governments alone, a matter to be adjusted in various ways at First Ministers conferences; instead, the *Charter* has recognized and set in motion forces that involve citizens in all further deliberations. Recognized groups and the citizenry as a whole have been mobilized as never before, and they now view the *Constitution Act* and especially the *Charter* as "theirs."

Status seeking naturally followed the *Charter,* and it takes place primarily within the judicial branch of government. Some refer to status seeking as rights talk, a type of political discourse that privileges the law and courts in sorting out political problems (Smith 1999, 74). Stimulated by the *Charter,* "the whole ethos of rights-talk has saturated Canadian politics and society" (Hutchinson 1995, 24). Consider the case of Aboriginal peoples (Cairns 2000, 175): "Section 35 of the Constitution Act, S. 25 of the *Charter,* an awakened legal community (both academic and practicing), reinforced by and reinforcing the growing rights consciousness of Aboriginal peoples, have generated a proliferation of court cases, law journal articles, and commentaries on judicial decisions." These conflicts begin in localities, but the most important rise to the federal level – even to the Supreme Court. The interests of *Charter* groups such as Aboriginal peoples therefore end up at the macro level, where they add a further layer of complexity to any process of constitutional revision.

The citizens' constitution brings out deep contradictions within the constitutional order, and those contradictions are powerful enough to put into motion processes that push reform in opposing directions. On the one hand, governments seek to resolve the inevitable problems of federalism, which generally revolve around division of powers. On the other hand, the *Charter* created a new system in which the trials and tribulations of federalism could no longer unfold without large-scale public involvement. Cairns (1991a, 17) states: "There are only three possible explanations for the quarter-of-a-century-long addiction of Canadians to constitutional reform: an overpowering necessity based on intolerable shortcomings of the existing constitutional order; an optimistic naiveté based on short memories; or the inability to stop a reform movement that once begun can only be brought to a close by some kind of resolution." With so many actors involved – and even constitutionally entrenched – it is only natural to echo the questions posed by Cairns (1995, 289): "What can we legitimately expect a constitution to do for us? Have we been asking too much?" The answer to the first question may be open, but it is clear that from the standpoint of citizens' constitution theory the answer to the second question is yes.

Critics might ask, how does citizens' constitution theory, as explained here, fit within the communitarian paradigm? The theory's classification, like that of the others, is a matter of emphasis. As will be seen, Cairns prioritizes minority rights and recognition over individual rights. This is evident, for example, in the title of his major work on Aboriginal peoples, *Citizens Plus* (2000).

Figure 5.2 shows the constitutional system through the lens of citizens' constitution theory. The process begins with an external definition of political order through the *BNA Act* and Confederation. Nation building at the national level leads to rival nation-building programs at the provincial level, and this development took on a particularly threatening form in Quebec, which quarrelled with Ottawa, long before the days of the Parti Québécois, over the boundaries between federal and provincial authority.

As the figure shows, exogenous international forces once again influenced constitutional affairs in Canada. According to Cairns (1992, 30),

*Figure 5.2*

**Citizens' constitution**

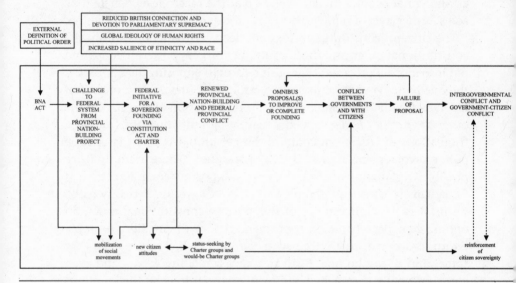

international influences – most notably loosening ties with England and a lower level of devotion to parliamentary supremacy, a global ideology of human rights, and the increased salience of ethnicity and race – over the course of several decades had an important influence on constitutional politics. These factors combined and put pressure on the federal government to develop an initiative that would take the place of a sovereign founding event – something that was still absent well over a century after Confederation.

This connection takes three forms in the figure – one direct and two indirect. First, in a direct exogenous-macro linkage, the federal pursuit of an initiative for a sovereign founding event via the *Constitution Act* and *Charter* was part of a more general trend around the world toward democratization.[5] In particular, the rise of the global ideology of human rights put pressure on governments of all kinds to respond positively or risk international censure. The possibility of censure was obviously a matter of great concern to Canada because it had established an international reputation through peacekeeping, foreign aid, and the like.

The second, indirect, connection involves social movements within Canada. External forces influenced existing and future Canadian social movements. Ideas emanating from the UN and the international environment in general legitimized and encouraged mobilization (Cairns 1991b, 19; see also Hiebert 2002, 41, 208; Weinrib 2001, 701, 2003, 22). This influence appears in the figure as an exogenous-micro linkage from the global ideology of human rights to mobilization of social movements. These movements, it should be reiterated, antedated the *Charter* and sought equality through the courts prior to its existence (Smith 1998, 307; Brock 2005).[6] The Court Challenges Program, for example, came into being in 1978. Under this program, the federal government funded human rights-based litigation against governments, including *itself,* in an effort to put the new culture into action. With the advent of the *Charter,* Ottawa expanded the program to include cases about language rights.[7] A micro-macro connection from the mobililization of social movements to a federal initiative for a sovereign founding event, in turn, took hold. The federal initiative that resulted exhibited an obvious bent toward a specific kind of rebirth, one that favoured recognition of interests articulated in group-specific ways, namely, the *Charter.*

Third, at the macro level, these same exogenous forces encouraged Québécois to challenge the federal system with their own social movement or provincial nation-building project. The difference in this case is that, because they held a local majority in Quebec, Québécois also happened to control a provincial government. Unlike other social movements, the Québécois have a clear territorial basis. Consequently, even more pressure was placed on the system. In substantive terms, the federal government needed to respond to Quebec, which had held, for the first time in that province's history, a referendum on sovereignty in 1980. Although the referendum went down to defeat by nearly a 20 percent margin, the fact that it took place at all enhanced perceptions of the Quebec nationalist movement as a force to be reckoned with in and beyond that province.

The threat posed by Quebec's nation-building project to the federal system provided a further stimulus to Ottawa's pursuit of a sovereign arrangement via the *Constitution Act* and *Charter.* Cairns (1991c, 54), in fact, puts great emphasis on Quebec's influence on the political purposes of the federal government in 1981: "Although the *Charter* process drew sustenance from the global rights revolution, the impetus for its sponsors came from the high political purposes it was intended to serve." In return for rejecting sovereignty association, the Trudeau government promised the people of Quebec constitutional reform. From the perspective of citizens' constitution theory, a combination of direct and indirect exogenous forces translated naturally into a federal initiative.

Figure 5.2 continues with a bifurcated macro-micro connection to new citizen attitudes, on the one hand, and status seeking by *Charter* and would-be *Charter* groups, on the other. These macro-micro linkages are an indirect result of the mobilization of social movements noted earlier, that is, both the creation and the content of the *Charter* can be traced to these processes. In particular, as Cairns (1988a, 261) points out, the Constitution "is now about women, aboriginals, multicultural groups, equality, affirmative action, the disabled, a variety of rights, and so on." These groups received explicit constitutional affirmation in sections 15, 28, and 25 of the *Charter*. Faced with skeptical, in some cases hostile, provincial governments, Ottawa obtained popular support through the various forms of recognition just noted (Cairns 1991c). The *Charter* channelled pre-existing pressures into the constitutional arena (Brodie and Nevitte 1993b, 271), and would-be *Charter* groups attempted to obtain recognition. The circle of support for the new regime widened as the process added new groups to the list.

Synergy among new citizen groups played a major role in this process. After a decade of micro-level mobilization among members of the legal community (activists and others open to the idea of promoting multiple identities even in constitutional terms), the concept of a *Charter* Canadian came into being in the early 1980s. In politics, as the saying goes, timing is everything. Thus, the substantive content of the Constitution expanded to include many citizen-based, non-federal concerns; put differently, it added micro- to macro-level provisions. The *Charter* provided a closer link between the Canadian state and society (Cairns 1991a, 13-14).

At the macro level, the enactment of the *Constitution Act* and *Charter* led to renewed nation-building attempts and federal-provincial conflict. The *Charter* and *Constitution Act* offered no recognition to provincial nation-building projects, most notably that of Quebec. So the battle of Quebec continued: both Prime Minister Pierre Trudeau and Premier René Levesque – and each prime minister and premier of Quebec that followed – had an incentive to exaggerate national and provincial identities (Cairns 1992). Ottawa had to contend with continuing alienation in Quebec and, to a lesser degree, with other provincial premiers who saw the *Charter* and *Constitution Act* as a renewed attempt at centralization. Moreover, the constitutional regime change included only four items – resource ownership and interprovincial trade, equalization and regional disparities, patriation with an amendment formula, and the *Charter* – out of a possible twelve. The extensive list of items not covered included communications, the Senate, the Supreme Court, family law, fisheries, offshore resources, powers over the economy, and a statement of principles (Cairns 1983, 29). (It is therefore not surprising that Cairns and other analysts saw the *Constitution Act, 1982* and *Charter* as rather limited documents at the time of their arrival.) The incomplete constitutional order that Trudeau presided over became his legacy, namely, ongoing confrontation between the provinces and the federal government over a wide range of unresolved policy issues.

Incomplete federalism produces a macro-macro linkage from intergovernmental conflict to one or more omnibus proposals to improve or complete the founding of Canada. Cairns (1988b, 115) labelled the Meech Lake Accord "a product of the internal dynamics of the intergovernmental arena responding to a problem within the constitutional system itself." This conclusion would undoubtedly hold true for any process of negotiation that came about because of these pressures. Meech Lake, and later the Charlottetown Accord, arose because of a perception among governments that the system had become dysfunctional. The federal leadership's desire to cope simultaneously with the challenge of Quebec nationalism and western alienation led to the unsuccessful package deal.

At the micro level, status seeking by *Charter* and would-be *Charter* groups produces conflict with governments, both federal and provincial. This is both an ongoing process, realized through the accumulation of legal disputes, and a short-term phenomenon, manifested in *Charter* group objections to any omnibus initiatives related to the Constitution. As Cairns (1988b, 108; see also Smith 1990, 19, and McRoberts 1997, 197) points out, the Meech Lake process looked more like an effort by governments "to keep the citizens at bay than an acceptable process of constitution-making in one of the world's oldest liberal democracies." The tactic conflicted with a new political culture of open ratification (Manfredi 2005, 43). Elements of permanent conflict between citizens and government clearly exist, which raises the question: "How can the constitutional amending process be adapted so that the stalemate born of competing constitutional visions of citizens and governments can be overcome?" (Cairns 1995, 289; see also Brock 2006). Although they were written after both the Meech Lake and Charlottetown accords, these words are just as relevant to the events that preceded the accords and would be germane even if neither accord had ever been proposed.

Things do not get any easier at the macro level. An omnibus proposal, no matter how complete it might seem, will likely produce further intergovernmental conflict and conflict between government and citizens. Any constitutional initiative will stall out because of the need for unanimity about the key element: an amendment formula (Cairns 1988b, 112, 114). Regardless of what Quebec or other provinces might seem to gain, only one among their number would have to remain unsatisfied – or reverse course and claim dissatisfaction – for the proposal to fail.

There is synergy between these macro-macro and micro-macro linkages. Efforts on one front will necessarily aggravate matters on the other for one simple reason: the division of powers, whether in terms of an amendment formula in particular or issues within the Constitution in general, is a purely redistributive game. If all governments managed a gain in status, it would come at the expense of *Charter* groups. Sovereignty is, in a word, indivisible. Of course, the worst of all possible worlds is not only possible but likely: efforts to improve either the standing of governments or *Charter* groups are likely to meet with disappointment for those targeted and suspicion among those who are not. Expectations get higher with time, while the ability to meet demands is fixed and likely to be diminished by protracted and difficult negotiations.

Overall, these forces combine and result in the failure of the proposal. Cairns predicts (1991a, 15) that the "most likely outcome of a constitutional reform effort is failure." Failure of the proposal leads, through a macro-macro feedback effect, to the introduction of a new proposal. So far, the story includes the Meech Lake and Charlottetown accords, but citizens' constitution theory does not rule out further attempts, even if they are futile.

Eventually, failure of a proposal – whatever that proposal may be – will lead to intergovernmental strife and government-citizen conflict. Intergovernmental strife is likely because of unsettled claims regarding the recognition of provincially oriented agendas. This became clear when Ottawa and Quebec came into conflict over the *Clarity Bill* (see Chapter 4). Government-citizen conflict will be a likely outcome as the federal government attempts to keep up with demands for the recognition of collective rights (e.g., activity in the courts generated by section 15) and as provinces dispute claims based on individual rights as interpreted by their citizens (e.g., conflict over the sign law and use of the notwith-standing clause by Quebec).

The failed proposal, however, also fosters a macro-micro linkage from intergovernmental conflict and government-citizen conflict to the re-inforcement of citizen sovereignty. Citizens regard defeat of the pro-posal as a victory over attempts to alter the status granted by the *Charter*. Cairns observes a unity of purpose between so-called *Charter* Canadians and citizens in general: each can be expected to support *the Charter* against challenges that emanate from governments (Cairns 1993, 262). Furthermore, observers quickly concluded after the defeat of the Charlottetown Accord that a referendum would now be a required part of any effort to change the Constitution (see, for example, Monahan 1993, 243). If anything, that norm has become stronger with time.

A feedback loop between the reinforcement of citizen sovereignty at the micro level and intergovernmental conflict and government-citizen conflict at the macro level is implied in citizens' constitution theory. Cairns (1992, 81), for instance, forecasts the following: "Ultimately, the evolution of the future blend of the individual and collective aspects of the *Charter* will be a product of law and politics, particularly given that *Charter* clauses relating to sex, language, ethnicity, and aboriginal status are able to generate organizations devoted to their protection and strengthening much more than are clauses relating to the more traditional individual rights, even with the number of civil liberties organizations in Canada." His observation suggests that the interests of citizens as individuals, and even more so as collectivities, are likely to conflict with those of governments. Although his assessment was made over fifteen years ago, it appears to be true, particularly in the case of Aboriginal peoples (Cairns 2000). Moving in the other direction along the feedback loop, citizens' consciousness of constitutional sover-eignty has become so strong – one could say it is the norm – that a Meech-like attempt at reform through pure executive federalism is now unthinkable.

Among the theories examined in this book, citizens' constitution theory is most likely to use the language of equilibrium analysis ex-plicitly. Cairns (1992, 8), writing around the time of the Charlottetown Accord, observed that "the present location is not an equilibrium pos-ition." The rationale for his judgment was straightforward: a discourse of federalism, dominated by governments, needed to be reconciled with a democratizing *Charter* discourse that included "an extensive cast of citizen actors" (Cairns 1992, 4). Fifteen years later, however, it looks like an equilibrium has been established in the form of a low intensity version of the final feedback loop in Figure 5.2.

What, then, of stability? A decade ago Cairns (1995, 289) posed a series of questions about the constitutional order:

- How can the constitutional amending process be adapted so that the stalemate born of competing constitutional visions of our citizens and governments can be overcome?
- How can we accommodate our multinational reality and our federal system to suit each other?
- What can we legitimately expect a constitution to do for us? Have we been asking too much?

Cairns (1991b, 131) regarded the Constitution as a generally destabilizing influence in the era of the Meech Lake and Charlottetown accords. Today, these questions would likely generate mixed answers. The last two questions are the easiest to answer. Canadians have backed away from expecting everything of constitutional reform, and regardless of whether or not they are satisfied with the status quo, they have moved away from large-scale confrontation politics in recent years. Trends, of course, are not laws. However, Canada shows no imminent signs of collapse, and the most recent election in Quebec, which saw the Parti Québécois fall to third place in the provincial legislature and back off from a referendum, suggests that the feedback loop has become more stable, even if it is still conflict prone.

Finally, there is normative desirability to consider. Cairns is fair and balanced in his review of the evidence. On the negative side, the era of the citizens' constitution did not promote the growth of bridging social capital. Cairns (1991b, 261) refers to a culture of constitutional selfishness. In the period leading up to the failure of the Meech Lake Accord, Cairns (1991b, 171) could identify only one group, Canadians of Origins in India, that suggested discarding the identification of specific collectivities in the Constitution. On a more positive note, public belief systems now embrace the *Charter* as an integral aspect of identity. Given the *Charter*'s contents, this entails increasing acceptance, and even identification with, collective identities recognized in the *Charter* and in subsequent court battles. This positive dimension is identified in a specific example offered by Alexandra Dobrowolsky (2000, 196): "Feminist struggles helped to foster broader constitutional consciousness and in some cases a participatory ethos on the part of the citizenry." Thus, overarching support for the good treatment of vulnerable collectivities, as a part of emerging national character, has created bridging capital to complement the bonding capital already in place. This support could even have positive implications for generalized trust. It is therefore possible to remain neutral or even somewhat positive about the normative desirability of the citizens' constitution as an equilibrium.

## Conclusion

Asymmetrical federalism and the citizens' constitution, the two major communitarian theories of Canadian constitutional evolution, have points of convergence that reflect their place in the communitarian paradigm. Each theory points to the significant role that collective consciousness about rights, both territorial and non-territorial, has played in Canada's constitutional development. Both therefore focus on recognition-seeking social groups who perceive themselves as oppressed minorities within a dominant mainstream culture. A key concern for adherents of each theory is how to reconcile traditions of executive federalism with the presence of a truly distinct society, Quebec, on the one hand and energized *Charter* groups on the other. The theories differ in that federalism and the *Charter* constitute different facilitating structures, but both types of status seeking (i.e., territorial and non-territorial) use institutional arrangements under the Constitution to foster the same basic goals: change in the status quo and compensatory status.

Both theories have implied feedback loops, and one is somewhat more encouraging than the other. Asymmetrical federalism paints a generally positive picture: public support for deep diversity and federal accommodation at the micro and macro levels reinforce each other. The vision of citizens' constitution theory is more conflict-oriented, but at a relatively low and manageable level. As citizen sovereignty becomes more entrenched, it, in turn, leads to further intergovernmental and citizen-government conflict.

As might be expected from the preceding observations, the two theories offer different assessments of equilibrium in constitutional evolution. Asymmetrical federalism identifies an equilibrium based on shared values and acceptance of constitutional asymmetry. Although the equilibrium is increasingly in operation, its stability is open to question and depends upon the degree to which recognition of collective rights will expand to incorporate Quebec's nation-building project. The equilibrium is desirable in that positive social capital has accumulated as social diversity has become the norm in public thinking. This development, in turn, has enhanced bridging capital and possibly even generalized trust.

Citizens' constitution theory equivocates on the issue of equilibrium. With time, however, the existence of an equilibrium within which citizen sovereignty expands and government resistance diminishes will become more likely. Events suggest that the equilibrium is becoming more stable. It is at least marginally desirable in a normative sense because, although bonding social capital is the direct product of change, bridging social capital will likely accumulate as the public embraces diversity as a shared value. The implications for generalized trust are neutral or even positive.

# 6

# A Critique and Comparison of Liberal and Communitarian Theories

This chapter integrates insights derived from examination of the five theories of the evolution of constitutional politics in Canada. It offers critiques of the theories in the liberal and communitarian paradigms based on debates in the literature, but it also offers additional points in each theory's favour or disfavour. Not surprisingly, criticism of a theory from one paradigm can often be traced to beliefs associated with the other. This is most evident in the war of words between advocates of institutional imbalance and asymmetrical federalism. In order to answer the overarching questions introduced in Chapter 1, the theories are compared to one another along salient dimensions, and the analysis concludes with an assessment of how each theory has fared.

## Liberal Theories

Each of the liberal theories entails multiple causal linkages and interesting normative implications. A review of the literature reveals that critics of these theories have focused overwhelmingly on the theory of institutional imbalance. In particular, a spirited debate has emerged between advocates of the Court Party thesis and their critics. An interesting twist is that some critics agree that institutional imbalance exists, but not in the form of judicial supremacy. The other two theories – negative identity and megapolitics – have been subjected to, at most, limited and indirect challenges. This suggests that the possibilities for synthesis, at least within the boundaries of the liberal paradigm, are high.

Direct criticism of negative identity theory is rare and never by name because the theory itself is a product of the rational reconstruction of ideas that have pervaded both academe and popular culture for a long time. But an important challenge to the theory's key causal mechanism – the long-term impact of Canada's being defined in opposition to the

United States – exists within the literature on political sociology. Edward Grabb and James Curtis (2002, 38) focus on the founding of Canada and the role that the migration of United Empire Loyalists and other factors played in the creation of a country based on counter-revolution, collectivism, and the like.[1] Referring to the United States and Canada, they question whether "differences in the historical development of our national political structures correspond to differences in the two peoples themselves" (Grabb and Curtis 2002, 40). In other words, did the lack of a positive founding event in Canada, along with tendencies toward collectivism and counter-revolution, translate into Canada having significantly different values than the United States, values that are still evident to this day? To answer this question, Grabb and Curtis (2002) investigate certain values – attitudes toward change, civil dissent, desired qualities in children, the individual in relation to government, and employment opportunities – on both sides of the border. From a sociological standpoint, these are basic components of a given value system. The data reveal virtually no support for the argument, embedded within negative identity theory, that Americans are more democratic and individualist than Canadians. Canadians are supposed to hold deference to authority in high regard, yet the public rejected the Meech Lake and Charlottetown accords, even when political elites almost uniformly supported the latter initiative (Grabb and Curtis 2002, 49).

What are the more general implications of Grabb and Curtis's findings for negative identity theory? Since the data are recent, they may indicate a relatively new movement among Canadians toward individualism and democratic values, which are identified with the United States. Perhaps the concept of negative identity can only be applied to the Canada and Canadians of the past. (Some critics of the *Charter* have made exactly that observation in response to the increasing litigiousness of Canadian politics.) If so, the theory would need to be modified to incorporate the influence of events such as high-profile trade agreements – the Canada-US Free Trade Agreement and NAFTA – and globalization in general. These developments may have greatly reduced Canadian collectivism and deference in recent decades.

Data on value change does indeed reveal a decline in deference among Canadians in the 1980s. Survey research reveals that confidence in public institutions and general deference declined between 1981 and 1990. In addition, US and Canadian values are converging along both of these dimensions, with Canada leading the trend (Nevitte 1996, 286-87,

292-93). It is interesting to note that these changes occur at equal rates among English- and French-speaking respondents (Nevitte 1996, 296-97).

Anti-Americanism, perhaps the most prominent aspect of Canada's negative identity, however, seems to be intact. Although more restrained under the Harper government (at least in terms of government statements), anti-Americanism is conveyed periodically by political figures, especially those on the left who hope to gain public support. Jean Chrétien's embarrassing but undoubtedly honest admission about the use of this tactic, which was caught on tape in July 1997 when the former prime minister thought a microphone had been turned off, is one revealing example. While some aspects of negative identity may be in question, the ongoing presence of anti-Americanism in the catechism of Canadian politics is without question.

Critics of negative identity theory could also question its assertions about the accumulation of bonding, but not bridging, social capital. What about the *unity* experienced by those who belong to various social movements? Women's groups joined forces with Aboriginal peoples in 1982 and 1987 to alter and oppose constitutional initiatives. By doing so, they transcended racial and ethnic identification to form bridging capital. Consider also the *Charter*'s impact on individuals living throughout the country. Could not the *Charter*'s general popularity, even in Quebec, be regarded as a form of bonding capital? Perhaps, given sufficient time, the net effect of group articulation in conjunction with the *Charter* will be positive with regard to social capital. Such a result would directly challenge negative identity theory on normative grounds.

Rare is the theory that meets with general approval, but megapolitics, unlike negative identity theory, seems to have pulled this off. The closest thing to an objection available in the literature comes from Roger Gibbins (1991, 24): "But if there can't be a 'Quebec round,' can there be an 'everything round'? It is doubtful. Anyone who imagines that Quebec, Senate reform, aboriginal rights, and the federal deficit can be rolled into one tidy constitutional package should wake up and smell the coffee. But so too should someone who believes that we should tackle these things sequentially. We can't." This statement could be interpreted to mean that constitutional megapolitics is not very promising but must be tried because a piecemeal approach is even less likely to work. Peter Russell (2004, 228-73), however, points to a number of successes in the gradual process of reform since the era of major constitutional initiatives. Some of the changes are constitutional, while others involve recognition at a lower level – Parliament's recognition of Quebec as a distinct society, for instance – that is, nonetheless, significant. At the very least, Russell could claim that political processes since the advent of megapolitics have entailed more incrementalism and less of a sense of ongoing crisis than in preceding decades.

Some may say, in contrast to Gibbins and in agreement with Russell, that an incremental approach is already underway and works reasonably well. A commentator's position on this matter probably says more about his or her beliefs than anything else. On the positive side, it is possible to point to the relatively smooth process that put Nunavut into existence, recognition of Quebec in the House of Commons, and the long-term decline of the Parti Québécois since the 1970s. On the negative side, it is possible to point to tensions over fiscal imbalance, the questionable viability of renewed brokerage politics (i.e., can the Conservatives ever win a majority?), and the sustained strength of the Bloc Québécois. The glass is either half full or half empty when it comes to reviewing the influence of post-Charlottetown incrementalism on national unity.

Why is the basic idea behind megapolitics so well received?[2] The traumatic failures of the Meech Lake and Charlottetown accords, followed by the narrow escape of the Quebec Referendum, hardly support the idea of constitutional reform through large-scale initiatives. The belief that such efforts will fail is pervasive and well grounded in theory and practice (Lusztig 1994, 1999). Thus, the theory of megapolitics has the potential to bridge the gap between liberals and communitarians.

Among the liberal theories, institutional imbalance is the one most directly challenged on both empirical and normative grounds. Critics focus on two multifaceted issues. The first is whether the courts, as described by the theory, really play a dominant anti-democratic role within the post-*Charter* constitutional order. Aspects of this issue include the existence of the Court Party, the direction of cause and effect (macro-micro versus micro-macro), the *Charter*'s consistency with contemporary Canada, the competence of judges in comparison to legislators, and the role of judicial review. The second issue is the possibility that institutional imbalance theory could be right about one component of the government overpowering the others in the post-*Charter* era but misses the mark by focusing on the judiciary rather than the executive.

Does the Supreme Court of Canada, aided and abetted by the Court Party, dominate Canada? Miriam Smith (2002, 4-5, 8) throws down the gauntlet and challenges the concept of the Court Party, which is central to institutional imbalance theory:

> [T]he picture of organized lobbies of minorities circumventing our democratic parliamentary process through the mechanism of an undemocratic and elitist court has become a stock in trade of the study of law and politics in Canada, refreshed, once more, by the publication of an update and reprise of F.L. Morton and Rainer Knopff's classic attack on the Supreme Court ... The study of law and politics in Canadian political science is dominated by normative claims about the Charter's impact on Canadian democracy at the expense of empirical explorations ... where empirical claims are made [by Morton and Knopff], they are not subjected to reasonable tests, or even formulated in a falsifiable fashion, the empirical evidence to substantiate the claims is not presented and the evidence that is presented does not substantiate their empirical claims.

Various critics expand on details in Smith's comprehensive overview. In particular, they challenge institutional imbalance theory's normative implications and its description of how post-*Charter* institutions operate.

One specific line of criticism about cause and effect concerns the role of forces operating at the macro and micro levels. A key question is "the extent to which the decisions of the courts are driving social change or reflecting social change" (Smith 2002, 21). In other words, is the connection macro-micro, as institutional imbalance would suggest, with the courts influencing society's values, or is the linkage micro-macro, in the sense that the courts reflect beliefs that have welled up from the public itself? Smith (2002, 28) provides an answer: An agent-centred social movement assessment "connects to the structural approach in that both social movement analysis and various structural theories of social change" suggest that "social movement organizations are connected to broad movements of social change that, while they may have been influenced by states, were not created by them." The causal story, in other words, is primarily $m \to M$ rather than $M \to m$, that is, members of society influence political institutions. Note the communitarian subtext in the emphasis on social movements as significant pre-*Charter* developments (see Chapter 5).

This account is backed up by Charterphiles such as Lorraine Weinrib (2003, 28, 31-32), who assert that the majority of Canadians in

1981 saw the constitutional status quo as flawed and wanted change. The passing of the *Charter* itself was, therefore, more consistent with democratic principles than institutional imbalance theory suggests. In addition, Charterphiles also argue that Canadians in general wanted a strong *Charter* to protect rights previously trampled on by governments. A poll in September 1980, for example, reported that 81 percent of Canadians favoured an entrenched *Charter* (Kelly 2005, 72). And what about the present? Is this description of Canadian society still accurate? *Charter* advocates point to the continuing popularity of the document. One representative poll revealed that 82 percent of Canadians support the *Charter* and nearly two-thirds agree that the Court should have the final say on legislation (Behiels 2003, 171). In other words, even if the Court is in a position of greatly enhanced power, one that surpasses even that of Parliament, so what? The Court's position reflects the wishes of an impressive supramajority within the public.

Why is the *Charter* so popular with Canadians? People who live in democracies typically take pride in some kind of declaration regarding human rights as a basic trait of their country. The *Charter*, however, is an exceptional document and will likely be the subject of long-term conflict because of its recent creation relative to analogous documents in other advanced democracies, the absence of Quebec's consent, and the conflict over its creation still residing in living memory. Despite these problems, proponents offer a straightforward answer in response to the question regarding the *Charter*'s popularity: its basic content. Michael Behiels (2003, 159) asserts that the *Charter* is "uniquely Canadian. Why? Because it is a hybrid document combining conventional fundamental freedoms with minority collective rights." Section 15.1 protects individual rights, while other components, such as section 15.2, recognize traditionally disadvantaged groups via collective rights. Thus, contrary to the assertions of institutional imbalance theory, the *Charter* suits contemporary Canada (Weinrib 2003, 34):

> For the most extreme Charter rejectionists, the greatest outrage is the way in which the Charter empowers rights-holders to engage in judicial review to reformulate public policy rooted in traditional socially conservative mores and encapsulated in statute. The underlying claim is that conservative approaches to social life must enjoy a special substantive immunity from legal, even constitutional, change. This demand may have been acceptable when the role of supreme legislatures was perceived to be the preservation of a homogeneous population's religious

and cultural heritage and common social norms. This claim presupposes that the moral categories contain no interests that a court could recognize as fundamental within a liberal democracy, even when constitutional amendment is designed to produce such a result.

For critics of institutional imbalance theory, all of this represents a shift toward constitutional *balance*, because the *Charter* has produced a less deferential judicial branch. A more balanced constitutional system has replaced traditional majoritarian parliamentary supremacy, which is now obsolete. Critics of institutional imbalance theory, such as Lorraine Weinrib, draw attention to the fact that Canadian society, in both demographic and ideational terms, is evolving away from English and French Canada and toward diversity. The *Charter*, therefore, is in line with a new Canada that no longer remotely resembles a pact between previously warring factions. Parliamentary supremacy, executive federalism, and a generally top-down process of constitutional reform play horse and buggy to the *Charter*, a fast-moving, modern vehicle that reflects a new citizen-centred regime.

Because a new Canada needs a revised constitutional system, critics of institutional imbalance theory argue that democracy must become more than simple majority rule (Iacobucci 2003, 390). Supreme Court Justice Frank Iacobucci takes this position as his point of departure in his reflection on the *Charter* two decades after it came into being. He regards the *Charter* as a positive development because it checks the excesses of majority rule and increases sensitivity to the rights of all Canadians (Iacobucci 2003, 381), particularly the ability of minorities to pursue redress for grievances regardless of majority preferences. Canada always had more diversity than was acknowledged, and that component of its character is still on the rise.

Institutional imbalance theory also raises the issue of whether legislatures or courts are more competent decision makers. In response to Charterphobes, who argue that the Supreme Court lacks the knowledge necessary to render valid judgments on complex socio-political issues, Justice Iacobucci (2003, 388-89) observes that the academic and professional community is consulted on a regular basis in the process of decision making. He also believes that the increasing role of interveners in the Court has had a positive effect because they offer a "richer understanding of the context" (Iacobucci 2003, 385). Given that a distinguished career is required to obtain one of the nine seats on the Supreme Court, Iacobucci could have added that the average level of intellectual ability among members of the Court is likely higher than among members of Parliament. (This is not to demean parliamentarians but instead to praise justices as exceptionally capable and accomplished people.) Furthermore, because interveners provide expert consultations and data, the Court – with its highly trained, experienced, and intellectually sophisticated membership – may even be in a better position than Parliament to make judgments about complex social issues.

The issue of judicial review is at the forefront of challenges to institutional imbalance theory. Consider the observations of Iacobucci and Weinrib:

> [C]ritics overlook the numerous restrictions that limit the capacity of the judiciary to dictate policy issues to the legislature; judicial review does not constitute a veto that allows courts to impose their own views for those of Parliament. Rather, judicial review is but one component of a dialogue that ensures that government is sensitive to the rights and interests of all Canadians. (Iacobucci 2003, 402-3)

> Judicial review does not lead courts into the open-ended world of political debate and policy formation, but allows them to operate as the independent and legally expert institution that safeguards the basic constitutional structure. (Weinrib 2001, 709)

Judicial review provides the basis for discussion, not dictatorship. To support this argument, critics of institutional imbalance theory can point to numerous instances of legislative sequels, that is, the passing of laws previously struck down but revised to achieve compliance with court rulings. Thus judicial review, which counteracts parliamentary supremacy, brings the system into balance.

Other critics of institutional imbalance theory likewise point out that courts can only go so far to refashion Canada. Consider these observations from Allan Hutchinson and Peter Russell, a decade apart, on the Court:

> In the first few years of the Charter, the court upheld many more claims than it rejected and struck down laws with relative abandon. More recently, the Supreme Court has settled into a more measured pace and has begun to worry about the legitimate scope and thrust of its mandate; the weight of democratic propriety has begun to rest a little heavier on the courts' constitutional shoulders. (Hutchinson 1995, 19)

[F]ear-mongering about a Canadian juristocracy borders on the hysterical ... from the beginning of Canada's constitutional odyssey the country's courts have had an important, although not a dominating or dictatorial influence, on the country's constitutional development. (Russell 2004, 268)

Constraints on the Court include the resources available to it and society's values in a given era. For example, in response to a series of successes for Aboriginal peoples, public opinion shifted and pressured the Court to restrain itself by the late 1990s. The Court's decision in the 1999 *Marshall* case, for example, emphasized that federal sovereignty should set justifiable limits on the rights of Aboriginal peoples. Violence between Natives and non-Natives in Atlantic Canada over fisheries likely influenced the decision (Russell 2004, 263-64).

Judicial supremacy is also criticized on the grounds of feasibility. Brian Slattery argues that only a small percentage of laws can be effectively subjected to judicial review because of the time and expense involved (Slattery 1987, 714), and this observation is as true today as it was two decades ago. In addition, judges who attempt to designate rights that lack fundamental consensus in society will find it difficult to secure compliance with their decisions (Hiebert 2002, 201). The study of bureaucratic politics reveals that it is difficult for those at the top of a pyramid to be certain that their orders, particularly when they are out of line with society, will be implemented faithfully by those below them. Jaywalking and the placing of small private bets are just two examples of behaviour that continues regardless of what the courts – or, for that matter, the government – might prefer. The same is true of Supreme Court rulings that are seriously out of line with a supramajority of citizens that includes members who also play a role in the implementation of government policy. As rational actors, judges undoubtedly can be expected to take the values of society as a whole into account during their deliberations.

This leads naturally into another objection to the story told by institutional imbalance, which critics associate with a politically conservative agenda: Is the theory guilty of overstating the ability of judicial power to effect a left-wing, even extremist, shift in public policy? For example, the success rate for the judicial invalidation of statutes in the *Charter* era is only 33 percent. Moreover, in a number of significant *Charter* cases, the Court has shot down efforts by rights claimants to increase social policy spending by government. Even the high-profile gay rights victory in *Vriend v. Alberta* did not obligate the state to address discrimination through public spending (Kelly 2005). For James Kelly (2005), the vision of the legislature as passive, fearful, and inhibited from acting is simply off base: "I conceive of judicial activism as part of a mutually reinforcing activist approach to *Charter* values that originates within the legislative arena. Thus, the *Charter* debate has largely discounted the ability of legislative activism to ensure that the parliamentary arena can engage in significant institutional and cultural reform to advance the values of the *Charter* that both supersedes and marginalizes judicial activism as the primary force behind the presence of *Charter* values in public policy." Ironically, Kelly argues that there *is* institutional imbalance, but not as conceived by critics of the post-*Charter* Supreme Court: the imbalance is an unintended effect of the *Charter* on the bureaucracy.

Critics therefore disagree with the causal story told by institutional imbalance theory in Figure 4.3. They argue that the courts needed greater power, granted by the *Charter*, to deal with injustices that had accumulated under majority rule. Thus, the legislative role has not been distorted in the *Charter* era. Later proposals for reform have failed because a pro-*Charter* public, now energized by the new constitutional order, is in a position to object to any watering down of hard-won rights. In sum, rather than being criticized as interest groups, collectivities defending the *Charter* should be praised for carrying out activities that represent enhanced democracy.

Imbalance may exist, critics acknowledge, but who, institutionally speaking, is out of control? Is it really the judiciary? Although he criticized the *Charter* for giving too much power to the courts, former prime minister Brian Mulroney (2007, 347) describes the judiciary as a moderate and centrist player in government. This observation, which comes from an ideologically conservative source who is hardly in league with Trudeau's vision of Canada, undermines the anti-court thesis. Perhaps instead the problem lies with the Prime Minister's Office (Russell 2004, 266). James Kelly (2005, 6-8) begins his authoritative study of *Charter*-era governance with these assertions:

> This study [Governing with the Charter] challenges the judicial-centric analyses that have dominated the Charter debate among legal and political analysts ... executive supremacy, not judicial supremacy, has been the primary outcome of the Charter's introduction, as bureaucratic-driven legislative activism has further marginalized Parliament and the

provincial legislatures as policy actors ... A central claim in this book is that the present debate over judicial activism in Canada is sterile and has established a false dichotomy, where judicial activism is said to undermine democracy and judicial deference serves to advance it.[3]

Kelly (2005) provides convincing evidence in favour of his new vision of the constitutional order. He points to the greater tendency of the courts over time to use suspended declarations to invalidate legislation. The Supreme Court suspended two pieces of legislation in the period from 1982 to 1992 and eleven pieces of legislation in the period from 1993 to 2003 (Kelly 2005, 137-38, 175). This pattern does not reflect the actions of an imperial judiciary. The sheer rate of judicial activity in the post-1982 era is also of interest. Among the sixty-four statutes that were invalidated before 2003, only forty-four, or about two per year, were passed after the *Charter*. These figures tend to confirm Mary Dawson's (1992, 603) prediction that "the government will get better at finding its way through *Charter* issues on the road to achieving important public policy goals."

Kelly's statistics, which do not paint a picture of a judiciary run amok, reflect the "general success of Charter-vetting by departments of justice" prior to legislation reaching the floor (Kelly 2005, 149; see also Dawson 1992, 599). And herein lies the darker side of the new story of constitutional change: the growing power of the executive at the expense of Parliament. The Department of Justice emerges as a central agency in the *Charter* era (Kelly 2005, 222; see also Dawson 1992, 599). Scrutiny of the *Charter* is institutionalized in the Department of Justice, and dialogue starts within the Cabinet. There is a "nearly invisible aspect of legislative activism within the machinery of government that is rarely exposed to critical commentary when the Supreme Court invalidates legislation" (Kelly 2005, 256). The net result, documented by Kelly (2005, 222-57), is the centralization of power in the Cabinet and the Prime Minister's Office.[4]

Advocates of institutional imbalance theory have responded vigorously to their critics. Rainer Knopff and F.L. Morton (1996, 70-71) object to Iacobucci's (2003) characterization of the process of consultation by the Courts: "[F]ar from respecting the collective wisdom of the many, as embodied in such mechanisms as prices and traditions, the unconstrained vision emphasizes the role of the intellectual élite in reconstructing the unenlightened many. In other words, it flatters precisely the defining characteristics of the postmaterialist knowledge class." Janet Hiebert (2002, 59) confronts Charterphilia less directly in her response but suggests that members of the Court may lack the expertise required for discretionary judgment across the board. Put simply, can the judiciary really know everything relevant? Its connection with certain members of the public, as Knopff and Morton observe, could be interpreted as evidence of biased sampling. Those consulted regularly by the Court tend to be on the political left. This could have important implications, from the perspective of institutional imbalance theorists, for the quantity and quality of social engineering that emerges from the Court.

In this context, consider the observations of the Honorable Vic Toews (2003, 348, 349), member of Parliament for Provencher, regarding the Supreme Court of Canada and jurisprudence on sexually explicit material that glorifies the violent sexual exploitation of children. Toews refers in particular to the Court's judgment in favour of John Robin Sharpe, who justified the production of this material on grounds of freedom of expression and artistic merit. By making this judgment, the Court rejected morality as the basis for assessments of artistic merit. But without a moral standard, Toews (2003) asks, how will the Court decide section 15 cases put before it? There must be some moral judgment involved in decisions about who is disadvantaged and in need of protection. But to return to the specific court case at hand – who possibly could be more disadvantaged and in need of protection than the victims of child abuse? This question needs to be asked in light of the judgment reached by the Court. It leads to the more general and troubling observation that the judiciary may indeed be ideologically biased .

Exponents of institutional imbalance theory could contrast outcomes of individual cases, which generally do not receive much media coverage, with the more general presumption that Canadians are fond of the *Charter*. Canadians are generally pro-*Charter*, but they would perhaps answer survey questions about the *Charter* differently if they were made aware of the implications of specific Supreme Court rulings. It is unlikely, for example, that Canadians in general, if made aware of the Sharpe decision and the basis for it, would prefer to see art that depicts child abuse protected more than the victims themselves. Ironically, citing the *Charter*, the victims might in turn appeal for relief.

It could be argued that the Court simply renders superior judgments and the occasional anomaly. Brian Slattery and Rainer Knopff have disputed this position at different stages of the *Charter*'s existence:

This view of the Charter should give us pause. It suggests in effect that the judiciary is the only "principled" branch of government, that legislatures and executive bodies have no mandate to uphold the Constitution and so may be expected to violate it as a matter of course. (Slattery 1987, 728)

[O]ne cannot easily sustain the stark (and facile) distinction often drawn between reasonable/principled judges (keepers of the keys) and impassioned/interested legislatures (would-be drunk drivers). The image of legislatures as responding in a knee-jerk fashion to every impassioned majority is as overdrawn as the image of disinterested judges above the fray. (Knopff 2003, 205)

These observations effectively turn discussion toward basic beliefs about the character of Canada's past. How good or bad was Canada before it had the *Charter*? The answer given to this question affects responses to all others. Those who see Canadian history as primarily a tale of excess power in Ottawa and the discriminatory treatment of the weak and the poor will insist that something like the *Charter* had to be put in place to allow the courts to rectify injustices of long standing. Others – advocates of institutional imbalance theory fall into this category – will acknowledge that Canadian history before the *Charter* included some shameful events, but on balance they believe the nation's past is something of which to be proud. Their answer to the question would include the observation that Canada enjoyed very high rankings from the UN and other organizations in the categories "freedom" and "respect for human rights" – before and after the *Charter*. Opposing views on the quality of the constitutional order before and after the *Charter* undoubtedly signal paradigmatic allegiances. Liberals emphasize individual rights, for which Canada has a nearly spotless record by world standards, while communitarians point to long-term suffering of disadvantaged collectivities, which still needs to be addressed.

Critics of institutional imbalance theory, as noted earlier, question whether the Court truly dominates Canada's political institutions. Christopher Manfredi and James Kelly (1999, 515, 516, 517) take exception to the idea that the *Charter* created a dialogue between the courts and the legislature as equals. They point out that simply counting the nullification of statutes is an inadequate way to assess the Court's impact on the legislature. The number of instances may be limited, but the

importance of the cases chosen for nullification may not be in propor-
tion to their numbers. Manfredi and Kelly (1999, 521) also point out
that legislative sequels do not, generally speaking, suggest a dialogue
between equals: "[M]ost legislative sequels do not involve minor amendments, but require major legislative responses on the part of elected
officials, such as repealing sections or replacing entire Acts." Kelly's
(2005) data on Court activity, considered a bit later, tends to offer more
support to the critics of institutional imbalance theory on this issue,
albeit with one important exception.

Defenders of the *Charter* point to the existence of section 33, the notwithstanding clause, as a check on judicial supremacy (Iacobucci 2003,
404). However, adherents of institutional imbalance theory point out a
harmful side effect of the clause (Knopff 2003, 213): "Under assumptions
of judicial finality in interpretation, the use of section 33 clearly implies
that legislatures are *infringing rights* rather than reasonably *disagreeing*
about their proper meaning and scope." This is evident in Robert Bourassa's use of the notwithstanding clause (see Chapter 2). There is a
stigma attached to the clause that has driven it into virtual non-use over
the last two decades. According to Russell, this excessive deference to
the Court needs to change (Russell 2004, 269).

Proponents of institutional imbalance theory have also responded to
criticisms about majoritarianism, a potential bane of democracy when
it is unconstrained. Knopff (2003, 210, 217) points out that the Supreme
Court itself operates on the basis of majority rule. Critics therefore could
be accused of exercising a double standard. Knopff advocates representative government as a means to constrain simple majoritarianism.
His argument reaffirms the fundamental importance of popular sovereignty. Elected leaders are not the product of mob rule; instead, they act
as agents of the public who exercise authority through legislation.

Some of those involved in debates over political institutions and the
distribution of power among them have searched for a middle ground
between advocates of institutional imbalance and defenders of the Court.
Their arguments to some degree resemble that of Knopff. Debate over
rights should not occur as an autonomous discourse: they should be a
natural part of democratic governance rather than "a precondition or
boundary to the legitimate realm of contested politics" (Hutchinson
1995, 55). Hiebert (2002, 45, 51, 55) offers a relational understanding
of the *Charter* as an alternative to the heavily disputed idea of a dialogue
between the courts and Parliament.[5] The basic idea is that "Parliament's
constitutional judgment may have a different focus than legal opinion,

reflecting its distinct responsibilities and different vantage point, relative to *Charter* issues." This goes beyond a limited role in *Charter*-proofing legislation ahead of time (Hiebert 2002, 71-72, 70, 144):

> I like to think of the Charter as embodying the Canadian polity's code of conduct, or its philosophical ethos, which expresses the normative values that should influence decisions about the exercise of state power, the benefits and burdens to which citizens are subject, and the recognition of status and allocation of entitlements ... Just as the government should respect judicial concerns when the court rules that legislation violates a right, and reflect seriously upon the normative message that may be convened in a judicial ruling, judges should similarly have respect for political judgments about how best to pursue complex social-policy objectives ... The idea that judicial answers are necessarily correct implies judicial infallibility, which has no basis in human and historical experience.

A less sweeping interpretation of the rights of the courts should be applied to avoid excess intrusions in the policy-making domain (Hiebert 2002, 83). At the same time, Parliament should be more assertive in its legislative role. Just like the Court, Parliament is capable of principled judgment. It should *share* responsibility with the Supreme Court in deciding the "merits of legislative decisions." Unfortunately, Hiebert (2002, 226, 227) asserts, this idea remains far from the reality of existing practice.

### Communitarian Theories

Communitarian theories have also been subject to criticism, and the theory of asymmetrical federalism has borne more of the criticism. The critique of asymmetrical federalism can be viewed as the flip side of the debate about institutional imbalance. Critics in that debate tend to reappear as defenders of asymmetrical federalism.

Asymmetrical federalism has been criticized on a number of grounds. The most basic case against it was summed up by Premier Clyde Wells during the Meech Lake debates at the Government Conference Centre in June 1990 (Mulroney 2007, 1029): "In every federal state there are two equalities: the equality of citizens and the equality of the component parts of the federation. A constitutional provision which accords a special legislative status to one of the component parts of the federation, a status that the other component parts do not have, upsets the essential balance of the federation." Asymmetrical federalism has also been criticized on a number of specific grounds, including the basis of collective recognition, intergovernmental strife as a function of asymmetries in practice, government expansion as a by-product of asymmetry, the meaning and value of a multination federation, and the potential for open-ended extremism in pursuit of constitutional status.

One key issue is the basis of recognition: "When is a person sufficiently disadvantaged to qualify for special treatment? When does he cease to qualify?" (Selick 1996, 112; see also Lusztig 2002). Should recognition be granted for special contributions to society, in response to systemic discrimination, or for some combination of the two? As it is currently formulated, asymmetrical federalism theory cannot answer these questions easily.

Consider, for example, Brian Walker's (1997) analysis of cultures, which is written as an explicit critique of Will Kymlicka's (1993, 1995) exegesis of asymmetrical federalism based on collective rights. Walker (1997, 211) associates Kymlicka and other advocates of asymmetrical federalism with a theoretical position "aimed at justifying a devolution of state powers to members of cultural groups so that they might maintain the integrity of their cultures." He raises an interesting question: why are *ethnic* communities privileged by culturalists who seek the means of cultural preservation for designated minorities (Walker 1997, 214)? Other cultures could just as easily be singled out for attention, including those that are not ethnic but that have been disrupted or even destroyed (Walker 1997, 218-19): "The family farm and the urban neighborhood are just two institutions singled out from a vast number which are undergoing intensive change under conditions of advanced modernity. Such institutional changes cut people off from crucial forms of cultural membership." To take things a step further, cultural deprivation among the groups just noted can be documented. For ethnic groups, however, special status is awarded in recognition of the *possibility* of cultural loss (Walker 1997, 218-19). The tendency to privilege ethnic groups, moreover, is not restricted to academic apologists: governments also seem to follow the same logic. As Walker (1997, 225) points out, recognition may reflect political efficacy more than a genuine need of protection: "[G]iven the tremendous resilience of ethnic communities and the deep attachment which most ethnic groups show to their institutions and communities, it might well be thought that ethnic communities are *less* vulnerable than many other groups." Rainer Knopff (2003, 210) reinforces this specific point by observing that, in practice, it may be more difficult than is suggested at an abstract level to decide who is disadvantaged.

Some criticize asymmetrical federalism theory vis-à-vis its future prospects.[6] In the case of Quebec, Steven Rockefeller (1994, 89) worries about "the danger of an erosion over time of fundamental human rights growing out of a separatist mentality that elevates ethnic identity over universal human identity." Michael Walzer (1994, 103) expresses similar concerns about the denigration of rights under more extreme conditions, that is, "if we were to treat our minorities as endangered species in need of official sponsorship and protection." One observer of the Constitution even described the language laws and government interventions of Canada, and especially Quebec, as oppressive (Gairdner 1994, 72).

This negative perception of asymmetrical federalism may be a by-product of basic tensions within the *Charter* itself. Karen Selick (1996, 112; see also Hutchinson 1995, 47) draws attention to sections 15.1 and 15.2 and argues that individual and collective rights are contradictory. Put differently, these provisions highlight the classic conflict between equality and liberty (Hutchinson 1995, 44). It is interesting to consider, in that context, the words of Justice Iacobucci (2003, 383), who asserts that liberty and equality "complement and reinforce each other" because the *Charter* monitors legislation for both. This is a puzzling observation because liberty does *not* reinforce equality. In fact, the more freedom people have, the more likely it is that their destinations in life will not work out to be the same as one another. Iacobucci must mean equality of *opportunity*, given the *Charter*'s actual content and especially its endorsement of affirmative action. But it must then be acknowledged that liberty is not the priority here, at least as understood in terms of the individual's freedom from external control.[7]

Kathy Brock (2005, 2006, 2007), in a series of studies, draws attention to the harmful consequences that asymmetrical federalism could have on intergovernmental relations. Brock reviews recent accords on health and equalization at the national level, both signed in 2004, and finds significant asymmetries at the time of signing and after the fact. Aboriginal peoples, Quebec, and even other provinces are singled out for special recognition. According to Brock (2005, 8), this recognition helps to redistribute power to the federal government because it permits, and even encourages, intrusions into areas previously designated as provincial jurisdictions. This is exactly what Ottawa wants because it seeks a key macro-micro shift, namely, it wants to justify its existence to an increasingly skeptical and impatient public that no longer sees the federal government as able to provide for its needs (Brock 2005). Ironically, this redistribution of power can exacerbate tensions between the federal government and the provinces because the latter are (1) tempted to give Ottawa more authority in return for relief from fiscal imbalance but (2) still resentful of its perceived meddling.

Asymmetrical federalism is also criticized on the grounds that legislative sequels lead to the expansion of government. Peter Hogg and Allison Bushell (1997, 81), as *Charter* advocates, draw attention to something that they see as a positive development. If the Court strikes down a law for not being inclusive enough, the government is free to either extend the benefit or reduce (or even eliminate) it. From the standpoint of the *Charter's* critics, this provision shows the legal mindset in action. To what extent would it be feasible politically to *reduce or eliminate* a benefit after it has been approved even once by Parliament? In fact, as Hogg and Bushell (1997, 91) point out, there are no cases in which a legislature has decided to eliminate rather than extend a benefit to an excluded group. Therefore, an expansion of government will occur because even the partial extension of a benefit creates a high probability of more rather than less activity in the future. Whether that is a good or bad thing is a normative judgment: Hogg and Bushell would perhaps reply that equality is being pursued uniformly, while critics would perhaps express a preference for more liberty and less government.

Practical considerations motivate a line of criticism directed at Kymlicka's articulation of a multination federation as the answer to Canada's problems (Meadwell 2002, 224-25):

> On the one hand, Kymlicka argues, we can conclude optimistically that these states will endure as multination federations; on the other hand, they may be terminally unstable because some of their parts are moving toward independence. Perhaps they can be construed as moving toward independence because they are not yet genuine multination federations. In that case, however, the claim that these cases demonstrate remarkable resilience should be abandoned. On the other hand, if they are resilient, and are not the genuine thing (a true multination federation), then surely we can ask why we need a true multination federation.

The idea of multinational federalism as a viable option is backed more by rhetoric than hard evidence. Kymlicka calls for greater asymmetry to complete the process of creating a multination federation. It is not clear, however, where the dividing line is between a viable multination federation and a situation that simply calls for secession (Meadwell 2002).

Some critics are skeptical about where it all ends when it comes to the politics of recognition. They see a process potentially without end and replete with harmful side effects. Barry Cooper (1996a), in a critique of Charles Taylor's vision of asymmetrical federalism, is uncertain about where to draw the line regarding deep diversity. Could Iranian Canadians, Ukrainian Canadians, and (of course) many other possible collectivities qualify as exhibiting deep diversity? Cooper's reading of Taylor is that, unlike the Québécois, the identities of these groups would be regarded as shallow. A natural by-product of this attempt to classify allegiances would be confusion and resentment. Moreover, constitutionalizing the politics of interest groups will virtually guarantee zero-sum competition; if anything, it will likely create a coalition of interests against any additional power for Quebec. Claims for asymmetry are likely to be competing rather than complementary. Cooper's story line is consistent with the outcomes of both Meech Lake and Charlottetown and tends to discourage further efforts toward asymmetrical federalism. It is, in essence, a liberal critique of the feasibility of a stable and effective communitarian constitutional order.

Self-government plays a central role in asymmetrical federalism at the level of policy prescription. But even Alan Cairns (2000, 187), who is known for putting forward very positive arguments for the rights of Aboriginal peoples, expresses skepticism for the viability of self-government: "[O]verlooked are terribly important practical problems of what is possible for small populations to achieve even if financial and other support from the larger society is very generous." A legal approach that emphasizes rights is unlikely to pay heed to governing capacity. Hudson Meadwell's critique comes to mind here. What do advocates of self-government envisage as being the optimal mixture of autonomy and allegiance within an entity such as Nunavut? At a more prosaic level, what about money? Nunavut is impoverished and highly dependent on federal largesse for its survival. (Of course, that could change if Nunavut obtains control over its natural resources, especially given that the federal government is building a port.) What is the presumed upper limit on support that Nunavat reasonably can expect from the rest of the country to ensure its continuation? Asymmetrical federalism theory must answer these questions.

Defenders of asymmetrical federalism have considered the problems described above and have proposed some tentative solutions. One thoughtful attempt to address what is perhaps the most central and vexing issue – designating status as a disadvantaged group – is carried out by Joseph Eliot Magnet (2003). He derives a set of questions to ask of any group that may put forward a maintenance claim, that is, an argument in favour of granting it autonomy that, in turn, puts some limits on the rights of other people. Magnet (2003, 302-3) is clearly a pragmatist: "A well-fashioned theory of equality between communities would require *at least* that the proponents of any package of minority rights demonstrate that the benefits of the package (in terms of main-tenance of the interior nation) outweigh the costs imposed on dissent-ers (in terms of coercion, loss of liberty, or fiscal imposition)." Consider the thoroughness of the list of questions Magnet (2003, 307) proposes to ask:

- Is the claim advanced by an "interior nation," or a community analo-gous thereto?
- Is that community's identity under pressure because of the state's "na-tion building" exercises?
- Was the community promised, at some constitutional moment, that it would be enabled to maintain its distinctive culture intact?
- Is the community sufficiently numerous so as to have reasonable prospects to keep its distinctive identity intact, assuming institu-tional support is provided?
- How much coercive power over others will the community need to use?
- Does accommodation of the community's claim pose a real, palpable existential threat to the unity of the larger polity?

The first and fourth questions pertain to feasibility. The second question properly focuses on whether a real need for recognition exists. The third question pertains to normative justification, while the fifth and sixth questions suggest reasonable limits for claims. Although it is arguably complete in the dimensions it covers, the set of questions may prove difficult to answer in practice. As with the issue of how Canadian con-stitutional history is to be perceived, answers to these questions may simply reflect liberal versus communitarian belief systems. It is not dif-ficult to imagine an inter-paradigmatic stalemate on anything but the extreme cases.

What about the situation in Canada today? Have incremental asym-metries made Canada better or worse? Brock (2005, 2006, 2007) has pointed out their potentially pernicious effects on federalism. In reply, defenders of asymmetrical federalism could point to the situation in Quebec today, as opposed to 1995, as evidence that their theory is on the right track. The influence of the Bloc Québécois is at a relatively low ebb in federal politics. Consider also the dreadful showing of the Parti Québécois in the election of March 2007: a third-place finish. The Parti Québécois' leader stepped down as a result, and his replacement, Pauline Marois, called for (1) reflection on why sovereignty is desirable in the first place and (2) unity rather than squabbling over the issue of when a referendum should occur (*The Economist*, 18 May 2007, 40, 41). With the gradual decline of the Parti Québécois and the rise of the autonomist-oriented Action démocratique du Québec to second place in the legislature on at least one occasion, advocates of asymmetrical federalism could claim that the gradual increase in recognition for Quebec is having the desired effect.

Advocates of asymmetrical federalism could question the implications of intergovernmental squabbling as depicted by Brock vis-à-vis national unity. Fiscal imbalance and like matters lack the emotional content of issues such as language rights, but they can still lead to heated debate. Consider, for instance, conflict between and among Nova Scotia, Newfoundland, and Ottawa over revenue sharing from offshore oil and natural gas. Although governments may engage in battles over jurisdiction, will any of this translate to the micro level and influence citizens' beliefs? Will Canadians exhibit a lower level of allegiance to their country as a by-product of intergovernmental quarrels over equalization payments or health care? It is just as reasonable to answer no to either or both of these questions.

Another point in favour of asymmetrical federalism follows from the advent of the Council of the Federation. Created in 2003, this body comprises the leaders of provinces and territories. It meets to coordinate relations with Ottawa, especially those that concern financial issues. This entity could be regarded as a safety valve for dissatisfaction and a welcome addition, from the viewpoint of asymmetrical federalism theory, to the constitutional system. It provides a structure for the orderly recognition of power sharing between Ottawa and the provinces and territories. Of course, the subnational units have some common interests to put forward to Ottawa, but the council's existence may also allow deconstitutionalized, and therefore less threatening, asymmetries to develop along desired dimensions.

Adherents of asymmetrical federalism also have an answer for their critics on the subject of self-government, particularly that of Aboriginal peoples. The example of Nunavut, for instance, suggests that self-government for Aboriginal peoples can succeed. It still faces many challenges, including inadequate housing, lack of education, a poorly trained workforce, and other social problems (Brock 2006). But Nunavut continues to make strides forward, and its very existence creates a voice, even an ally, for Aboriginal peoples at the federal level. This enhanced sense of involvement among Aboriginal peoples with their government may dissipate conflict.

Citizens' constitution theory, like the theory of asymmetrical federalism, has been criticized on several grounds. One ground for criticism – constitutional selfishness – is anticipated to some degree by Cairns himself (see Chapter 5). But the problem is discussed at greater length and in a more encompassing way by Knopff and Morton (1992, 80): "[T]he citizens' constitution can be understood as an arena for competitive 'status' building in much the same way that the constitution of federalism provides the background for the rival phenomena of nation building and province building." Examples of such competition are legion: even as early as 1980-81, the National Action Committee tried but failed to exclude age from the list of prohibited grounds for discrimination (Knopff and Morton 1992, 87-88). Eight years later, Morton and Knopff offered a tougher judgment of interest group activity, identifying Cairns's *Charter* Canadians as part of the Court Party coalition: "They all seek to constitutionalize policy preferences that could not easily be achieved through the legislative process" (2000, 25). The overlapping sets of participants include national unity advocates, civil libertarians, equality seekers, social engineers, and postmaterialists (Morton and Knopff 2000, 31). All are problematic in that there is no evidence that their views are representative of society as a whole.

Another point of criticism concerns the representativeness of groups who have obtained status in the *Charter*. Jennifer Smith (1991, 76) points out that the leaders of women's groups who presented briefs on the Meech Lake Accord, for instance, represent only a small fraction of Canadian women. Without exception, these groups are from the left wing of the political spectrum. Socially conservative women's organizations – REAL (Realistic, Equal, Active for Life) Women is the most prominent example – have been refused government financial support that more liberal variants have come to take for granted. Moreover, by nurturing *Charter* groups via the Court Challenges Program and in other ways, the government effectively ignores "citizens who do not identify with any one group" (Smith 1991, 77).

This observation leads into a more general critique derived from Mancur Olson's (1965; see also Sandler 1992) classic exposition of the asymmetrical organization of societal groups. The logic of collective action is that large groups with general interests will tend to remain unorganized, whereas more specialized collectivities, which can provide each of their members with a greater overall share of the total amount of benefits obtained from lobbying or other activities, are likely to crystallize into effective actors. The *Charter*, within the context of this reasoning, aggravates an already asymmetrical situation. Among the obvious groups to consider as under-represented, as a rule, are consumers and the poor. Each group is substantial in number but lacks the infrastructure to effectively influence the political process. This is particularly true in a situation such as that of the *Charter*'s creation, in which the ability to exert quick and visible pressure strongly affected the likelihood of recognition.

This set of problems is summed up by James (2006) as the Rawlsian paradox. Rawlsian (1971) thinking about how to maximize the interests of those worst off in society requires among those deliberating on a constitution a so-called veil of ignorance. This veil will ensure that the deliberators do not focus on themselves but on the lot of those who will be worst off in the constitutional order to come, which could turn out to be anyone. In a process such as occurred in 1982, however, discourse on the rights and privileges to be constitutionalized tends to occur in a situation in which everyone is already aware of his or her position in society. Rather than the idealized situation predicted by Rawls, what develops is a situation ripe for interest group politics. The logic of collective action (Olson 1965) then ensures a biased – and, unfortunately, constitutionally entrenched – outcome.

Given the preceding asymmetry, James Kelly's (2005) observations about the evolution of the *Charter* as an example of legitimate tactics by interest groups is not convincing. History does support Kelly's (2005) assertion that the federal government did not hand pick pro-*Charter* interest groups – but that is not what matters. The situation itself ensured an imbalance in who could get their messages across – and the general public interest, whatever it may be, stands as the most obvious example of what came to be excluded.

Cairns's citizen constitution theory puts a very positive emphasis on the shift from executive federalism to public empowerment with regard to constitutional change. Michael Lusztig (1994), however, points out that legitimized mass input (through referendums or whatever means) combined with existing constitutional agendas from Quebec and elsewhere in Confederation make it virtually certain that constitutional reform will fail in the future. This is troubling when Olson's argument is taken into consideration. Smaller, more easily organized interests had the ability to come together and be heard at the decisive stage that led to the *Charter*. They were also able to coordinate opposition to constitutional change from that point onward. More encompassing interests, by contrast, may be shut out forever.

Perhaps the most negative reaction to the citizens' constitution concerns its potential impact on the national psyche. Allan Hutchinson (1995, 37-38) sees the potential for an open-ended and pernicious process: "The danger of this almost limitless proliferation of rights is that people try to express all their claims and aspirations in its one-dimensional vocabulary, i.e., rights-talk becomes almost infinite in its scope." According to Anthony Peacock (1996, 123; see also 2002), the *Charter* created not a citizens' constitution but instead a "victim's constitution, a constitution concerned with ameliorating the conditions of disadvantaged groups." Peacock (2002) takes this a step further in his assessment of the Canadian government as a therapeutic state. As a long-term effect of the *Charter*, the idea that the state is supposed to take care of its citizens replaces the assumption of personal responsibility. Minorities are manufactured (see Knopff 1985), and virtually anyone can make a case for status as a victim. Thus, an unintended macro-micro consequence of the *Charter* is that it has changed personal values in a harmful way. The tendency toward collectivism inherent in Canadians is reinforced by a norm that rewards groups that seek compensation from the state rather than those who overcome obstacles through personal achievement.

Another criticism of the citizens' constitution pertains to the impact of multiculturalism on the political spectrum. Neil Bissoondath (2002, 65) claims that multiculturalism is a failed policy because of its role in "eradicating the centre." Canada, as a result, lacks a "new and definable centre" (Bissoondath 2002, 71). The policy, constitutionalized since 1982, evokes "uncertainty as to what and who is a Canadian" and diminishes "all sense of Canadian values."[8] Paradoxically, by embracing everything, Canada becomes nothing – a receptacle for whatever interest groups can pour into it, politically speaking. By implication, this weakens the political centre and opens the door to regional or more narrowly based entities that eschew brokerage politics.

Unlike the case of institutional imbalance, there is no ongoing dialogue between critics and defenders of the citizens' constitution. However, that does not prevent a response to the preceding observations. Take, for example, constitutional selfishness. A simple response would be that, with time, it should dissipate. As *Charter* rulings accumulate, and under an assumption of valid and reliable judgments by the Supreme Court, aggrieved parties should exhibit a lower intensity of preference about status.

Evidence suggests that engagement and dialogue have improved in the *Charter* era. The relationship between the government and Aboriginal peoples is one example. The passing of Bill C-34 tends to support the argument of those who support the citizens' constitution that favourable attitudes toward Aboriginal peoples as a part of national identity, along with increasingly constructive engagement on the part of Aboriginal peoples themselves with government, have been the product of constitutional change. Bill C-34, introduced by the western-oriented Conservative government – not the Liberals, who brought the *Charter* into existence – serves as human rights legislation for Aboriginal peoples. This fact alone suggests that Canadians now hold a more positive view of cooperation with Aboriginal peoples.

Conflict did ensue over Bill C-34's contents. Aboriginal leaders in particular wanted more consultation. Liberal MPs, with the support of the Association of First Nations (AFN), stalled a clause-by-clause reading of the bill (*Hill Times*, 30 July 2007). But even this incident can be viewed as a favourable development because it lacked extremist rhetoric and even a hint of violence. Instead, a review of the debate gives the impression that it proceeded according to politics as usual and in no way resembled the angry constitutionalized politics of Meech Lake and Charlottetown or the violent confrontations between Aboriginal peoples and government that preceded them. Public discussions along the way included the input of both the AFN and the Native Women's Association of Canada (*Hill Times*, 30 July 2007).

What about the argument that events brought on by the *Charter* have led to constitutional paralysis? This is certainly true of megapolitics: many years have passed since the last omnibus constitutional initiative. However, advocates of the citizens' constitution could point to the creation of Nunavut, recognition of Quebec as a distinct society in the House of Commons, and a series of accumulating constitutional asymmetries (see Chapter 5) as evidence that constitutional paralysis has not occurred. Joining forces with adherents of megapolitics across the paradigmatic divide, proponents of the citizens' constitution could adopt an incremental position, in both normative and empirical terms. The Constitution is evolving, but in a gradual way that does not seem to put national unity at risk.

Another point to consider is the impact of the *Charter* on individual Canadians, which has been highly damaging, according to Anthony Peacock (2002). Charles Epp (1998) and James Kelly (2005) provide data that suggests otherwise, at least in terms of Court activity. Pursuit of this kind of therapy does not seem to have escalated significantly in the *Charter* era. The only exception, hinted at earlier, is Kelly's (2005, 175) observation that judicial remedies in *Charter* cases have shown a tendency to read-in or read-down with time: whereas there was only one instance from 1982 to 1992, there were nine from 1993 to 2003. Obviously, this is not definitive evidence in favour of or against Peacock's assertions. At the level of the individual, of course, it is difficult to render judgment regarding the impact of *Charter* decisions either for specific groups or in general. Nevertheless, evidence that there has been an increased tendency to legislate from the bench gives credence to at least some aspects of Peacock's argument.

Has the political centre in Canada declined as a result of constitution-alized multiculturalism? Advocates of the citizens' constitution could argue that the *Charter* does more than simply recognize collectivities – it has also established a tradition of individual rights. Moreover, its group-based provisions could be viewed as creating through the legal system a mechanism to rectify injustices that otherwise may persist and create an even greater threat to Canada's viability. Brokerage politics, while diminished in an era of mobilized rights seeking, may resume as the polity deals with its principal grievances in an incremental manner.

### Conclusion: A Brief Comparison

Figure 6.1 compares the five theories in the liberal and communitarian paradigms along key dimensions: the primary means of identification, key causal variables, implications for social capital, three aspects of equilibrium (existence, stability, and normative desirability), and major challenges.

Three theories are primarily the result of a magnum opus, while two are the products of rational reconstruction. With regard to key causal variables, two of the three liberal theories emphasize aspects of the founding event: negative identity theory stresses the long-term effects of collectivism and anti-Americanism, while megapolitics theory, which

*Figure 6.1*

## A summary comparison of theories

| Paradigm | Theory | Primary means of identification | Key causal variables | Implications for social capital | Equilibrium | | | Major challenges |
|---|---|---|---|---|---|---|---|---|
| | | | | | Stability | Normative desirability | (Dis)integration? | |
| LIBERAL | Negative identity | Rational reconstruction | Lack of positive founding event; collectivism; proximity to United States | Yes – accumulating negative social capital; conflict within Confederation | Low | Low, with declining trust | Centrifugal > centripetal forces | Data showing similar values for United States |
| | Mega-politics | Magnum opus | Absence of sovereign founding event; package-style attempts to complete founding | Yes – accumulating negative social capital; cycles of conflict within Confederation | Low | Low, with declining trust | Centrifugal > centripetal forces | Lasting reform without mega-politics |
| | Institutional imbalance | Magnum opus | Judicial dominance; Court Party | Yes – accumulating negative social capital; judicial supremacy with continuing conflict | Low | Low, with declining trust | Centrifugal > centripetal | Public support for *Charter*; executive dominance |

▼ *Figure 6.1*

| Paradigm | Theory | Primary means of identification | Key causal variables | Implications for social capital | Equilibrium | | | Major challenges |
|---|---|---|---|---|---|---|---|---|
| | | | | | Stability | Normative desirability | (Dis)integration? | |
| COMMUNITARIAN | Asymmetric federalism | Rational reconstruction | Tension in symmetrical federalism; status seeking by excluded territorial collectivities | Yes – dynamic but convergent | Moderate | High, with increasing trust | Centripetal > centrifugal | Criteria for recognition; asymmetry-induced conflict |
| | Citizens' constitution | Magnum opus | Provincial nation-building challenge; *Charter* Canadians | Yes – low intensity conflict | Moderate | Moderate, with possible increasing trust | Centripetal > centrifugal | Constitutional selfishness; decreasing self-reliance |

focuses on package-style attempts to complete the founding event, is concerned more with forces exerted in the short term. Institutional imbalance theory concentrates most directly on the effects of the *Charter;* it stresses judicial dominance and the Court Party to explain where things are headed. Both of the communitarian theories, by contrast, emphasize problems with federalism: asymmetrical federalism theory stresses tension in symmetrical federalism and status seeking by excluded territorial collectivities, while citizens' constitution theory is concerned more with provincial nation-building challenges from Quebec. The latter theory also identifies the creation of *Charter* Canadians as a key causal variable.

All five theories identify a state of equilibrium for the system. Within the liberal theories, equilibrium is established or maintained by accumulating negative social capital. And proponents of each theory predict that, as a result, conflict will continue in the future. Megapolitics theory emphasizes the cyclical character of conflict, while institutional imbalance theory points toward judicial dominance. By contrast, proponents of communitarian theories see less conflict inherent in the equilibrium. Within asymmetrical federalism theory, the equilibrium is dynamic but convergent, while within citizens' constitution theory equilibrium consists of low intensity conflict.

All three liberal theories regard the equilibrium as being low in normative desirability. They predict that generalized trust will decline. The communitarian theories are more positive: adherents of asymmetrical federalism characterize the equilibrium as highly desirable, while adherents of citizens' constitution theory characterize it as only moderately so. Each of these theories predicts that generalized trust will be a long-term product of the *Charter.* Although none of the theories predicts imminent collapse for Canada, liberal theories point toward more centrifugal than centripetal forces within Confederation, whereas communitarian theories see it the other way around.

Although this chapter identifies points of agreement among the five theories, plenty of controversy remains. Differences between the theories often reflect the basic emphases – for instance, the individual versus collectivities – of the liberal and communitarian paradigms. And all five theories face challenges. For negative identity theory, it is troubling that recent data show so much similarity between Canadian and American values. Megapolitics theory must consider the issue of whether lasting reform can take place through a gradual approach, that is, in the absence of the package-style constitutional deals that it sees as the kiss of death.

High levels of public support for the *Charter* and the possibility of executive rather than judicial dominance are issues that the proponents of institutional imbalance theory must consider, while the criteria for recognition and asymmetry-induced conflict are issues that must be confronted by proponents of asymmetrical federalism. Finally, proponents of citizens' constitution theory need to consider constitutional selfishness and decreased self-reliance as possible harmful side effects of the *Charter*. These challenges create the opportunity for more to be learned as each complication is addressed.

# 7
# Conclusion

I have noticed that asking scholars to care about Canadian politics is like asking them to get a physical and eat more vegetables. Everyone agrees these are probably good ideas, but there is often a certain reluctance to comply. If you want someone to look at you quizzically, just say "I've become interested in Canada lately."

– David L. Leal, "Canada: The Unknown Country"

It is easy to relate to Leal's humorous reflections after studying the vast range of issues – and divided opinion about them – that surrounds constitutional evolution in Canada. Canada *is* interesting to study, but the country's generally peaceful and prosperous nature can be off-putting. Paradoxically, it is a common belief that the better a place is to live, the less interesting it must be to study. Although Canada is obviously a great success in many ways, its unity in the future is by no means certain and understanding constitutional evolution, the subject of the theories studied in this book, is the key to comprehending the direction in which the country is headed. This book concludes by addressing the following questions: Do the theories tend to agree about the direction of constitutional affairs in Canada? Is Canada headed toward some form of renewal? Is the end of Confederation in sight? Is the constitutional status quo the most likely future for a still-united Canada? What relevance do these findings have for policy, and what is the significance of the Canadian case of constitutional evolution to the world in general?

Using systemism as a frame of reference, this study identifies five theories of constitutional evolution in Canada. At first glance this might seem like a small number. The standards set by systemism, even when not fully implemented (recall that theories have been excused from meeting the requirement that functional form be specified for each linkage entailed), are quite demanding. Further research based on existing sources could turn up additional theories through rational reconstruction, and new publications may offer additional theories. The good faith effort at a comprehensive review of the literature undertaken in this study, however, led to the identification of only five theories – and that effort included rational reconstruction in at least one case (i.e., negative identity theory). A reasonable conclusion to reach, given the small number of theories identified, is that the study of constitutional politics in Canada does not generally include a self-conscious specification of a general equilibrium theory either cumulatively or in a given exposition. If the standards imposed by systemism are reasonable, then further work on constitutional politics in Canada should emphasize (1) the elaboration of existing theories and (2) the development of new competitors.

Although a systematic review of the evidence about the future of national unity in Canada is beyond the scope of this study, it is possible to sample opinion on the subject and assess it in the context of the preceding review of theories about constitutional evolution. In general, opinions about state-society relations vary. Those who view this issue in a positive light tend to focus on data about social capital and generalized trust, the place of Quebec in Canada, and the *Charter's* effects on personal beliefs. Those who view it in a negative light tend to focus on the political landscape, the electoral system, and the legal system.

One difference between liberal and communitarian theories pertains to social capital. Liberals argue that negative social capital is accumulating and leading to declining levels of generalized trust; by contrast, communitarians regard increased bonding capital as an asset that could stimulate more bridging capital over time. It may even have done so already. Data from Douglas Baer, James Curtis, and Edward Grabb (2001, 260) are at least neutral and perhaps even positive on the subject of social capital. In a comparison of the years 1981-83 and 1991-93, they found no decline in voluntary association membership among Canadians. Although this data does not cover recent years, it does pertain to the first decade of the *Charter's* existence and suggests that social capital was stable over that period – a result that sits somewhere between the expectations of liberal and communitarian theories.

Social capital, as demonstrated by Eric Uslaner (2002), can serve as an indirect indicator of generalized trust. What about trust itself? Using data from the World Values Survey, Dietlind Stolle and Eric Uslaner (2003, 2) report that Canadians are "among the most trusting people in the world." In response to the statement "most people can be trusted," 53 percent of Canadians responded *yes*. Their positive response was high by world standards, placing fourth behind citizens of Norway, Sweden, and the Netherlands. And the fact that Canada's ranking remained high in 1981, 1990, and 1995 suggests a high level of continuity among Canadian attitudes (Stolle and Uslaner 2003). In addition, survey data in 2003 shows that Canadians' trust in others stands at 56 percent. Only the very low figure of 35 percent recorded for Quebec stands out as a problem among the more fine-grained data (*Statistics Canada* 2004).

Another major consideration of theories of constitutional evolution is provincial nation building and the possibility of separation from Canada. Quebec, which is in the forefront of these concerns, stands out positively within a cross-national study of minorities at risk (Gurr 2000, 106, 112, 116, 120). The Québécois now number among the 33 (within a total of 273) ethnic minorities who are free from economic, political, or cultural disadvantages. Their presence among this small group suggests either that no problems ever existed (which is unlikely) or that things have improved in the decades since the Quiet Revolution (which is highly probable). If you add to this the incremental steps that have been made toward recognizing Quebec as a distinct society, the *Constitutional Veto Act*, the increased popularity of the *Charter* (Weinrib 2003, 30), the recent uneven performance of the Parti Québécois, and the lack of public interest in a third referendum (*Hill Times*, 10 September 2007), it is not hard to be optimistic about national unity. Perhaps Quebec nationalism as a centrifugal force is in long-term or even permanent decline. Or perhaps the incremental gains achieved in recent years have diminished interest in outright secession and will continue to do so.

Another positive development has been the popularity of the *Charter*. Values embodied by that document seem to be more in evidence over time and point toward higher national integration, which suggests that the *Charter* has had at least some influence. Perhaps it has even indirectly caused bridging capital to build up – an outcome desired by communitarian theorists. Although this connection cannot be proven, it is worthy of consideration.

Consider also Miriam Smith's (2007, 35-36) observations on the place of the *Charter* in Canadian life more than twenty-five years after its creation: "[T]he *Charter* has become an important factor in structuring political mobilization and debate, encouraging civil society organizations to stake their political claims in terms of *Charter* rights (for better or ill) and contributing to the partisan competition between political parties in federal politics." Smith offers a generally positive judgment on the *Charter's* integration into Canadian political life. She emphasizes the *Charter's* role in ongoing political, as opposed to dramatically constitutional, processes. The *Charter's* activation of civil society organizations could be regarded as an implicit argument in favour of the *Charter* vis-à-vis social capital in the sense that its mobilizing properties counteract alienation.

Some observers, however, are less optimistic about Canada in the post-*Charter* era. Aboriginal peoples and Quebec continue to be concerns. Kathy Brock (2006), for one, sees the path ahead as a rocky one. She cites polls that show "continuing deep ambivalence in Quebec towards Canada" (Brock 2006, 4). Quebec's annoyance stems from federal intrusions and fiscal imbalance, along with the sponsorship scandal, which obviously also troubles Canadians in general. Moreover, Canadians remain skeptical about political actors and the system as a whole a decade after megapolitics, and the level of trust in government in particular is at a low ebb (Brock 2006, 21). Canadians also tend to view rising expectations among Aboriginal peoples as a problem. Demands for self-government today are more intense than they were in the era of the Charlottetown Accord (Brock 2006). And Kathy Brock (2006, 28) enumerates other centrifugal forces: "A weakened Ontario, a stronger West, and growing resentments in both, not to mention the eastern provinces or neglected mid-west, bode ill for future discussions of national unity." With an emphasis on the conduct of federalism rather than the perception of individual citizens, Brock does not paint the prospect of governments working together to meet the country's needs in a positive light.

Evidence in favour of Brock's overarching position can be found in the electoral system. According to one recent study, Canada's electoral system is now more fragmented than at any other time in Canadian history (Carty 2006). This observation meshes well with Brock's description of a system with rising confrontation. Neither brokerage party seems to be able to obtain a majority, and each party is almost entirely shut out of certain provinces. Tom Flanagan's (2007, 192) observations about the 2004 federal election, which reflect the point of view of the Conservative Party, are revealing in this sense: "In regional terms, our greatest achievement was to make a long-awaited breakthrough in Ontario, where we won 31.5 percent of the vote and twenty-four of 106 seats." This quotation shows just how far things have fragmented when a high-ranking official in one of the brokerage parties describes a vote of less than one-third in Canada's most populous province as a major achievement.[1] Moreover, the Bloc Québécois's staying power in Quebec during the post-Charlottetown era, which takes a significant number of seats out of play, makes it much more difficult for anyone to form a majority government. A series of minority governments would not bode well for the development of a clear policy on constitutional affairs.

Fragmentation in the electoral system at the macro level has been accompanied by dissatisfaction at the micro level. Mebs Kanji and Antoine Bilodeau (2006) have discovered that differences in values increased significantly across a wide range of issues between 1990 and 2000. And this diversity provides the key to unlocking the mystery of electoral fragmentation. The rise of completely new parties – the Bloc Québécois, the Reform Party (later reintegrated to form the Conservative Party), and the Green Party – is a significant development. It suggests that the brokerage parties will be unable to regain sufficient support to obtain majorities and govern from the centre.

Although they provide ample evidence of trust at a general level, Stolle and Uslaner (2002, 8) also report an anomaly among Canadian attitudes – Canadians do not have a high level of trust in their legal system. Canada is merely average among 42 countries in this respect. The result is especially interesting in light of other survey results that suggest a high level of public confidence in the Supreme Court – even belief that the judiciary should have the final say on constitutional matters.

Evidence regarding key issues such as the role of Quebec and Aboriginal peoples and levels of social capital and trust reinforces the mixed message offered by analyses in the preceding chapters. *Canada is subject to centrifugal forces that perhaps exceed centripetal forces, but the likelihood of de-Confederation in the foreseeable future is very low.* In the fast-moving world of the new millennium, this prediction may be bolder than it appears. The fact that major forces are operating in both directions, toward integration as well as disintegration, suggests that Canadians face a situation in which they can control their own destiny. Put differently, there is some truth in the stories told by both liberal and communitarian theories. Canada may be headed toward some form of renewal, but whether it will be achieved depends on government policies at the macro level as well as millions of decisions by citizens at the micro level. The presence of both centrifugal and centripetal forces suggests that the end of Confederation is not in sight, and the most likely scenario for the future is an incrementally adjusted version of the status quo.

Several priorities for future research emerge as a natural extension of this book's review of theorizing on the evolution of constitutional politics in Canada. One priority comes out of the simple and honest acknowledgment that there may be more theories out there or will be in the future. A magnum opus could come out tomorrow, rational reconstruction could produce a new theory out of existing studies, or a previously unidentified school of thought could reach critical mass and generate another theory.[2] Therefore, one priority for future work should be the identification of additional theories from which to learn new things. Existing theories should also be subjected to further study to produce additional hypotheses. Every linkage in each of the five theory-conveying figures in this book is, in principle, a hypothesis to be tested. This could help to develop a means by which to aggregate centripetal and centrifugal forces in the same way. Moreover, new connections can be generated in every diagram – the only limit is the imagination. New theorizing may produce better answers to central questions about constitutional evolution.

This study's findings are also relevant to the small but expanding literature on systemism and the social sciences. Diagrammatic exposition via systemism facilitates a full understanding of the complexity within a given theory. It also helps to uncover connections that are excluded but important to the theory's development. In conjunction with a solid micro foundation – that is, rational choice – systemism can be used to convey seemingly incommensurable theories in a manner that facilitates dialogue and even some degree of synthesis. For example, contrary to what may have been expected, communitarian and liberal theories can be expressed in terms of rational choice, as long as the different goals assigned to actors by each paradigm are acknowledged. Systemism, given its inclusive nature, yields significant insights about state-society relations by giving an explicit place to macro-micro and micro-macro linkages in the explication of theories.

This study also introduces other innovations at the level of interdisciplinary theorizing about the evolution of constitutional politics in Canada. For example, it borrows the concept of equilibrium from economics and evaluates it in terms of existence, stability, and normative desirability. In addition, the concepts of social capital and generalized trust are imported from sociology to help assess Canadian constitutional affairs. This book therefore offers an interdisciplinary contribution that transcends the discipline's normative reliance on philosophy, law, and history as the wellspring of ideas.

Canadians and their government are in a position to influence the overall direction of the country. Neither the achievement of full national integration nor de-Confederation is inevitable. Given the importance of generalized trust and social capital for achieving an effective political order, some recommendations about policy are called for. Brock (2007), in a critique of asymmetrical federalism and perceived federal meddling in provincial jurisdictions, calls for a sharper federal focus on areas more truly within Ottawa's purview. It is interesting to see that Brock's two major policy recommendations are consistent with the creation of bridging capital. She (2007, 19) recommends reinvestment in the Canadian Broadcasting Corporation as a "national vehicle of information and education" that can promote a higher degree of national integration. She also calls for rebuilding the transportation system, "especially the trains, to encourage Canadians to visit each other and to get to know their land." Both of these suggestions are consistent with a vision of national unity based on the accumulation of bridging capital. Greater contact among citizens would also likely enhance generalized trust and shared knowledge and understanding.

Another recommendation addresses Anthony Peacock's (2002) troubling observations about self-reliance versus dependency on government. A key weakness in the Canadian economy – namely, Canada's level of productivity – seems to be in line with Peacock's assertions. In spite of record growth, Canadian productivity lags by world standards. Statistics by the Organisation for Economic Co-operation and Development for the period from 1981 to 2005 put Canada in last place for productivity growth in developed economies with populations over ten million (*Hill Times*, 30 July 2007). One notable editorial commentary has urged political leaders to take heed and mobilize public opinion and policy to improve weak productivity. What makes this recommendation especially credible is that it comes from Robin V. Sears, who is a former national campaign director of the NDP and hardly a shill for corporate interests. Sears urges policy makers to pay more attention to the size of the economic pie, metaphorically speaking, and less to how it should be divided. All of this is consistent with Peacock's assertion that Canadians need to develop more initiative and shake off an increasing tendency to depend on their government. A productivity revolution would seem to be in order.

Policies that build generalized trust as a micro-level foundation for macro-level accommodation of constitutional interests, such as those described regarding interpersonal contact and enhanced productivity, should also be a priority. To be sure, Canada's ability to cope with its problems, constitutional and otherwise, is of great importance to the rest of the world: "[H]ow the issue of ethnicity and multinationalism is handled in what has been one of the models for Western democracies has implications for the regroupings now occurring in Europe and for the ethnic and racial conflicts which dog much of the Third World" (Sanders 1991, 4). These words ring just as true today as they did when they were written in the early 1990s. The United States, in particular, wants Canada to survive intact: "In the twenty-first century, the final battle of democracy faced by the individual may be the battle for cultural tolerance, that is, for the mature type of political association described by the label 'democratic pluralism'" (Doran 2001, 35; see also Dion 1999, 132). The observations of Peter Russell (2004, 236), a great critic of constitutional wrangling in Canada, should also be considered: "In the long term, the example of that tradition [i.e., civility] – of avoiding violence in accommodating the very deep differences of identity and national sentiment that animate our people – may be our country's greatest contribution to human civilization." In that sense, the successful management of diversity in Canada complements the military might of the United States and the ability of its other powerful allies to bring about a more secure world.

Depending on the context, the Canadian exercise of this special form of power could take on added significance. In a tour de force on Canadian public diplomacy, *Branding Canada* (2008), Evan Potter demonstrates the potential value of the country's external presence in facilitating human development. Making the world more aware, through international education and broadcasting, of Canada's ability to achieve cooperation and avoid violence under conditions of relatively high diversity should be one of the most important priorities of any Canadian government.

This book offers a new approach to the subject of the evolution of constitutional politics in Canada. It uses systemism to articulate leading theories in a way that facilitates understanding of the points of agreement and controversy between and among them. To some extent, responding with uncertainty to the question, in which direction is Canada headed? may seem somewhat disappointing after so much effort. But the truth, when the arguments and evidence from the liberal and communitarian paradigms are taken together, lies somewhere between unity and disintegration. That is the reality of Canada today.

# Notes

**Chapter 1: Constitutional Politics in Canada**

1 *Aboriginal peoples* will be used throughout this volume to refer to First Nations, Métis, and Inuit because the term is the appropriate constitutional construct for the analysis that follows.

2 See Stevenson (1982); Banting and Simeon (1983a, 1983b, 1983c); Cairns (1983); Norrie, Simeon, and Krasnick (1986); Courchene (1988); Caplan (1989); Lederman (1989); Scott (1989); Simeon and Robinson (1990); Campbell and Pal (1991); Fry (1991); Reuber (1991); Smith (1991a, 1991b); Young (1991a; 1991b); Christian (1992); Gibson (1992); LaSelva (1993); McBride (1993); Sproule-Jones (1993); Taylor (1993); Jérôme-Forget (1994); Milne (1994); Archer et al. (1995); Hueglin (1995); Meisel (1995); Lachapelle (1996); Flanagan (1996, 1998, 2002); McRoberts (1997); Kymlicka (1998); Laforest (1998a, 1998b, 2000); Nöel (1998); Brooks (2000); Dyck (2002); Meadwell (2001); Behiels (2004); Russell (2004); and Brock (2005, 2006, 2007). Some of the items in this note and those that follow (e.g., Norrie et al. 1986) may appear in more than one list.

3 Studies of the courts include Flanagan (1985); Gibson (1985a, 1985b); Knopff (1985, 1996, 2001); Russell, Knopff, and Morton (1990); Knopff and Morton (1992, 1996); Brodie (1993, 1996, 2001); Manfredi (1993, 2001); Roach (1993); Mandel (1994); Morton (1994); Darby and Emberly (1996); Martin (1996); Peacock (1996b, 1996c, 2002); Young (1998); Morton and Knopff (2000); Kelly (2002, 2005); Hiebert (2002); Rush (2002); and Smithey (2002).

4 In this book *the West* refers to British Columbia, Alberta, Saskatchewan, and Manitoba, but it is understood that, for some issues, it makes more sense to distinguish between British Columbia and the Prairie provinces. Examples from a vast literature on the problems of national unity include Stevenson (1982, 1991); Banting and Simeon (1983a, 1983b, 1983c); Trudeau (1989, 1992); Lipset (1990); Valaskakis (1990); Cairns (1991c); Courchene (1991); Coyne (1991); Fraser (1991); Greschner (1991); Martin (1991); McDougall (1991); Palmer (1991); Robertson (1991); Russell (1991a, 1991d, 1991e, 1992, 1993a, 1993b, 1993c); Sanders (1991); Whittaker (1991); Whyte (1991); Wintrobe and Young (1991); Young (1991a, 1991b); Weaver (1992a, 1992b, 1993); Beatty (1993); Meekison (1993); McRoberts (1993, 1997); Thomas (1993, 1997); Cook (1994); Lenihan,

Robertson, and Tassé (1994); Lusztig (1994); Webber (1994); Barnes (1995); Jockel (1995); Cooper (1996a, 1991b, 2000); Stein (1997); Flanagan (1998); Gibbins (1998a); Gibbins and Laforest (1998a, 1998b); Jenson (1998); Laforest (1998a, 1998b); Watts (1998a, 1998b); James (1999); Lusztig (1999); Bissoondath (2000); Granatstein (2000a, 2000b); Griffiths (2000); Ignatieff (2000a, 2000b); James, Abelson, and Lusztig (2002a, 2002b); and Chrétien (2008).

5 Because the issue is long-standing, many treatments from the francophone perspective and varying points of view are available in English. See, for instance, Morton (1985); Breton (1988); Latouche (1990, 1998); Banting (1991); Bercuson and Cooper (1991); Blais (1991); Dion (1991, 1993); Fortin (1991); Gibson (1991); Laforest (1991); Resnick (1991); Imbeau and Laforest (1991-92); Leeson (1991); McRoberts (1991-92, 1997, 1998); Orban (1991); Schneiderman (1991); Blais and Nadeau (1992); Laxer (1992); Richler (1992); Scott (1992); Heard (1993); Meadwell (1993); Gairdner (1994); Martin (1994, 1995); Carens (1995); Usher (1995a, 1995b); Vipond (1995); Watson (1995); Young (1995, 1998, 1999); James and Lusztig (1996, 1997a, 1997b); Lachapelle (1996); Turp (1996); Thomas (1997); Gibbins (1998b); Howe (1998); Jenson (1998); Nöel (1998); Norrie and Percy (1998); Rocher (1998); Newman (1999); and Courchene (2004).

6 See Gibbins (1983, 1991, 1996); McLellan (1992); Cooper (1994); and Lusztig (1995).

7 Some examples from the vast literature on the *Constitution Act, 1982* and the *Charter of Rights and Freedoms* are Banting and Simeon (1983a, 1983b, 1983c); Cairns (1983); Gibbins (1983); Smiley (1983); Morton (1985); Slattery (1987); Imbeau (1990, 1992); Simeon and Robinson (1990); Coyne (1991); Lederman (1991); Martin (1991); Manfredi (1993, 2001); Pal (1993a, 1991b); Roach (1993); Sigurdson (1993); Gairdner (1994); Mandel (1994); Hutchinson (1995); Selick (1996); Hogg and Bushell (1997); McRoberts (1997); Schneiderman (1998); Weinrib (2001, 2003); Manfredi and Kelly (1999); Flanagan (2002); James, Abelson, and Lusztig (2002a, 2002b); Hiebert (2002); Behiels (2003); Iacobucci (2003); Knopff (2003); Magnet (2003); Toews (2003); Kelly (2005); and Kelly and Manfredi (2009).

8 Although Canada lacked a domestic amending formula, it did have a procedure for constitutional change prior to 1982. If a matter rested under exclusive federal authority, Parliament could ask the Westminster Parliament to amend the *British North America Act, 1867* in accordance with its views. In cases involving issues that affected both levels of government, a different procedure was followed. If the provincial governments agreed to a proposed change, Parliament could ask Westminster to change the *BNA Act* accordingly. Thus, an amending procedure existed within an imperial context prior to the *Constitution Act, 1982*.

9 Studies of the Meech Lake Accord and its aftermath include Breton (1988, 1992); Cairns (1988a, 1988b, 1991a); Chamberlin (1988); Courchene (1988, 1991); Gibbins (1988a, 1988b, or 1988c); Simeon (1988a, 1988b); Smith (1988); Swinton (1988); Cohen (1990); Meekison (1990); Simeon and Robinson (1990); Smith (1990); Blakeney (1991); Brock (1991); Cloutier (1991); Fournier (1991); Fraser (1991); Imbeau (1991); McLellan (1991); Milne (1991); Monahan (1991); Owram (1991); Palmer (1991); Peacock (1996b); Scott (1991); Smith and Courtney (1991);

Tupper (1991, 1993); Whittaker (1991); Vipond (1995); McRoberts (1997); Stein (1997); and James (1998). Studies of the Charlottetown Accord and its aftermath include Leeson (1992); Meekison (1992); Scott (1992); Brock (1993); Crowley (1993); Jhappan (1993); Johnston (1993); Monahan (1993); Gairdner (1994); Lusztig (1994); Morton (1994); Manfredi (1995, 1996); Pammett and LeDuc (1995); Peacock (1996a); Stein (1997); and Dickerson and Flanagan (1998).

10  For studies of the referendum, see, for example, Cairns (1996, 1998); Denis (1996); Jenson (1996); Peacock (1996a); and Tupper (1996).

11  See, for instance, Cloutier (1991); Smith (1991); Abu-Laban and Stasiulis (1992); Kornberg and Clarke (1992); Clarke and Kornberg (1994); Levine (1994); LeDuc and Pammett (1995); Pammett and LeDuc (1995); Howe and Fletcher (2000); Johnston (2000); Uslaner (2001); and Carty (2006).

12  See Norrie, Simeon, and Krasnick (1986); Boothe and Harris (1991); Fortin (1991); Furtan and Gray (1991); Harris and Purvis (1991); McDougall (1991); Wintrobe and Young (1991); Howlett and Ramesh (1992); Landry (1993); McBride (1993); Martin (1994, 1995); Turp (1996); Norrie and Percy (1998); McMahon (2000); Crowley (2000, 2001); James and Lusztig (2001); Courchene (2004); and Brock (2005).

13  A diverse literature touches on the acquisition of values (most notably in relation to rights) and interest groups. See, for instance, Cairns (1988a, 1988b, 1991a, 1991b, 1992, 1993, 1995, 2000); Kymlicka (1989, 1993, 1995, 1998); Greschner (1991); Pocklington (1991); Smith (1991); Stevenson (1991); Brodie and Nevitte (1993a, 1993b); Hiebert (1993); Pal (1993a, 1993b); Taylor (1993, 1994); Ajzenstadt (1995); Walker (1997); Bateman (1998); M. Smith (1998); Howe and Fletcher (2000); Klein (2000); Bissoondath (2002); James, Abelson, and Lusztig (2002a, 2002b); Lusztig (2002); and Smithey (2002). The literature on women includes Smith (1990); Baines (1991); Smith (1991); Greschner (1993); Krosenbrink-Gelissen (1993); Vickers (1993); and Manfredi (2005). Treatments of Aboriginal peoples and constitutional change include Morton (1985); Chamberlin (1988); Mercredi (1991, 2000); Courchene and Powell (1992); Flanagan (1992, 1998, 2000); Jhappan (1993); and Cairns (2000).

14  For studies of the media, see Fraser (1991); Meisel (1991); Palmer (1991); Raboy (1991); Taras (1991); and Antecol and Enbersby (1999). Studies of commissions and task forces include Cameron (1993); Oliver (1993); and Abelson (2002).

15  Systemism is a method for the articulation of theory, not a theory in and of itself. It is therefore important to distinguish it from systems theory in political science. Easton's (1953, 1965a, 1965b) high-profile behavioural theory differs significantly from systemism as developed by Bunge (1996). Chapter 2 discusses the legacy of Easton's theory as it relates to systemism.

### Chapter 2: Systemism and Canadian Constitutional Politics

1  Although the description and analysis that follows relies on Easton (1965a), it could just as easily proceed on the basis of the other two works noted, which also convey Easton's basic concept formation and arguments.

2  A literature review revealed no significant attempt to reformulate Easton's systems analysis after the early 1970s, although it would be fair to say that many frame-

works from that decade and beyond owe at least an indirect intellectual debt to Easton's call for rigor and diagrammatic emphasis. Leslie's (1972, 169-70) attempts to reformulate the approach based on an expansive set of variables, which fall under four headings (system attributes, regime characteristics, characteristics of political community, and characteristics of the authorities), stands as an isolated attempt to continue to work under the rubric of systems analysis.

3   See Sproule-Jones (1993) for an effective application in the context of Canadian federalism. It is ironic that Bunge (1996), the creator of systemism, is also an outspoken critic of rational-choice models as they have been conceived to date. Among the most glaring faults of these models are undefined or arbitrary utility functions (i.e., what actors want and why); static specification; lack of context; a narrow focus on exchange; the omission of a wider range of motives for action; and a lack of descriptive, explanatory, and predictive power (Bunge 1996, 393-94). Although the list would become even longer if other critics were consulted, it is worth pointing out that even Bunge (1996, 394), who has a systemist orientation, sees some potential for rational-choice models: they can (1) help in the preliminary formulation of problems, (2) show a connection between self-interest and the collective problems that result, (3) suggest useful experiments, and (4) show the limits of rationality as an explanation for behaviour. For these reasons, a project that uses self-interest as the micro foundation for applying systemism to the study of constitutional politics in Canada is not regarded as a contradiction in terms.

4   A wide range of successful applications in normative theory and comparative and international politics have already appeared (Booth, James, and Meadwell 1993). It is interesting to note that only two book-length applications of rational choice to Canadian politics have been written so far (Sproule-Jones 1993; Flanagan 1998). Other studies that use game theory, expected utility, and related approaches in this substantive field include Kilgour (1983, 1985); Kilgour and Levesque (1984); Levesque and Moore (1984); Mintz (1985); Imbeau (1990, 1991, 1992); Flanagan (1992); Brodie (1993, 1996); James (1993, 1998, 1999); and James and Lusztig (1996, 1997a, 1997b).

5   Three qualifications must be made about Figure 2.2, which guides analysis of the notwithstanding clause and its aftermath. First, the figure does not include a functional form for each respective linkage, as is advocated by systemism and conveyed in Figure 2.1. For purposes of simplification, it is assumed that each connection is either direct (e.g., Quebec's use of the clause restored Bill 178) or monotonically increasing (e.g., as public opinion shifted against the Meech Lake Accord, individual and group mobilization increased). Although they are not ruled out, more complex, non-linear functions – for example, logarithmic or exponential functions – are not considered. Second, the figure does not include exogenous inputs to the system because they are non-existent in the example – that is, neither Quebec's use of the notwithstanding clause nor subsequent events connected to it were affected by external forces during the period in question. In other words, the processes occurred strictly within the Canadian constitutional system, although environmental effects would play a role at some point if the story were extended forward or backward in time. Third, the arrows in the

figure are not drawn to scale to convey the passing of time. Some connections, such as "Supreme Court of Canada Finds Bill 178 Unconstitutional → Notwithstanding Clause Invoked by Bourassa," are rapid and occur within a few days or weeks. Others, such as "Public Opinion Outside of Quebec Shifts against Meech Lake Accord → Individual and Interest Group Mobilization (e.g., Trudeau)," can take place over months (as was the case in this example), years, or even decades.

6  Figures 2.1 and 2.2 do not have the same structure because Figure 2.1 represents an ideal type that covers a cycle of cause and effect with precisely one linkage from each of the four possibilities in the system, along with exogenous input and output. Tracing out the linkages in a real series of events, as is represented in Figure 2.2, creates a more complex configuration as connections shift back and forth across the macro and micro levels. The figure would be even more elaborate if it were extended to include environmental effects.

7  Under the rules of the Manitoba legislature, a fixed number of days are required before a vote on a bill can be introduced. This process can be skipped only if a unanimous vote takes place. Rather than preventing a vote on Meech Lake, Harper refused to allow the rules to be altered to reduce the number of days required for public hearings. Thus, the three-year limit on the accord expired before a vote could be taken.

8  Manfredi (2001, 115) refers to macro- and micro-constitutional politics as, respectively: "[P]olitical bargaining conducted according to the constraints found in the formal rules of the Canadian amending process" and "constitutional rule-making through litigation." Although applied clearly and effectively throughout his study, the definitions from Manfredi are more restrictive than those used here. The macro and micro levels in this context refer more inclusively to processes beyond those covered by formal rules of amendment and litigation.

9  The example of Trudeau is used because it is especially difficult to classify. It could be argued that the former prime minister would still qualify as a macro-level entity during the Meech Lake controversy because of his position as a statesman and his overall prominence. However, if this line of reasoning were followed, the status of every given individual acting outside of a formal government role would need to be evaluated. This alternative, subjective approach toward classification would be unworkable.

## Chapter 3: Identifying Concepts and Theories

1  This review of the literature is not exhaustive, but because explicit definitions are somewhat uncommon, it is likely representative. (This is not surprising because concept formation at the most basic level generally takes an implicit form within a given research paradigm, regardless of discipline [James 2002].)

2  Hogg (1977, 5-11) observes that Canada does not have a single comprehensive constitutional document. Instead, he enumerates the imperial statutes, Canadian statutes, case law, and conventions that collectively make up the Constitution. The *BNA Act* is an example of an imperial statute, while the *Constitution Act, 1982* and the *Charter of Rights and Freedoms* are the most prominent Canadian statutes. (The *Charter* is part of the *Constitution Act, 1982,* but the latter is identified separately to prevent confusion because the *BNA Act* became the *Constitution*

*Act, 1867,* at the time of repatriation in 1982.) Conventions are time-honoured rules not enforced by the courts, while case law represents ongoing judicial interpretation.

3  Alternative concept formations, which are generally consistent with the definition of theory put forward here, are summarized in James (2002). The definition from Bunge (1996) works in tandem with the other theoretical apparatuses that have been borrowed from his landmark reassessment of the social sciences.

4  For an extremely accessible and informative exegesis of the concepts, see Sandler (2001, 130-45). The discussion that follows relies primarily on this source.

5  Uniqueness, a fourth issue enumerated by Sandler (2001), does not have an analogue with regard to constitutional evolution.

6  The discussion that follows is based on Uslaner (2002). Research reveals that generalized trust is a function primarily of parental influence. It therefore makes sense to focus on social capital as an indicator of generalized trust.

7  It is true that the *BNA Act* included references to Aboriginal peoples in the language of the times. One example is section 91.24. Yet, there is no way that Aboriginal peoples can be regarded as being present, literally or figuratively, at the bargaining table.

8  During the Lubicon Lake dispute, for instance, the federal government attempted to undermine the Lubicon band's claims by recognizing and dealing with new bands such as the Woodland Cree. The conflict centred on whether the Lubicon would be able to obtain more lucrative Aboriginal rights as opposed to the limited benefits provided by territorial entitlement. See Flanagan (1992, 288, 290).

9  Flanagan (2000) provides an extensive critique of the Aboriginal orthodoxy that is beyond the scope of this study.

10  Canadian politics as a field of study, whether the focus is on the Constitution in particular or matters in general, does not emphasize theory per se. Theory, when it does appear, is generally borrowed and applied from other disciplines. This is true even of classic works. One example is John Porter's *Vertical Mosaic* (1965), which uses a quasi-Marxist class analysis to come to grips with the Canadian political system. Porter (1965, 3-28) refers to class and power as major themes, but does not claim to be producing a theory about Canadian society.

11  And how much is enough? Perhaps the best answer is to fall back on Justice Potter Stewart's definition of pornography – "I know it when I see it." More seriously, objective criteria, such as citation counts, could be worked out, but that type of assessment is beyond the scope of this study, which focuses on substantive issues in the evolution of Canadian constitutional politics rather than the sociology of knowledge.

12  See Flanagan (1985, 1992, 1996, 2000); Knopff (1985, 1996, 2001); Knopff and Morton (1992, 1996); Brodie (1993, 1996, 2001); Cooper (1994, 1996a, 1996b, 2000); Lusztig (1994, 1995, 1999, 2002); James and Lusztig (1996, 2001); and James (1999).

13  For example, at its biennial meeting in San Antonio in November 2001, the Association for Canadian Studies in the United States held a panel in honour of the Calgary School.

14  Something should be said about what might seem to be an obvious alternative to this multifaceted, and perhaps even cumbersome, way of identifying theories: why

not begin simply with the question, what are the principal features of Canadian constitutional evolution that require explanation? Answering this question would presuppose a sense of the major causal mechanisms at work in the Canadian polity. The paradox is that to embark on that path with any prospect for success would require the development of a theory *a priori*. What else, after all, could provide a sense of direction? To reply that the path is obvious is not a compelling argument. In short, this exercise would be fundamentally different than the one conducted in this book, which seeks to identify what passes for theory and assess its potential for development.

15 It could be argued that identity-based theories are the hallmark of communitarianism, while liberals favour a more interest-based understanding of political behaviour and back away from the idea that conduct is predicated on shared identity. The proper classification of negative identity, which focuses on aspects of identity that operate within the constitutional system, will be explored further in Chapter 4.

**Chapter 4: Liberal Theories**

1 Because a government report granted some recognition to women in 1970, it could be said that the *Charter* reinforced status.

2 It would be more accurate to say that First Nations leaders called for a boycott and additional time for deliberation.

3 Because negative identity is largely a product of rational reconstruction, significant aspects of the preceding discussion, notably the equilibrium analysis, derive from that process.

4 This articulation of megapolitics as a theory relies heavily on the writings of Peter Russell (1991a, 1991b, 1991c, 1991d, 1991e, 1992, 1993a, 1993b, 2004), who put forward its basic arguments in reviewing the failures of the Meech Lake and Charlottetown accords. Although Russell did not refer to megapolitics as a theory per se, he did introduce the terms *macro-constitutional politics* and *mega-constitutional politics* into the debate and put forward virtually all of the causal linkages conveyed in Figure 4.2.

5 Russell's observations, of course, turned out to be prescient, particularly his identification of the potential for mobilization of homosexuals in response to section 15 of the *Charter*. This issue became quite visible in the courts from the 1990s onward (Manfredi 2002; Rush 2002).

6 Emphasis on the *Constitution Act, 1982* and the *Charter* as an anchor event does not deny the existence of previous efforts toward constitutional sovereignty. The Fulton-Favreau formula and the Victoria Charter are two examples that come to mind. Neither figures into the existing discourse of the theory because these initiatives did not cover issues as comprehensively as the *Charter*, Meech Lake, and Charlottetown. See Behiels (2003, 151).

7 The Canadian Supreme Court granted 30 percent of *Charter*-based requests to nullify federal or provincial statutes between 1984 and 2001. In contrast, the US Supreme Court "overturned only one federal statute and 18 state laws during the first *34 years* that it claimed to exercise judicial review" (Manfredi 2001, 23). Although this difference can be accounted for in many ways – perhaps as a result of better-written legislation in the United States – the sheer magnitude

of Canadian judicial review tends to support the assertion that the *Charter* ushered in an era of qualitatively greater activity per se.

8 This connection is implicit in the treatments associated with the Court Party and Ian Brodie's *Friends of the Court* and explicit in the work of Robert Martin (1994), whose assessment is critical of judicial supremacy for very different substantive reasons. Martin's attack on the *Charter* as a tool of corporations seeking to avoid regulation by elected officials is at the opposite end of the ideological spectrum from Court Party analysts, but it also bemoans the negative effect that post-*Charter* judicial activism has had on democracy.

### Chapter 5: Communitarian Theories

1 See Watts (1998b) for a classification of constitutional asymmetries in the context of Canadian federalism.

2 Along with the work of Kymlicka (1989, 1993, 1995, 1998), see Taylor (1993); Meisel (1995); Jenson (1998); Laforest (1998a, 1998b); and Magnet (2003).

3 Kymlicka (1995, 191) uses data from Quebec after Meech Lake to establish this point: "[W]hile over half of Quebeckers attach priority, in their self-identity, to their status as Quebec citizens, compared with just under 30 percent who attach priority to Canadian citizenship, still 70 percent of Quebeckers say they would be willing to make personal sacrifices that would benefit only Canadians outside of Quebec."

4 Some tension exists within asymmetrical federalism between liberal versus communitarian values and their role in the construction of an argument in favour of the recognition of collective rights. This issue will be addressed further in Chapter 6.

5 This is summed up by Huntington (1993) with the term *third wave*. Huntington argues that democracy rises and falls in waves over long periods that can be measured in decades. Thus, although Canada was already a constitutional democracy in the era leading up to the *Charter*, it can be expected to move even further in that direction.

6 Charles Epp (1998, 6-7) produces considerable evidence that a rights revolution, led and supported by the federal government, existed prior to the *Constitution Act* and *Charter*. Consider the following data on the Supreme Court from 1960 to 1990: while the percentage of cases about civil rights and liberties increased after the *Charter*, requests for judicial review went up dramatically before its advent. In addition, third-party interventions also increased significantly before the *Charter* (Epp 1998, 172-75).

7 The Harper government cancelled the Court Challenges Program at one point but reinstated a more limited version in response to criticism from the commissioner of official languages. Ottawa provides financial support to groups that seek to challenge government policy, but only in the area of minority language rights. The Harper government introduced the Program to Support Linguistic Rights in June 2008.

### Chapter 6: A Critique and Comparison of Theories

1 Grabb and Curtis (2002), in reviewing the literature on the subject, refer directly to the political sociology of Seymour Martin Lipset (1990), who put forward

influential ideas about the essential differences between Canada and the United States (see Chapter 4).

2 Because Russell does not present megapolitics as a theory, as defined by this study, it is more appropriate to study reactions to megapolitics as a guiding idea or general hypothesis about the harmful effects of package-style constitutional proposals.

3 The discussion that follows is based primarily on Kelly (2005).

4 It is interesting to note that even Knopff and Morton (2002, 37), who first put forward the idea of the Court Party, agree that parliamentary institutions are executive dominated.

5 Hiebert (2002) effectively operationalizes Slattery's (1987, 707, 710) coordinate model, in which the branches of government share responsibility and relate as equals within a "continuing dialogue between the courts and legislatures." The basis for dialogue is the existence of section 33.

6 A comprehensive critique of a rights-based regime at an operational level appears in Hutchinson (1995, 28-56).

7 Gairdner (1994, 60) makes the following observation about the Charlottetown Accord: "The words 'equality,' 'equal,' or 'equalization' appeared in this document twenty-three times; the word 'authority' eight times; the word 'liberty' – not at all." Critics might draw attention to this difference in priorities as being a reflection of the equality-seeking forces set in motion by the *Charter,* even if the accord itself did not pass into law.

8 Bissoondath (2002) does not mention the citizens' constitution in his analysis of multiculturalism. The argument made here is derived from that exposition.

**Chapter 7: Conclusion**

1 In this context, note also one of the fundamental lessons of the 2004 election identified by Flanagan (2007, 196, emphasis added): "Our advertising had to become *more regionally diverse* and responsive to attacks from other parties."

2 Consider just one possible source for a new theory: the vast literature on welfare economics (Kaldor 1939; de Scitovsky 1941). Welfare economics focuses on prescribing policy and could easily be adapted to the Canadian context vis-à-vis ideas about what an optimal constitutional system would look like and how it might be pursued. Still other disciplines, such as sociology, could be sources of new theory.

# References

Abelson, Donald E. 2002. "Think Tanks, Public Policy and Constitutional Politics in Canada." In Patrick James, Donald E. Abelson, and Michael Lusztig, eds., *The Myth of the Sacred: The Charter, the Courts and the Politics of the Constitution in Canada*, 171-87. Montreal and Kingston: McGill-Queen's University Press.

Abu-Laban, Yasmeen, and Daiva Stasiulis. 1992. "Ethnic Pluralism under Siege: Popular and Partisan Opposition to Multiculturalism." *Canadian Public Policy* 18, 4: 365-86.

Ajzenstat, Janet. 1995. "Decline of Procedural Liberalism: The Slippery Slope to Secession?" In Joseph H. Carens, ed., *Is Quebec Nationalism Just? Perspectives from Anglophone Canada*, 120-36. Montreal and Kingston: McGill-Queen's University Press.

Antecol, Michael, and James W. Endersby. 1999. "Newspaper Consumption and Beliefs about Canada and Quebec." *Political Communication* 16, 1: 95-112.

Archer, Keith, Roger Gibbins, Rainer Knopff, Heather McIvor, and Leslie A. Pal. 2002. *Parameters of Power: Canadian Political Institutions*. 3rd ed. Scarborough: Thomson Nelson.

Archer, Keith, Roger Gibbins, Rainer Knopff, and Leslie A. Pal. 1995. *Parameters of Power: Canada's Political Institutions*. Toronto: Nelson Canada.

Archer, Margaret A. 1996. *Culture and Agency: The Place of Culture in Social Theory*. Rev. ed. Cambridge: Cambridge University Press.

Baer, Douglas, James Curtis, and Edward Grabb. 2001. "Has Voluntary Association Activity Declined? Cross-National Analyses from Fifteen Countries." *Canadian Review of Sociology and Anthropology* 38, 3: 249-74.

Baines, Beverly. 1991. "After Meech Lake: The Ms/Representation of Gender in Scholarly Spaces." In David E. Smith, Peter MacKinnon, and John C. Courtney, eds., *After Meech Lake: Lessons for the Future*, 205-18. Saskatoon: Fifth House Publishers.

Banting, Keith G. 1991. "If Quebec Separates: Restructuring Northern North America." In R. Kent Weaver, ed., *The Collapse of Canada?* 159-78. Washington, DC: Brookings Institution.

Banting, Keith, and Richard Simeon. 1983a. "Federalism, Democracy and the Constitution." In Keith Banting and Richard Simeon, eds., *And No One Cheered: Federalism, Democracy and the Constitution Act*, 2-26. Toronto: Methuen.

–. 1983b. "Federalism, Democracy and the Future." In Keith Banting and Richard Simeon, eds., *And No One Cheered: Federalism, Democracy and the Constitution Act*, 348-60. Toronto: Methuen.

–, eds. 1983c. *And No One Cheered: Federalism, Democracy and the Constitution Act*. Toronto, Methuen.

Barnes, Thomas G. 1995. "There'll Always Be a Canada and a Canadian Constitutional Crisis." *Annals of the American Academy of Political and Social Science* 538: 27-39.

Bateman, Thomas M.J. 1998. "Rights Application of Doctrine and the Clash of Constitutionalisms in Canada." *Canadian Journal of Political Science* 31, 1: 3-29.

Beatty, David. 1993. "Amending the Canadian Constitution." *Constitutional Forum* 4, 2: 53-54.

Behiels, Michael D. 2004. *Canada's Francophone Minority Communities: Constitutional Renewal and the Winning of School Governance*. Montreal and Kingston: McGill-Queen's University Press.

–. 2003. "Pierre Elliott Trudeau's Legacy: The Canadian Charter of Rights and Freedoms." In Joseph Eliot Magnet, Gérald-A. Beaudoin, Gerald Gall, and Christopher P. Manfredi, eds., *The Canadian Charter of Rights and Freedoms: Reflections on the Charter after Twenty Years*, 139-73. Markham: Butterworths.

Bercuson, David J., and Barry Cooper. 1991. *Deconfederation: Canada without Quebec*. Toronto: Key Porter Books.

Bissoondath, Neil. 2002. 2nd ed. *Selling Illusions: The Cult of Multiculturalism in Canada*. Toronto: Penguin Books.

–. 2000. "Dreaming of Other Lands." In Rudyard Griffith, ed., *Great Questions of Canada*, 27-31. Toronto: Stoddart.

Blais, André. 1991. "The Constitutional Game in Quebec: Options, Interests, Strategies, Outcomes." In Robert A. Young, ed., *Confederation in Crisis*. Toronto: James Lorimer and Company.

Blais, André, and Richard Nadeau. 1992. "To Be or Not To Be Sovereigntist: Quebeckers' Perennial Dilemma." *Canadian Public Policy* 18, 1: 89-103.

Blakeney, Allan E. 1991. "Commentary." In David E. Smith, Peter MacKinnon, and John C. Courtney, eds., *After Meech Lake: Lessons for the Future*, 61-64. Saskatoon: Fifth House Publishers.

Booth, William James, Patrick James, and Hudson Meadwell, eds. 1993. *Politics and Rationality*. Cambridge: Cambridge University Press.

Boothe, Paul, and Richard Harris. 1991. "The Economics of Constitutional Change: Dividing the Federal Debt." *Canadian Public Policy* 17, 4: 434-44.

Brecher, Michael. 1999. "International Studies in the Twentieth Century and Beyond: Flawed Dichotomies, Synthesis, Cumulation." *International Studies Quarterly* 43, 2: 213-64.

Breton, Albert. 1989. "The Theory of Competitive Federalism." In Garth Stevenson, ed., *Federalism in Canada: Selected Readings*, 457-502. Toronto: McClelland and Stewart.

Breton, Raymond. 1992. *Why Meech Failed: Lessons for Canadian Constitution Making*. Toronto: C.D. Howe Institute.

–. 1988. "The Concept of 'Distinct Society' and 'Identity' in the Meech Lake Accord." In Katherine E. Swinton and Carol J. Rogerson, eds., *Competing Constitutional Visions: The Meech Lake Accord*, 3-10. Toronto: Carswell.

Brock, Kathy L. 2007. "Open Federalism, Section 94, and Principled Federalism: Contradictions in Vision." Paper presented at the annual meeting of the Canadian Political Science Association, 29 May-1 June, London, Ontario.
–. 2006. "Surviving as Canadians: Tracking New and Continuing Tensions in the Federation." Unpublished manuscript.
–. 2005. "Accords and Discord: The Politics of Asymmetrical Federalism and Intergovernmental Relations." Paper presented at the annual meeting of the Canadian Political Science Association, London, Ontario.
–. 1993. "Learning from Failure: Lessons from Charlottetown." *Constitutional Forum* 4, 2: 29-33.
–. 1991. "Commentary." In David E. Smith, Peter MacKinnon, and John C. Courtney, eds., *After Meech Lake: Lessons for the Future*, 65-66. Saskatoon: Fifth House Publishers.
Brodie, Ian. 2001. *Friends of the Court*. Albany, NY: SUNY Press.
–. 1996. "The Market for Political Status." *Comparative Politics* 28, 3: 253-71.
–. 1993. "Competition for Charter Equality Rights Status: The Rational Choice Dynamic." Paper presented at the annual meeting of the Canadian Political Science Association.
Brodie, Ian, and Neil Nevitte. 1993a. "Clarifying Differences: A Rejoinder to Alan Cairn's Defence of the Citizens' Constitution Theory." *Canadian Journal of Political Science* 26, 2: 269-72.
–. 1993b. "Evaluating the Citizens' Constitution Theory." *Canadian Journal of Political Science* 26, 2: 235-59.
Brooks, Stephen. 2000. *Canadian Democracy: An Introduction*. 3rd ed. Toronto: Oxford University Press.
Bunge, Mario. 1998. *Social Science under Debate: A Philosophical Perspective*. Toronto: University of Toronto Press.
–. 1996. *Finding Philosophy in Social Science*. New Haven, CT: Yale University Press.
Cairns, Alan C. 2000. *Citizens Plus: Aboriginal Peoples and the Canadian State*. Vancouver: UBC Press.
–. 1998. "The Quebec Secession Reference: The Constitutional Obligation to Negotiate." *Constitutional Forum* 10, 1: 26-30.
–. 1996. "The Legacy of the Referendum: Who Are We Now?" *Constitutional Forum* 6, 2-3: 35-59.
–. 1995. "Citizens, Scholars and the Canadian Constitution." *International Journal of Canadian Studies* 12 (Fall): 285-89.
–. 1993. "A Defence of the Citizens' Constitution Theory: A Response to Ian Brodie and Neil Nevitte." *Canadian Journal of Political Science* 26, 2: 261-67.
–. 1992. *Charter versus Federalism: The Dilemmas of Constitutional Reform*. Montreal and Kingston: McGill-Queen's University Press.
–. 1991a. "The Charter, Interest Groups, Executive Federalism, and Constitutional Reform." In David E. Smith, Peter MacKinnon, and John C. Courtney, eds., *After Meech Lake: Lessons for the Future*, 13-32. Saskatoon: Fifth House Publishers.
–. 1991b. *Disruptions: Constitutional Struggles, from the Charter to Meech Lake*. Ed. Douglas E. Williams. Toronto: McClelland and Stewart.

–. 1991c. "Roadblocks in the Way of Constitutional Change." *Constitutional Forum* 2, 2: 54-58.

–. 1988a. "The Limited Constitutional Vision of Meech Lake." In Katherine E. Swinton and Carol J. Rogerson, eds., *Competing Constitutional Visions: The Meech Lake Accord*, 247-62. Toronto: Carswell.

–. 1988b. "Ottawa, The Provinces, and Meech Lake." In Roger Gibbins, ed., *Meech Lake and Canada: Perspectives from the West*. Edmonton: Academic Printing and Publishing.

–. 1983. "The Politics of Constitutional Conservatism." In Keith Banting and Richard Simeon, eds., *And No One Cheered: Federalism, Democracy and the Constitution Act*, 28-58. Toronto: Methuen.

Cameron, David R. 1993. "Not Spicer and Not the B and B: Reflections of an Insider on the Workings of the Pepin-Robarts Task Force on Canadian Unity." *International Journal of Canadian Studies* 7-8: 333-57.

Campbell, Robert M., and Leslie A. Pal. 1991. *The Real Worlds of Canadian Politics: Cases in Process and Policy*. Toronto: Broadview Press.

Caplan, Neil. 1989. "Some Factors Affecting the Resolution of a Federal-Provincial Conflict." In Garth Stevenson, ed., *Federalism in Canada: Selected Readings*, 417-34. Toronto: McClelland and Stewart.

Cardozo, Andrew. 1994. "Reform Is Here to Stay." *Canadian Forum* 8-9 (December): 8-9.

Carens, Joseph H. 1995. "Liberalism, Justice, and Political Community: Theoretical Perspectives on Quebec's Liberal Nationalism." In Joseph H. Carens, ed., *Is Quebec Nationalism Just? Perspectives from Anglophone Canada*, 3-19. Montreal and Kingston: McGill-Queen's University Press.

Carty, R.K. 2006. "Political Turbulence in a Dominant Party System." *PS: Political Science and Politics* 37, 4, http://www.apsanet.org/.

Chamberlin, J. Edward. 1988. "Aboriginal Rights and the Meech Lake Accord." In Katherine E. Swinton and Carol J. Rogerson, eds., *Competing Constitutional Visions: The Meech Lake Accord*, 11-20. Toronto: Carswell.

Chrétien, Jean. 2008. *My Years as Prime Minister*. Toronto: Vintage Canada.

Christian, Timothy J. 1992. "Canada in the 90's: A Constitutional Overview." *Annual Review of Canadian Studies* 12: 90-101.

Clarke, Harold D., and Allan Kornberg. 1994. "The Politics and Economics of Constitutional Choice: Voting in Canada's 1992 National Referendum." *Journal of Politics* 56, 4: 940-62.

Cloutier, Édouard. 1991. "We the People: Public Opinion, Sovereignty and the Constitution." In Robert A. Young, ed., *Confederation in Crisis*, 9-18. Toronto: James Lorimer and Company.

Cohen, Andrew. 1990. *A Deal Undone: The Making and Breaking of the Meech Lake Accord*. Vancouver: Douglas and McIntyre.

Coleman, James S. 1990. *Foundations of Social Theory*. Cambridge, MA: Belknap Press of Harvard University.

Cook, Curtis. 1994. "Introduction: Canada's Predicament." In Curtis Cook, ed., *Constitutional Predicament: Canada after the Referendum of 1992*, 3-24. Montreal and Kingston: McGill-Queen's University Press.

Cooper, Barry. 2000. "The Unfounded Country." In Rudyard Griffiths, ed., *Great Questions of Canada*, 55-59. Toronto: Stoddart.

–. 1996a. "Taylor-Made Canada." *Literary Review of Canada* 5 (February): 19-22.

–. 1996b. "Theoretical Perspectives on Constitutional Reform in Canada." In Anthony A. Peacock, ed., *Rethinking the Constitution: Perspectives on Canadian Constitutional Reform, Interpretation, and Theory*, 217-32. Toronto: Oxford University Press.

–. 1994. "Looking Eastward, Looking Backward: A Western Reading of the Never-Ending Story." In Curtis Cook, ed., *Constitutional Predicament: Canada after the Referendum of 1992*, 89-107. Montreal and Kingston: McGill-Queen's University Press.

Courchene, Thomas J. 2004. "The Changing Nature of Quebec-Canada Relations: From the 1980 Referendum to the Summit of the Canadas." Working Paper 2, Institute for Intergovernmental Relations, Queen's University, Kingston, Ontario.

–. 1991. "Forever Amber." In David E. Smith, Peter MacKinnon, and John C. Courtney, eds., *After Meech Lake: Lessons for the Future*, 33-60. Saskatoon: Fifth House Publishers.

–. 1988. "Meech Lake and Federalism: Accord or Discord?" In Katherine E. Swinton and Carol J. Rogerson, eds., *Competing Constitutional Visions: The Meech Lake Accord*, 121-44. Toronto: Carswell.

Courchene, Thomas J., and Lisa M. Powell. 1992. "A First Nations Province." Political Economy Research Group, Papers in Political Economy, no. 26, University of Western Ontario.

Coyne, Deborah. 1991. "Commentary." In David E. Smith, Peter MacKinnon, and John C. Courtney, eds., *After Meech Lake: Lessons for the Future*, 139-45. Saskatoon: Fifth House Publishers.

Crowley, Brian L. 2001. "Incentives Matter and All the Rest Is Commentary: Nova Scotia and Equalization." Address to the Annual General Meeting of the Liberal Party of Nova Scotia, 21 April, Halifax, Nova Scotia.

–. 2000. "Atlantic Canada and the Zero Sum Economy." Address to the Founding Convention of the United Alternative, 28 January, Halifax, Nova Scotia.

–. 1993. "Banquo's Ghost and Other Constitutional Incubuses: Some Lessons from the Charlottetown Process." *Constitutional Forum* 4, 2: 50-52.

Darby, Tom, and Peter C. Emberley. 1996. "'Political Correctness' and the Constitution: Nature and Convention Re-examined." In Anthony A. Peacock, ed., *Rethinking the Constitution: Perspectives on Canadian Constitutional Reform, Interpretation, and Theory*, 233-48. Toronto: Oxford University Press.

Dawson, Mary. 1992. "The Impact of the Charter on the Public Policy Process and the Department of Justice." *Osgoode Hall Law Journal* 30, 3: 595-603.

Denis, Claude. 1996. "Sovereignty Postponed: On the Canadian Way of Losing a Referendum, and Then Another." *Constitutional Forum* 6, 2-3: 44-49.

de Scitovsky, T. 1941. "A Note on Welfare Propositions in Economics." *Review of Economic Studies* 9, 1: 77-88.

Devlen, Balkan, Patrick James, and Özgur Özdamar. 2005. "The English School, International Relations, and Progress." *International Studies Review* 7, 2: 171-97.

Dickerson, Mark O., and Tom Flanagan. 1998. *An Introduction to Government and Politics*. 5th ed. Toronto: ITP Nelson.

Dion, Stéphane. 1999. *Straight Talk: Speeches and Writings on Canadian Unity*. Montreal and Kingston: McGill-Queen's University Press.

–. 1993. "The Quebec Challenge to Canadian Unity." *PS: Political Science and Politics* 26, 1: 38-43.

–. 1991. "Explaining Quebec Nationalism." In R. Kent Weaver, ed., *The Collapse of Canada?* 77-117. Washington, DC: Brookings Institution.

Dobrowolsky, Alexandra. 2000. *The Politics of Pragmatism: Women, Representation, and Constitutionalism in Canada*. Don Mills: Oxford University Press.

Doran, Charles F. 2001. *Why Canadian Unity Matters and Why Americans Care: Democratic Pluralism at Risk*. Toronto: Toronto University Press.

Dyck, Rand. 2002. *Canadian Politics: Critical Approaches*. 3rd ed. Peterborough, ON: Nelson.

Easton, David. 1965a. *A Framework for Political Analysis*. Englewood Cliffs, NJ: Prentice Hall.

–. 1965b. *A Systems Analysis of Political Life*. New York: Wiley.

–. 1953. *The Political System: An Inquiry into the State of Political Science*. New York: Alfred A. Knopf.

Epp, Charles R. 1998. *The Rights Revolution: Lawyers, Activists, and Supreme Courts in Comparative Perspective*. Chicago: University of Chicago Press.

Flanagan, Tom. 2007. *Harper's Team: Behind the Scenes in the Conservative Rise to Power*. Montreal and Kingston: McGill-Queen's University Press.

–. 2002. "Canada's Three Constitutions: Protecting, Overturning, and Reversing the Status Quo." In Patrick James, Donald E. Abelson, and Michael Lusztig, eds., *The Myth of the Sacred: The Charter, The Courts and the Politics of the Constitution in Canada*, 125-46. Montreal and Kingston: McGill-Queen's University Press.

–. 2000. *First Nations? Second Thoughts*. Montreal and Kingston: McGill-Queen's University Press.

–. 1998. *Game Theory and Canadian Politics*. Toronto: University of Toronto Press.

–. 1996. "Amending the Canadian Constitution: A Mathematical Analysis." *Constitutional Forum* 6, 2-3: 97-101.

–. 1992. "The Lubicon Lake Dispute." In Allan Tupper and Roger Gibbins, eds., *Government and Politics in Alberta*, 269-304. Edmonton: University of Alberta Press.

–. 1985. "The Manufacture of Minorities." In Neil Nevitte and Allan Kornberg, eds., *Minorities and the Canadian State*, 107-23. Oakville, ON: Mosaic Press.

Fortin, Pierre. 1991. "How Economics Is Shaping the Constitutional Debate in Quebec." In Robert A. Young, ed., *Confederation in Crisis*, 35-44. Toronto: James Lorimer and Company.

Fournier, Pierre. 1991. *A Meech Lake Post-Mortem: Is Quebec Sovereignty Inevitable?* Trans. Sheila Fischman. Montreal and Kingston: McGill-Queen's University Press.

Franks, C.E.S. 2000. "Rights and Self-Government for Canada's Aboriginal Peoples." In Curtis Cook and Juan D. Lindau, eds., *Aboriginal Rights and Self-Government: The Canadian and Mexican Experience in North American Perspective*, 101-34. Montreal and Kingston: McGill-Queen's University Press.

Fraser, Graham. 1991. "Commentary." In David E. Smith, Peter MacKinnon, and John C. Courtney, eds., *After Meech Lake: Lessons for the Future*, 201-3. Saskatoon: Fifth House Publishers.

Fry, Earl H. 1991. "The Canadian Political System." *The ACSUS Papers*. Washington, DC: Association for Canadian Studies in the United States.

Furtan, W.H., and R.S. Gray. 1991. "The Constitutional Debate: Some Issues for Agriculture." *Canadian Public Policy* 17, 4: 445-55.

Gairdner, William D. 1994. *Constitutional Crack-Up: Canada and the Coming Showdown with Quebec*. Toronto: Stoddart.

Gibbins, Roger. 1996. "Western Canadian Nationalism in Transition." *Constitutional Forum* 6, 2-3: 52-57.

–. 1991. "Constitutional Politics in the West and the Rest." In Robert A. Young, ed., *Confederation in Crisis*, 19-27. Toronto: James Lorimer and Company.

–. 1998a. "Getting There from Here." In Roger Gibbins and Guy Laforest, eds., *Beyond the Impasse: Toward Reconciliation*. Montreal: Institute for Research on Public Policy.

–. 1998b. "The Institutional Parameters of a Canada-Quebec Partnership." In Roger Gibbins and Guy Laforest, eds., *Beyond the Impasse: Toward Reconciliation*, 275-300. Montreal: Institute for Research on Public Policy.

–. 1988. "A Sense of Unease: The Meech Lake Accord and Constitution-Making in Canada." In Roger Gibbins, ed., *Meech Lake and Canada: Perspectives from the West*. Edmonton: Academic Printing and Publishing.

–. 1983. "Constitutional Politics and the West." In Keith Banting and Richard Simeon, eds., *And No One Cheered: Federalism, Democracy and the Constitution Act*, 119-32. Toronto: Methuen.

Gibbins, Roger, and Guy Laforest. 1998a. "Conclusion." In Roger Gibbins and Guy Laforest, eds., *Beyond the Impasse: Toward Reconciliation*, 429-36. Montreal: Institute for Research on Public Policy.

–. 1998b. "Introduction." In Roger Gibbins and Guy Laforest, eds., *Beyond the Impasse: Toward Reconciliation*, 1-10. Montreal: Institute for Research on Public Policy.

Gibson, Dale. 1992. "Federal Symmetry: Constitutional Uniformity and the Federal Amendment Proposals." *Constitutional Reform* 3, 3: 54-56.

–. 1991. "Now What?" *Constitutional Forum* 3, 1: 10.

–. 1985a. "Protection of Minority Rights under the Canadian Charter of Rights and Freedoms: Can Politicians and Judges Sing Harmony?" In Neil Nevitte and Allan Kornberg, eds., *Minorities and the Canadian State*, 31-55. Oakville, ON: Mosaic Press.

–. 1985b. "Stereotypes, Statistics and Slippery Slopes: A Reply to Professors Flanagan and Knopff and Other Critics of Human Rights Legislation." In Neil Nevitte and Allan Kornberg, eds., *Minorities and the Canadian State*, 125-38. Oakville, ON: Mosaic Press.

Grabb, Edward G., and James E. Curtis. 2002. "Comparing Central Political Values in the Canadian and American Democracies." In Douglas E. Baer, ed., *Political Sociology: Canadian Perspectives*, 37-54. Toronto: Oxford University Press.

Granatstein, Jack. 2000a. "History as Victimology." In Rudyard Griffiths, ed., *Great Questions of Canada*, 3-6. Toronto: Stoddart.

–. 2000b. "Postscript." In Rudyard Griffiths, ed., *Great Questions of Canada*, 12-18. Toronto: Stoddart.

Gray, Charlotte. 2000. "Heroes and Symbols." In Rudyard Griffiths, ed., *Great Questions of Canada*. Toronto: Stoddart.

Green, Leslie. 1985. "Support for the System." *British Journal of Political Science* 15, 2: 127-42.

Greschner, Donna. 1993. "It's the Law of the Land: Gender and the Geography of Hope." *Constitutional Forum* 4, 4: 97-101.

–. 1991. "Commentary." In David E. Smith, Peter MacKinnon, and John C. Courtney, eds., *After Meech Lake: Lessons for the Future*, 223-25. Saskatoon: Fifth House Publishers.

Grey House Publishing. 2000. *Nations of the World: A Political, Economic, and Business Handbook*. Lakeville, CT: Grey House Publising.

Griffiths, Rudyard. 2000. "Introduction." In Rudyard Griffiths, ed., *Great Questions of Canada*, ix-xiii. Toronto: Stoddart.

Gurr, Ted Robert. 2000. *People versus States: Minorities at Risk in the New Century*. Washington, DC: United States Institute of Peace Press.

Guy, James John. 1998. *People, Politics, and Government: A Canadian Perspective*. 4th ed. Scarborough, ON: Prentice Hall Allyn and Bacon.

Harris, Richard G., and Douglas D. Purvis. 1991. "Constitutional Change and Canada's Economic Prospects." *Canadian Public Policy* 17, 4: 379-94.

Heard, Andrew D. 1993. "Québec Courts and the Canadian Charter of Rights." *International Journal of Canadian Studies* 7-8: 153-66.

Hiebert, Janet L. 2002. *Charter Conflicts: What Is Parliament's Role?* Montreal and Kingston: McGill-Queen's University Press.

–. 1993. "Rights and Public Debate: The Limitation of a 'Rights Must Be Paramount' Perspective." *International Journal of Canadian Studies* 7-8: 117-35.

Hirschl, Ran. 2004. *Toward Juristocracy: The Origins and Consequences of the New Constiutionalism*. Cambridge, MA: Harvard University Press.

Hogg, Peter W. 1977. *Constitutional Law of Canada*. Toronto: Carswell Company.

Hogg, Peter W., and Allison A. Bushell. 1997. "The *Charter* Dialogue between Courts and Legislatures (Or Perhaps the *Charter of Rights* Isn't Such a Bad Thing after All)." *Osgoode Hall Law Journal* 35, 1: 75-124.

Howe, Paul. 1998. "Rationality and Sovereignty Support in Quebec." *Canadian Journal of Political Science* 31, 1: 31-59.

Howe, Paul, and Joseph Fletcher. 2000. "The Evolution of Charter Values." Paper presented at the "Conference on the Transformation of Canadian Political Culture and the State of the Federation," Institute of Intergovernmental Relations, October, Queen's University, Kingston, Ontario.

Howlett, Michael, and M. Ramesh. 1992. *The Political Economy of Canada: An Introduction*. Toronto: McClelland and Stewart.

Hueglin, Thomas O. 1995. "New Wine in Old Bottles? Federalism and Nation States in the Twenty-First Century: A Conceptual Overview." In Karen Knop, Sylvia Ostry, Richard Simeon, and Katherine Swinton, eds., *Rethinking Federalism: Citizens, Markets, and Governments in a Changing World*. Vancouver: UBC Press.

Huntington, Samuel P. 1993. *The Third Wave: Democratization in the Late Twentieth Century*. Norman: University of Oklahoma Press.

Hutchinson, Allan C. 1995. *Waiting for Coraf: A Critique of Law and Rights*. Toronto: University of Toronto Press.

Iacobucci, Frank. 2003. "The Charter: Twenty Years Later." In Joseph Eliot Magnet, Gérald-A. Beaudoin, Gerald Gall, and Christopher P. Manfredi, eds., *The Canadian Charter of Rights and Freedoms: Reflections on the Charter after Twenty Years*, 381-420. Markham, ON: Butterworths.

Ignatieff, Michael. 2000a. "The History that Matters Most." In Rudyard Griffiths, ed., *Great Questions of Canada*, 7-11. Toronto: Stoddart.

–. 2000b. "Postscript." In Rudyard Griffiths, ed., *Great Questions of Canada*, 18-24. Toronto: Stoddart.

Imbeau, Louis M. 1992. "Procedural Constraints and Conflictual Preferences in Collective Decision-Making: An Analysis Based on the Constitutional Decision of November 1981 in Canada." Unpublished manuscript.

–. 1991. "Le compromis est-il encore possible: La négociation constitutionnelle de l'aprés-Meech á la lumière de la théorie de jeux." In Louis Balthazar, Guy Laforest, and Vincent Lemieux, eds., *Le Quebec et la restructuration du Canada, 1980-1992*. Sillery, QC: Septentrion.

–. 1990. "Voting Games and Constitutional Decision: The 1981 Constitutional Negotiation in Canada." *Journal of Commonwealth and Comparative Politics* 28, 1: 90-105.

Imbeau, Louis M., and Guy Laforest. 1991-92. "Quebec's Distinct Society and the Sense of Nationhood in Canada." *Quebec Studies* 13: 13-26.

James, Patrick. 2006. "The Rawlsian Paradox and the Governance of Canada." *British Journal of Canadian Studies* 19, 2: 177-90.

–. 2002. *International Relations and Scientific Progress: Structural Realism Reconsidered*. Columbus: Ohio State University Press.

–. 1999. "The Chain Store Paradox and Constitutional Politics in Canada." *Journal of Theoretical Politics* 11, 1: 5-36.

–. 1998. "Rational Choice? Crisis Bargaining over the Meech Lake Accord." *Conflict Management and Peace Science* 16, 2: 51-86.

–. 1993. "Energy Politics in Canada, 1980-1981: Threat Power in a Sequential Game." *Canadian Journal of Political Science* 26, 1: 31-59.

James, Patrick, Donald E. Abelson, and Michael Lusztig. 2002a. "Introduction: The Myth of the Sacred in the Canadian Constitutional Order." In Patrick James, Donald E. Abelson, and Michael Lusztig, eds., *The Myth of the Sacred: The Charter, the Courts, and the Politics of the Constitution in Canada*, 3-16. Montreal and Kingston: McGill-Queen's University Press.

–, eds. 2002b. *The Myth of the Sacred: The Charter, the Courts, and the Politics of the Constitution in Canada*. Montreal and Kingston: McGill-Queen's University Press.

James, Patrick, and Michael Lusztig. 2001. "Say Goodbye to the Dream of One Canada: The Costly Failure to Purchase National Unity." In Harvey Lazar and Hamish Telford, eds., *Canada: State of the Federation 2001*, 83-109. Kingston: Queen's University Institute of Intergovernmental Relations.

–. 1997a. "Assessing the Reliability of Predictions on the Future of Quebec." *Quebec Studies* 24 (Fall): 197-210.

–. 1997b. "Quebec's Economic and Political Future with North America." *International Interactions* 23, 3 & 4: 283-98.

–. 1996. "Beyond the Crystal Ball: Modeling Predictions about Quebec and Canada." *American Review of Canadian Studies* 26 (December): 559-75.

Jenson, Jane. 1998. "Recognizing Difference: Distinct Societies, Citizenship Regimes and Partnership." In Roger Gibbins and Guy Laforest, eds., *Beyond the Impasse: Toward Reconciliation*, 215-40. Montreal: Institute for Research on Public Policy.

–. 1996. "After 30 October 1995." *Constitutional Forum* 6, 2-3: 40-43.

Jérôme-Forget, Monique. 1994. "Brinkmanship and Renewal of Canadian Federalism: A High Stakes Game." In F. Leslie Seidle, ed., *Seeking a New Canadian Partnership: Asymmetrical and Confederal Options*, 19-26. Toronto: Institute for Research on Public Policy.

Jhappan, Radha. 1993. "Inherency, Three Nations and Collective Rights: The Evolution of Aboriginal Constitutional Discourse from 1982 to the Charlottetown Accord." *International Journal of Canadian Studies* 7-8: 225-59.

Jockel, Joseph T. 1995. "On Watching, from across the Border, the Canadian Game of Chicken." *Annals of the American Academy of Political and Social Science*, 538: 16-26.

Johnston, Richard. 2000. "Canadian Elections at the Millennium." *Choices: Strengthening Canadian Democracy* 6, 6: 4-36.

–. 1993. "An Inverted Logroll: The Charlottetown Accord and the Referendum." *PS: Political Science and Politics* 26, 1: 43-48.

Kaldor, Nicholas. 1939. "Welfare Propositions of Economics and Interpersonal Comparisons of Utility." *Economic Journal* 49, 195: 549-52.

Kanji, Mebs, and Antoine Bilodeau. 2006. "Value Diversity and Support for Electoral Reform in Canada." *PS: Political Science and Politics* 37, 4: 829-36. http://www.apsanet.org/.

Kelly, James B. 2005. *Governing with the Charter: Legislative and Judicial Activism and Framers' Intent*. Vancouver: UBC Press.

–. 2002. "The Supreme Court of Canada and the Complexity of Judicial Activism." In Patrick James, Donald E. Abelson, and Michael Lusztig, eds., *The Myth of the Sacred: The Charter, the Courts and the Politics of the Constitution in Canada*, 97-125. Montreal and Kingston: McGill-Queen's University Press.

Kelly, James B., and Christopher P. Manfredi, eds. 2009. *Contested Constitutionalism: Reflections on the Canadian Charter of Rights and Freedoms*. Vancouver: UBC Press.

Kilgour, D. Marc. 1985. "Reply: Distributing the Power to Amend to Canada's Constitution." *Canadian Journal of Political Science* 18, 2: 389-96.

–. 1983. "A Formal Analysis of the Amending Formula of Canada's *Constitution Act, 1982*." *Canadian Journal of Political Science* 16, 4: 771-77.

Kilgour, D. Marc, and Terrence J. Levesque. 1984. "The Canadian Constitutional Amending Formula: Bargaining in the Past and the Future." *Public Choice* 44, 3: 457-80.

Klein, Naomi. 2000. "Boats, Not Birthrights." In Rudyard Griffiths, ed., *Great Questions of Canada*, 32-36. Toronto: Stoddart.

Knopff, Rainer. 2003. "How Democratic Is the Charter? And Does It Matter?" In Joseph Eliot Magnet, Gérald-A. Beaudoin, Gerald Gall, and Christopher P. Manfredi, eds., *The Canadian Charter of Rights and Freedoms: Reflections on the Charter after Twenty Years*, 199-218. Markham, ON: Butterworths.

–. 2001. "A Delicate Dance: The Courts and the Chrétien Government." Unpublished manuscript, University of Calgary.

–. 1996. "Courts and Character." Paper presented at the annual meeting of the Canadian Political Science Association, 1-4 June, St. Catharines, Ontario.

–. 1985. "The Statistical Protection of Minorities: Affirmative Action Policy in Canada." In Neil Nevitte and Allan Kornberg, eds., *Minorities and the Canadian State*, 87-106. Oakville, ON: Mosaic Press.

Knopff, Rainer, and F.L. Morton. 1996. "Canada's Court Party." In Anthony A. Peacock, ed., *Rethinking the Constitution: Perspectives on Canadian Constitutional Reform, Interpretation, and Theory*, 63-87. Toronto: Oxford University Press.

–. 1992. *Charter Politics*. Scarborough, ON: Nelson Canada.

Kornberg, Allan, and Harold D. Clarke. 1992. *Citizens and Community: Political Support in a Representative Democracy*. Cambridge: Cambridge University Press.

Krosenbrink-Gelissen, Lilianne E. 1993. "The Canadian Constitution, the Charter, and Aboriginal Women's Rights: Conflicts and Dilemmas." *International Journal of Canadian Studies* 7-8: 207-24.

Kuhn, Thomas S. 1962. *The Structure of Scientific Revolutions*. Chicago: University of Chicago Press.

Kymlicka, Will. 1998. "Multinational Federalism in Canada: Rethinking the Partnership." In Roger Gibbins and Guy Laforest, eds., *Beyond the Impasse: Toward Reconciliation*, 15-51. Montreal: Institute for Research on Public Policy.

–. 1995. *Multicultural Citizenship: A Liberal Theory of Minority Rights*. Oxford: Clarendon Press.

–. 1993. "Group Representation in Canadian Politics." In F. Leslie Seidle, ed., *Equity and Community: The Charter, Interest Advocacy and Representation*, 91-118. Ottawa: Institute for Research on Public Policy.

–. 1989. *Liberalism, Community, and Culture*. Oxford: Clarendon Press.

Lachapelle, Guy. 1996. "The Three Failures in Modern Canadian Federalism: Why Is It Impossible to Find a New Québec-Canada Partnership?" *Constitutional Forum* 6, 2-3: 86-90.

Laforest, Guy. 2000. "The Reality Principle." In Rudyard Griffiths, ed., *Great Questions of Canada*, 105-9. Toronto: Stoddart.

–. 1998a. "The Need for Dialogue and How to Achieve It." In Roger Gibbins and Guy Laforest, eds., *Beyond the Impasse: Toward Reconciliation*, 413-28. Montreal: Institute for Research on Public Policy.

–. 1998b. "Standing in the Shoes of the Other Partners in the Canadian Union." In Roger Gibbins and Guy Laforest, eds., *Beyond the Impasse: Toward Reconciliation*, 51-82. Montreal: Institute for Research on Public Policy.

–. 1995. *Trudeau and the End of a Canadian Dream*. Trans. Paul Leduc Browne and Michell Weinroth. Montreal and Kingston: McGill-Queen's University Press.

–. 1991. "Interpreting the Political Heritage of André Laurendau." In David E. Smith, Peter MacKinnon, and John C. Courtney, eds., *After Meech Lake: Lessons for the Future*, 99-107. Saskatoon: Fifth House Publishers.

Landes, Ronald G. 1998. *The Canadian Polity*. 5th ed. Scarborough, ON: Prentice Hall Allyn and Bacon Canada.

Landry, Réjean. 1993. "Interest Groups and the Political Economy of the Constitutional Debates in Canada." *Business and the Contemporary World* 5 (Winter): 116-29.

LaSelva, Samuel V. 1993. "Federalism as a Way of Life: Reflections on the Canadian Experiment." *Canadian Journal of Political Science* 26, 2: 219-34.

Latouche, Daniel. 1998. "Projecting a Canada-Quebec Partnership on the International Stage: Some Logical Speculations." In Roger Gibbins and Guy Laforest, eds., *Beyond the Impasse: Toward Reconciliation*, 333-58. Montreal: Institute for Research on Public Policy.

–. 1990. "Quebec and Canada: Scenarios for the Future." *Business in the Contemporary World* 3: 58-70.

Laxer, Gordon. 1992. "Distinct Society Status for Québec: A Benefit to English Canada." *Constitutional Forum* 3, 3: 57-61.

Leal, David L. 2006. "Canada: The Unknown Country." *PSOnline* 37, 4 (October). http://www.apsanet.org/.

–. 1989. "Unity and Diversity in Canadian Federalism: Ideals and Methods of Moderation." In Garth Stevenson, ed., *Federalism in Canada: Selected Readings*, 142-64. Toronto: McClelland and Stewart.

Lederman, W.R. 1991. "Constitutional Reform: Charter Rights and Freedoms." In David E. Smith, Peter MacKinnon, and John C. Courtney, eds., *After Meech Lake: Lessons for the Future*. Saskatoon: Fifth House Publishers.

–. 1989. "Unity and Diversity in Canadian Federalism: Ideals and Methods of Moderation." In Garth Stevenson, ed., *Federalism in Canada: Selected Readings*. Toronto: McClelland and Stewart.

LeDuc, Lawrence, and Jon H. Pammett. 1995. "Referendum Voting: Attitudes and Behaviour in the 1992 Constitutional Referendum." *Canadian Journal of Political Science* 28, 1: 3-33.

Leeson, Howard. 1992. "Why Canadians Should Vote 'Yes.'" *Points of View, 3: Referendum Round-Table – Perspectives on the Charlottetown Accord*. Edmonton: Centre for Constitutional Studies.

–. 1991. "Comments on Symposium." *Constitutional Forum* 3, 1: 11.

Lenihan, Donald G., Gordon Robertson, and Roger Tassé. 1994. *Canada: Reclaiming the Middle Ground*. Montreal: Institute for Research on Public Policy.

Leslie, Peter. 1972. "General Theory in Political Science: A Critique of Easton's Systems Analysis." *British Journal of Political Science* 2, 2: 155-72.

Levesque, Terrence J., and James W. Moore. 1984. "Citizen and Provincial Power under Alternative Amending Formulae: An Extension of Kilgour's Analysis." *Canadian Journal of Political Science* 17, 1: 157-66.

Levine, Marc V. 1994. "The Quebec Election of 1994." *CSIS Western Hemisphere Election Study Series* 12: 1-13.

Lipset, Seymour Martin. 1993. "Canadian Studies in the United States: A Summary." In Karen Gould, Joseph T. Jockel, and William Metcalfe, eds., *Northern Exposures: Scholarship on Canada in the United States*, 397-416. Washington, DC: Association for Canadian Studies in the United States.

–. 1990. *Continental Divide: The Values and Institutions of the United States and Canada*. New York: Routledge.

Lusztig, Michael. 2002. "Deeper and Deeper: Deep Diversity, Federalism and the Rawlsian Paradox." In Patrick James, Donald E. Abelson, and Michael Lusztig, eds., *The Myth of the Sacred: The Charter, the Courts and the Politics of the Constitution in Canada*, 207-17. Montreal and Kingston: McGill-Queen's University Press.

–. 1999. "Canada's Long Road to Nowhere: Why the Circle of Command Liberalism Cannot Be Squared." *Canadian Journal of Political Science* 32, 3: 451-70.

–. 1995. "Federalism and Institutional Design: The Perils and Politics of a Triple-E Senate in Canada." *Publius* 25, 1: 35-50.

–. 1994. "Constitutional Paralysis: Why Canadian Constitutional Initiatives Are Doomed to Fail." *Canadian Journal of Political Science* 27: 747-71.

Maddex, Robert L. 1995. *Constitutions of the World*. Washington, DC: Congressional Quarterly.

Magnet, Joseph Eliot. 2003. "What Does 'Equality between Communities' Mean?" In Joseph Eliot Magnet, Gérald-A. Beaudoin, Gerald Gall, and Christopher P. Manfredi, eds., *The Canadian Charter of Rights and Freedoms: Reflections on the Charter after Twenty Years*, 277-308. Markham, ON: Butterworths.

Mahler, Gregory. 1993. "American Approaches to Canadian Domestic Politics: A Distinction without a Difference." In Karen Gould, Joseph T. Jockel, and William Metcalfe, eds., *Northern Exposures: Scholarship on Canada in the United States*, 49-68. Washington, DC: Association for Canadian Studies in the United States.

Malcolmson, Patrick, and Richard Myers. 1996. *The Canadian Regime*. Peterborough, ON: Broadview Press.

Mandel, Michael. 1994. *The Charter of Rights and the Legalization of Politics in Canada*. Rev. ed. Toronto: Thompson Educational Publishing.

Manfredi, Christopher P. 2005. *Feminist Activism in the Supreme Court: Legal Mobilization and the Women's Legal Education and Action Fund*. Vancouver: UBC Press.

–. 2002. "Strategic Behaviour and the Canadian Charter of Rights and Freedoms." In Patrick James, Donald E. Abelson, and Michael Lusztig, eds., *The Myth of the Sacred: The Charter, the Courts, and the Politics of the Constitution in Canada*, 147-70. Montreal and Kingston: McGill-Queen's University Press.

–. 2001. *Judicial Power and the Charter: Canada and the Paradox of Liberal Constitutionalism*. 2nd ed. Don Mills, ON: Oxford University Press.

–. 1996. "On the Virtues of a Limited Constitution: Why Canadians Were Right to Reject the Charlottetown Accord." In Anthony Peacock, ed., *Rethinking the Constitution: Perspectives on Canadian Constitutional Reform, Interpretation, and Theory*, 40-62. Toronto: Oxford Press.

–. 1995. "On the Virtues of a Limited Constitution: Why Canadians Were Correct to Reject the Charlottetown Accord." Unpublished manuscript.

–. 1993. *Judicial Power and the Charter: Canada and the Paradox of Liberal Constitutionalism*. Norman: University of Oklahoma Press.

Manfredi, Christopher P., and James B. Kelly. 1999. "Six Degrees of Dialogue: A Response to Hogg and Bushell." *Osgoode Hall Law Journal* 37, 3: 513-27.

Martin, Pierre. 1995. "Association after Sovereignty? Canadian Views on Economic Association with a Sovereign Quebec." *Canadian Public Policy* 21, 1: 53-71.

–. 1994. "Free Trade and Party Politics in Quebec." In Charles F. Doran and Gregory P. Marchildon, eds., *The NAFTA Puzzle: Political Parties and Trade in North America*, 143-72. Boulder, CO: Westview Press.

Martin, Robert. 2003. *The Most Dangerous Branch: How the Supreme Court of Canada Has Undermined Our Law and Our Democracy.* Montreal and Kingston: McGill-Queen's University Press.

–. 1996. "Reconstituting Democracy: Orthodoxy and Research in Law and Social Science." In Anthony Peacock, ed., *Rethinking the Constitution: Perspectives on Canadian Constitutional Reform, Interpretation, and Theory*, 249-70. Toronto: Oxford University Press.

–. 1991. "The Charter and the Crisis in Canada." In David E. Smith, Peter MacKinnon, and John C. Courtney, eds., *After Meech Lake: Lessons for the Future*, 121-37. Saskatoon: Fifth House Publishers.

McBride, Stephen. 1993. "Renewed Federalism as an Instrument of Competitiveness: Liberal Political Economy and the Canadian Constitution." *International Journal of Canadian Studies* 7-8: 187-205.

McDougall, John N. 1991. "North American Integration and Canadian Disunity." *Canadian Public Policy* 17, 4: 395-408.

McLellan, A. Anne. 1992. "The West: Myth or Reality in the Constitutional Reform Process?" *Constitutional Forum* 3, 3: 88-92.

–. 1991. "The Constitutional Politics of Language." *Constitutional Forum* 2, 2: 49-53.

McMahon, Fred. 2000. *Retreat from Growth: Atlantic Canada and the Negative Sum Economy.* Halifax: Atlantic Institute for Market Studies.

McRoberts, Kenneth. 1998. "Linguistic Minorities in a Canada-Quebec Partnership." In Roger Gibbins and Guy Laforest, eds., *Beyond the Impasse: Toward Reconciliation*, 187-214. Montreal: Institute for Research on Public Policy.

–. 1997. *Misconceiving Canada: The Struggle for National Unity.* Toronto: Oxford University Press.

–. 1993. "Constructing Canadian Identities." *Constitutional Forum* 4, 4: 93-96.

–. 1991-92. "Separate Agendas: English Canada and Quebec." *Quebec Studies* 13: 1-12.

Meadwell, Hudson. 2002. "Is a 'True' Multination Federation the Cure for Our Ills?" In Patrick James, Donald E. Abelson, and Michael Lusztig, eds., *The Myth of the Sacred: The Charter, the Courts, and the Politics of the Constitution in Canada*, 219-38. Montreal and Kingston: McGill-Queen's University Press.

–. 1993. "The Politics of Nationalism in Quebec." *World Politics* 45, 2: 203-41.

Meekison, J. Peter. 1993. "Canada's Quest for Constitutional Perfection." *Constitutional Forum* 4, 2: 55-59.

–. 1992. "The Agenda for Constitutional Reform." *Constitutional Forum* 3, 3: 75-78.

–. 1990. "The Meech Lake Accord: The End of the Beginning – Or the Beginning of the End?" *Constitutional Forum* 1, 2: 13-16.

Meisel, John. 1995. "Multinationalism and the Federal Idea: A Synopsis." In Karen Knop, Sylvia Ostry, Richard Simeon, and Katherine Swinton, eds., *Rethinking Federalism: Citizens, Markets, and Governments in a Changing World*, 341-46. Vancouver: UBC Press.

–. 1991. "Mirror? Searchlight? Interloper? The Media and Meech." In David E. Smith, Peter MacKinnon, and John C. Courtney, eds., *After Meech Lake: Lessons for the Future*, 147-68. Saskatoon: Fifth House Publishers.

Mercredi, Ovide. 2000. "Postscript." In Rudyard Griffiths, ed., *Great Questions of Canada*, 119-27. Toronto: Stoddart.

–. 1991. "Aboriginal Peoples and the Constitution." In David E. Smith, Peter MacKinnon, and John C. Courtney, eds., *After Meech Lake: Lessons for the Future*, 219-22. Saskatoon: Fifth House Publishers.

Milne, David. 1994. "Exposed to the Glare: Constitutional Camouflage and the Fate of Canada's Federation." In F. Leslie Seidle, ed., *Seeking a New Canadian Partnership: Asymmetrical and Confederal Options*, 107-32. Ottawa: Institute for Research on Public Policy.

–. 1991. *The Canadian Constitution*. Toronto: James Lorimer and Company.

Mintz, Eric. 1985. "Banzhaf's Power Index and Canada's Constitutional Amending Formula: A Comment on Kilgour's Analysis." *Canadian Journal of Political Science* 18, 2: 385-87.

Monahan, Patrick J. 1993. "The Sounds of Silence." In Kenneth McRoberts and Patrick J. Monahan, eds., *The Charlottetown Accord, the Referendum, and the Future of Canada*. Toronto: University of Toronto Press.

–. 1991. *Meech Lake: The Inside Story*. Toronto: University of Toronto Press.

Morton, F.L. 1994. "Judicial Politics, Canadian Style: The Supreme Court's Contribution to the Constitutional Crisis of 1992." In Curtis Cook, ed. *Constitutional Predicament: Canada after the Referendum of 1992*, 132-48. Montreal and Kingston: McGill-Queen's University Press.

–. 1985. "Group Rights versus Individual Rights in the Charter: The Special Cases of Natives and the Quebecois." In Neil Nevitte and Allan Kornberg, eds., *Minorities and the Canadian State*, 71-85. Oakville, ON: Mosaic Press.

Morton, F.L., and Rainer Knopff. 2000. *The Charter Revolution and the Court Party*. Peterborough, ON: Broadview Press.

Motyl, Alexander J. 1999. *Revolutions, Nations, Empires: Conceptual Limits and Theoretical Possibilities*. New York: Columbia University Press.

Mulroney, Brian. 2007. *Memoirs, 1939-1993*. Toronto: McClelland and Stewart.

Nevitte, Neil. 1996. *The Decline of Deference: Canadian Value Change in Cross-National Perspective*. Peterborough, ON: Broadview Press.

Newman, Warren J. 1999. *The Quebec Secession Reference: The Rule of Law and the Position of the Attorney General of Canada*. Toronto: Centre for Public Law and Public Policy, York University.

Noël, Alain. 1998. "The Federal Principle, Solidarity and Partnership." In Roger Gibbins and Guy Laforest, eds., *Beyond the Impasse: Toward Reconciliation*, 241-74. Montreal: Institute for Research on Public Policy.

Norrie, Kenneth, and Michael Percy. 1998. "A Canada-Quebec Partnership: The Economic Dimensions." In Roger Gibbins and Guy Laforest, eds., *Beyond the Impasse: Toward Reconciliation*, 83-110. Montreal: Institute for Research on Public Policy.

Norrie, Kenneth, Richard Simeon, and Mark Krasnick. 1986. *Federalism and Economic Union in Canada*. Toronto: University of Toronto Press.

Oliver, Michael. 1993. "The Impact of the Royal Commission on Bilingualism and Biculturalism on Constitutional Thought and Practice in Canada." *International Journal of Canadian Studies* 7-8: 315-32.

Olson, Mancur. 1965. *The Logic of Collective Action.* Cambridge, MA: Harvard University Press.

Olson, Susan M. 1990. "Interest-Group Litigation in Federal District Court: Beyond the Political Disadvantage Theory." *Journal of Politics* 52, 3: 854-82.

Orban, Edmond. 1991. "Constitutional and Regional Cleavages: A View from Quebec." In David E. Smith, Peter MacKinnon, and John C. Courtney, eds., *After Meech Lake: Lessons for the Future,* 83-97. Saskatoon: Fifth House Publishers.

Owram, Doug. 1991. "The Historical Context of Meech Lake." *Constitutional Forum* 2, 2: 23-26.

Pal, Leslie A. 1993a. "Advocacy Organizations and Legislative Politics: The Effect of the Charter of Rights and Freedoms on Interest Lobbying of Federal Legislation, 1989-91." In F. Leslie Seidle, ed., *Equity and Community: The Charter, Interest Advocacy, and Representation,* 159-88. Ottawa: Institute for Research on Public Policy.

–. 1993b. *Interests of State: The Politics of Language, Multiculturalism, and Feminism in Canada.* Montreal and Kingston: McGill-Queen's University Press.

–. 1990. "From Society to State: New Approaches to the Study of Politics." In Alain G. Gagnon and James P. Bickerton, eds., *Canadian Politics: An Introduction to the Discipline,* 17-41. Peterborough, ON: Broadview Press.

Palmer, Vaughn. 1991. "Commentary." In David E. Smith, Peter MacKinnon, and John C. Courtney, eds., *After Meech Lake: Lessons for the Future,* 199-200. Saskatoon: Fifth House Publishers.

Pammett, John H., and Lawrence LeDuc. 1995. "Referendum Voting: Attitudes and Behaviour in the 1992 Constitutional Referendum." *Canadian Journal of Political Science* 28, 1: 3-33.

Peacock, Anthony A. 2002. "Judicial Rationalism and the Therapeutic Constitution: The Supreme Court's Reconstruction of Equality and Democratic Process under the Charter of Rights and Freedoms." In Patrick James, Donald E. Abelson, and Michael Lusztig, eds., *The Myth of the Sacred: The Charter, the Courts, and the Politics of the Constitution in Canada,* 17-66. Montreal and Kingston: McGill-Queen's University Press.

–. 1996a. "The 1995 Quebec Referendum, Liberal Constitutionalism, and the Future of Canada." In Anthony A. Peacock, ed., *Rethinking the Constitution: Perspectives of Canadian Constitutional Reform, Interpretation, and Theory,* 271-75. Toronto: Oxford University Press.

–. 1996b. "Introduction: The Necessity of Rethinking the Constitution." In Anthony A. Peacock, ed., *Rethinking the Constitution: Perspectives of Canadian Constitutional Reform, Interpretation, and Theory.* Toronto: Oxford University Press.

–. 1996c. "Strange Brew: Tocqueville, Rights, and the Technology of Equality." In Anthony A. Peacock, ed., *Rethinking the Constitution: Perspectives of Canadian Constitutional Reform, Interpretation, and Theory,* 122-60. Toronto: Oxford University Press.

Pocklington, T.C. 1991. "Some Drawbacks of the Politics of Constitutional Rights." *Constitutional Forum* 2, 2: 42-43.

Porter, John. 1965. *Vertical Mosaic: An Analysis of Social Class and Power in Canada.* Toronto: University of Toronto Press.

Potter, Evan H. 2008. *Branding Canada: Projecting Canada's Soft Power through Public Diplomacy.* Montreal and Kingston: McGill-Queen's University Press.

Putnam, Robert D. 1993. *Bowling Alone: The Collapse and Revival of American Community.* New York: Simon and Schuster.

Raboy, Marc. 1991. "Canadian Broadcasting, Canadian Nationhood: Two Concepts, Two Solitudes, and Great Expectations." In David E. Smith, Peter MacKinnon, and John C. Courtney, eds., *After Meech Lake: Lessons for the Future,* 181-97. Saskatoon: Fifth House Publishers.

Rawls, John. 1971. *A Theory of Justice.* Cambridge, MA: Harvard University Belknap Press.

Reesor, Bayard. 1992. *The Canadian Constitution in Historical Perspective.* Scarborough, ON: Prentice Hall.

Resnick, Philip. 1991. *Toward a Canada-Quebec Union.* Montreal and Kingston: McGill-Queen's University Press.

Reuber, Grant L. 1991. "Federalism and Negative-Sum Games." In Robert A. Young, ed., *Confederation in Crisis,* 45-56. Toronto: James Lorimer and Company.

Richler, Mordecai. 1992. *Oh Canada! Oh Quebec! Requiem for a Divided Country.* Toronto: Penguin Books.

Riker, William H. 1962. *The Theory of Political Coalitions.* New Haven, CT: Yale University Press.

Roach, Kent. 1993. "The Role of Litigation and the Charter in Interest Advocacy." In F. Leslie Seidle, ed., *Equity and Community: The Charter, Interest Advocacy, and Representation.* Ottawa: Institute for Research on Public Policy.

Robertson, Gordon. 1991. "What Future for Canada?" In David E. Smith, Peter MacKinnon, and John C. Courtney, eds., *After Meech Lake: Lessons for the Future,* 227-35. Saskatoon: Fifth House Publishers.

Rocher, Francois. 1998. "Economic Partnership and Political Integration: Recasting Quebec-Canada's Economic Union." In Roger Gibbins and Guy Laforest, eds., *Beyond the Impasse: Toward Reconciliation,* 111-46. Montreal: Institute for Research on Public Policy.

Rockefeller, Steven C. 1994. "Comment." In Amy Gutmann, ed., *Multiculturalism: Examining the Politics of Recognition,* 87-98. Princeton, NJ: Princeton University Press.

Rosenau, James N. 1997. *Along the Domestic-Foreign Frontier: Explaining Governance in a Turbulent World.* Cambridge: Cambridge University Press.

–. 1990. *Turbulence in World Politics: A Theory of Change and Continuity.* Princeton, NJ: Princeton University Press.

Rush, Mark E. 2002. "Judicial Supervision of the Political Process: Canadian and American Responses to Homosexual Rights Challenges." In Patrick James, Donald E. Abelson, and Michael Lusztig, eds., *The Myth of the Sacred: The Charter, the Courts and the Politics of the Constitution in Canada,* 67-96. Montreal and Kingston: McGill-Queen's University Press.

Russell, Peter H. 2004. *Constitutional Odyssey: Can Canadians Become a Sovereign People?* 3rd edition. Toronto: University of Toronto Press.

–. 1993a. "Attempting Macro Constitutional Change in Australia and Canada: The Politics of Frustration." *International Journal of Canadian Studies* 7-8: 41-61.

–. 1993b. "The End of Mega Constitutional Politics in Canada?" *PS: Political Science and Politics* 26, 1: 33-37.

–. 1992. *Constitutional Odyssey: Can Canadians Become a Sovereign People?* Toronto: University of Toronto Press.

–. 1991a. "Can the Canadians Be a Sovereign People?" *Canadian Journal of Political Science* 24, 4: 691-709.

–. 1991b. "Commentary." In David E. Smith, Peter MacKinnon, and John C. Courtney, eds., *After Meech Lake: Lessons for the Future,* 67-68. Saskatoon: Fifth House Publishers.

–. 1991c. "Comments on Symposium." *Constitutional Forum* 3, 1: 14.

–. 1991d. "The Future Process of Canadian Constitutional Politics." In Robert A. Young, ed., *Confederation in Crisis,* 75-87. Toronto: James Lorimer and Company.

–. 1991e. "Interchange." In Robert A. Young, ed., *Confederation in Crisis,* 88-94. Toronto: James Lorimer and Company.

Russell, Peter H., Rainer Knopff, and F.L. Morton. 1990. *Federalism and the Charter.* Ottawa: Carleton University Press.

Sanders, Sol W. 1991. "The Canadian Crisis: Dilemmas and Options." Report on the Conference on Canada, Quebec and the United States, Wingspread Conference Center of the Johnson Foundation, Racine, Wisconsin.

Sandler, Todd. 2001. *Economic Concepts for the Social Sciences.* Cambridge, MA: Cambridge University Press.

–. 1992. *Collective Action: Theory and Applications.* Ann Arbor: University of Michigan Press.

Schneiderman, David. 1998. "Human Rights, Fundamental Differences? Multiple Charters in a Partnership Frame." In Roger Gibbins and Guy Laforest, eds., *Beyond the Impasse: Toward Reconciliation,* 147-86. Montreal: Institute for Research on Public Policy.

–. 1991. "Symposium Report: After Allaire and Bélanger-Campeau." *Constitutional Forum* 3, 1: 2-6.

Scott, F.R. 1989. "Centralization and Decentralization in Canadian Federalism." In Garth Stevenson, ed., *Federalism in Canada: Selected Readings,* 52-80. Toronto: McClelland and Stewart.

Scott, Ian. 1991. "After Meech Lake." In David E. Smith, Peter MacKinnon, and John C. Courtney, eds., *After Meech Lake: Lessons for the Future,* 251-57. Saskatoon: Fifth House Publishers.

Scott, Stephen A. 1992. "October 1992: Issues Relating to Quebec Independence." Remarks prepared for delivery as a guest speaker at a public meeting, Pointe Claire, Quebec.

Selick, Karen. 1996. "Rights and Wrongs in the Canadian Charter." In Anthony A. Peacock, ed., *Rethinking the Constitution: Perspectives on Canadian Constitutional Reform, Interpretation, and Theory,* 103-21. Toronto: Oxford University Press.

Shankar, S.G.. 1988. "Wittgenstein's Remarks on the Significance of Godel's Second Theorem." In S.G. Shanker, ed., *Godel's Theorem in Focus*. New York: Croom Helm.

Sigurdson, Richard. 1993. "Left- and Right-Wing Charterphobia in Canada: A Critique of the Critics." *International Journal of Canadian Studies* 7-8: 95-115.

Simeon, Richard. 1988a. "Meech Lake and Shifting Conceptions of Canadian Federalism." *Canadian Public Policy* 14 (supplemental): S7-S24.

–. 1988b. "Meech Lake and Visions of Canada." In Katherine E. Swinton and Carol J. Rogerson, eds., *Competing Constitutional Visions: The Meech Lake Accord*, 295-306. Toronto: Carswell.

Simeon, Richard, and Ian Robinson. 1990. *State, Society, and the Development of Canadian Federalism*. Toronto: University of Toronto Press.

Simon, Herbert A. 1978. "Rationality as a Process of Thought." *American Economic Review* 68: 1-16.

Simpson, Jeffrey. 1993. "The Referendum and Its Aftermath." In Kenneth McRoberts and Patrick J. Monahan, eds., *The Charlottetown Accord, the Referendum, and the Future of Canada*. Toronto: University of Toronto Press.

Slattery, Brian. 1988. "A Theory of the Charter." *Osgoode Hall Law Journal* 25: 701-47.

Smiley, Donald. 1983. "A Dangerous Deed: The Constitution Act, 1982." In Keith Banting and Richard Simeon, eds., *And No One Cheered: Federalism, Democracy and the Constitution Act*, 74-95. Toronto: Methuen.

Smith, Allan. 1994. *Canada – An American Nation? Essays on Continentalism, Identity, and the Canadian Frame of Mind*. Montreal and Kingston: McGill-Queen's University Press.

Smith, David E., and John C. Courtney. 1991. "Introduction." In David E. Smith, Peter MacKinnon, and John C. Courtney, eds., *After Meech Lake: Lessons for the Future*, 7-12. Saskatoon: Fifth House Publishers.

Smith, Jennifer. 1991. "Representation and Constitutional Reform in Canada." In David E. Smith, Peter MacKinnon, and John C. Courtney, eds., *After Meech Lake: Lessons for the Future*, 69-82. Saskatoon: Fifth House Publishers.

–. 1988. "Political Vision and the 1987 Constitutional Accord." In Katherine E. Swinton and Carol J. Rogerson, eds., *Competing Constitutional Visions: The Meech Lake Accord*, 271-77. Toronto: Carswell.

Smith, Lynn. 1990. "Could the Meech Lake Accord Affect the Protection of Equality Rights for Women and Minorities in Canada?" *Constitutional Forum* 1, 2: 12, 17-20.

Smith, Miriam. 2007. "The Impact of the *Charter*: Untangling the Effects of Institutional Change." *International Journal of Canadian Studies* 36: 17-40.

–. 2002. "Partisanship as Political Science: A Reply to Rainer Knopff and F.L. Morton." *Canadian Journal of Political Science* 35, 1: 48.

–. 1999. *Lesbian and Gay Rights in Canada: Social Movements and Equality-Seeking, 1971-1995*. Toronto: University of Toronto Press.

–. 1998. Social Movements and Equality Seeking: The Case of Gay Liberation in Canada." *Canadian Journal of Political Science* 31, 2: 285-309.

Smithey, Shannon Ishiyama. 2002. "Cooperation and Conflict: Group Activity in *R. v. Keegstra*." In Patrick James, Donald E. Abelson, and Michael Lusztig, eds., *The Myth of the Sacred: The Charter, the Courts, and the Politics of the Constitution in Canada,* 189-206. Montreal and Kingston: McGill-Queen's University Press.

Sproule-Jones, Mark. 1993. *Governments at Work: Canadian Parliamentary Federalism and Its Public Policy Effects.* Toronto: University of Toronto Press.

Statistics Canada. 2004. *2003 General Social Survey on Social Engagement, Cycle 17: An Overview of Findings.* Ottawa: Statistics Canada.

Stein, Michael B. 1997. "Improving the Process of Constitutional Reform in Canada: Lessons from the Meech Lake and Charlottetown Constitutional Rounds." *Canadian Journal of Political Science* 30: 307-38.

Stevenson, Garth. 1991. "Commentary." In David E. Smith, Peter MacKinnon, and John C. Courtney, eds., *After Meech Lake: Lessons for the Future,* 109-10. Saskatoon: Fifth House Publishers.

–. 1982. *Unfulfilled Union: Canadian Federalism and National Unity.* Rev. ed. Toronto: Gage Publishing.

Stolle, Dietlind, and Eric M. Uslaner. 2003. "The Structure of Trust in Canada." Paper presented at the biennial meeting of the Association for Canadian Studies in the United States, 19-23 November, Portland, Oregon.

Swinton, Katherine. 1988. "Competing Visions of Constitutionalism: Of Federalism and Rights." In Katherine E. Swinton and Carol J. Rogerson, eds., *Competing Constitutional Visions: The Meech Lake Accord,* 279-94. Toronto: Carswell.

Taras, David. 1991. "How Television Transformed the Meech Lake Negotiations." In David E. Smith, Peter MacKinnon, and John C. Courtney, eds., *After Meech Lake: Lessons for the Future,* 169-80. Saskatoon: Fifth House Publishers.

Taylor, Charles. 1994. "The Politics of Recognition." In Amy Gutmann, ed., *Multiculturalism: Examining the Politics of Recognition,* 3-24. Princeton, NJ: Princeton University Press.

–. 1993. *Reconciling the Solitudes: Essays on Canadian Federalism and Nationalism.* Ed. Guy Laforest. Montreal and Kingston: McGill-Queen's University Press.

Thomas, David M. 1997. *Whistling Past the Graveyard: Constitutional Abeyances, Quebec, and the Future of Canada.* Toronto: Oxford University Press.

–. 1993. "Turning a Blind Eye: Constitutional Abeyances and the Canadian Experience." *International Journal of Canadian Studies* 7-8: 63-79.

Toews, Vic. 2003. "The Charter in Canadian Society." In Joseph Eliot Magnet, Gérald-A. Beaudoin, Gerald Gall, and Christopher P. Manfredi, eds., *The Canadian Charter of Rights and Freedoms: Reflections on the Charter after Twenty Years,* 345-50. Markham, ON: Butterworths.

Trent, John. 1977. "Common Ground and Disputed Territory." In Richard Simeon, ed., *Must Canada Fail?* 139-41. Montreal and Kingston: McGill-Queen's University Press.

Trudeau, Pierre Elliott. 1992. "Trudeau Speaks Out." *Maclean's,* 28 September.

–. 1989. "Who Speaks for Canada? Defining and Sustaining a National Vision." In Michael D. Behiels, ed., *The Meech Lake Primer: Conflicting Views of the 1987 Constitutional Accord,* 60-99. Ottawa: University of Ottawa Press.

Tupper, Allan. 1996. "Reflections on the 1995 Québec Referendum: Problems and Possibilities." *Constitutional Forum* 7, 2-3: 29-34.

–. 1993. "English-Canadian Scholars and the Meech Lake Accord." *International Journal of Canadian Studies* 7-8: 347-57.

–. 1991. "Meech Lake and Democratic Politics: Some Observations." *Constitutional Forum* 2, 2: 26-31.

Turp, Daniel. 1996. "From an Economic and Political Partnership between Québec and Canada to a Canadian Union." *Constitutional Forum* 6, 2-3: 91-96.

Usher, Dan. 1995a. "The Interests of English Canada." *Canadian Public Policy* 21, 1: 72-84.

–. 1995b. "[Home Game: Comments on 'the Interests of English Canada']: A Reply." *Canadian Public Policy* 21, 1: 94-106.

Uslaner, Eric M. 2002. *The Moral Foundations of Trust*. Cambridge: Cambridge University Press.

–. 2001. "Strong Institutions, Weak Parties: The Paradox of Canadian Political Parties." Paper presented at the biennial meeting of the Association for Canadian Studies in the United States, 14-18 November, San Antonio, Texas.

Valaskakis, Kimon. 1990. *Canada in the Nineties: Meltdown or Renaissance?* Montreal: Gamma Institute Press.

Vickers, Jill. 1993. "The Canadian Women's Movement and a Changing Constitutional Order." *International Journal of Canadian Studies* 7-8: 261-84.

Vipond, Robert. 1995. "From Provincial Autonomy to Provincial Equality (Or, Clyde Wells and the Distinct Society)." In Joseph H. Carens, ed., *Is Quebec Nationalism Just? Perspectives from Anglophone Canada*, 97-119. Montreal and Kingston: McGill-Queen's University Press.

Walker, Brian. 1997. "Plural Cultures, Contested Territories: A Critique of Kymlicka." *Canadian Journal of Political Science* 30, 2: 211-34.

Walzer, Michael. 1994. "Comment." In Amy Gutmann, ed., *Multiculturalism: Examining the Politics of Recognition*, 99-103. Princeton, NJ: Princeton University Press.

Watson, William. 1995. "Home Game: Comments on 'the Interests of English Canada.'" *Canadian Public Policy* 21, 1: 85-93.

Watts, Ronald L. 1998a. "Examples of Partnership." In Roger Gibbins and Guy Laforest, eds., *Beyond the Impasse: Toward Reconciliation*, 359-96. Montreal: Institute for Research on Public Policy.

–. 1998b. "Federalism, Political Systems, and Federations." *Annual Review of Political Science* 1: 117-37.

Weaver, R. Kent. 1993. "The Canadian Constitutional Crisis: Canada's Constitutional Discontents." *PS: Political Science and Politics* 26, 1: 32.

–. 1992a. "Constitutional Conflict in Canada." In R. Kent Weaver, ed., *The Collapse of Canada?* 1-6. Washington, DC: Brookings Institution.

–. 1992b. "Political Institutions and Canada's Constitutional Crisis." In R. Kent Weaver, ed., *The Collapse of Canada?* 7-76. Washington, DC: Brookings Institution.

Webber, Jeremy. 1994. *Reimagining Canada: Language, Culture, Community, and the Canadian Constitution*. Kingston and Montreal: McGill-Queen's University Press.

Weinrib, Lorraine E. 2003. "The Canadian Charter's Transformative Aspirations." In Joseph Eliot Magnet, Gérald-A. Beaudoin, Gerald Gall, and Christopher P.

Manfredi, eds., *The Canadian Charter of Rights and Freedoms: Reflections on the Charter after Twenty Years*, 17-37. Markham, ON: Butterworths.

–. 2001. "The Supreme Court of Canada in the Age of Rights: Constitutional Democracy, the Rule of Law and Fundamental Rights under Canada's Constitution." *Canadian Bar Review* 80: 699-748.

Whittaker, Reg. 1991. "Commentary." In David E. Smith, Peter MacKinnon, and John C. Courtney, eds., *After Meech Lake: Lessons for the Future*, 111-13. Saskatoon: Fifth House Publishers.

Whyte, John D. 1991. "The Future of Canada's Constitutional Reform Process." In David E. Smith, Peter MacKinnon, and John C. Courtney, eds., *After Meech Lake: Lessons for the Future*, 237-49. Saskatoon: Fifth House Publishers.

Wintrobe, Ronald, and Robert A. Young. 1991. "Preface." In Robert A. Young, ed., *Confederation in Crisis*. Toronto: James Lorimer and Company.

Wolf, Susan. 1994. "Comment." In Amy Gutmann, ed., *Multiculturalism: Examining the Politics of Recognition*, 75-86. Princeton, NJ: Princeton University Press.

Young, Iris Marion. 1990. *Justice and the Politics of Difference*. Princeton, NJ: Princeton University Press.

Young, Oran R. 1968. *Systems of Political Science*. Englewood Cliffs, NJ: Prentice Hall.

Young, Robert A. 1999. *The Struggle for Quebec: From Referendum to Referendum?* Montreal and Kingston: McGill-Queen's University Press.

–. 1998. "A Most Politic Judgement." *Constitutional Forum* 10, 1: 14-18.

–. 1995. *The Secession of Quebec and the Future of Canada*. Montreal and Kingston: McGill-Queen's University Press.

–. 1991a. "Introduction." In Robert A. Young, ed., *Confederation in Crisis*, 1-8. Toronto: James Lorimer and Company.

–. 1991b. "In Summation." In Robert A. Young, ed., *Confederation in Crisis*. Toronto: James Lorimer and Company.

# Index

f = figure

Aboriginal orthodoxy, 39-41
Aboriginal peoples, 3, 56, 63, 69, 77, 143n1; eviction, 39, 40f; public support, 39-41; relations with government, 129; rising expectations, 94-95, 138; third order of government, 83-84. *See also* specific Aboriginal peoples
Aboriginal Women's Council, 57
accommodation: of constitutional interests, 141-42; of diversity, 81-82, 86f, 87-88, 91
Action démocratique du Québec, 125
activism: judicial, 70-71, 72, 130, 149n7, 150n8; judicial *vs.* legislative, 114-15
Alberta, 25, 143n4
anti-Americanism, 107
anti-patriotism, 50
Archer, Keith, 29f, 30, 30f, 31, 68
articulation, of groups, 53, 55f, 57-58, 107
Assembly of First Nations, 41, 83
assimilation, 39-40, 84
Association of First Nations (AFN), 129
asymmetrical federalism theory, 9-10, 46; diagrammatic analysis, 86-89, 90-91; equilibrium analysis, 91-93, 132f; key insight, 81, 83;
major challenges, 90, 91-93, 132f, 133, 134; predictions, 89, 91, 103

Baer, Douglas, 136
Behiels, Michael, 110
bias: *Charter,* 126-27; holistic/homeostatic, 13-14; ideological, 18, 116
Bill 99 (Quebec), 67-68
Bill 178 (Quebec), 20-25
Bill C-34, 129
Bilodeau, Antoine, 139
Bissoondath, Neil, 50, 128, 151n8
Blakeney, Allan, 82
Bloc Québécois, 4-5, 108, 125, 139
Bourassa, Robert, 8, 21, 23, 118
British Columbia, 143n4
*British North America Act* (1867). *See Constitution Act, 1867*
Brock, Kathy, 121, 124-25
Brodie, Ian, 150n8
Brooks, Stephen, 30f
Bunge, Mario, 14, 15-16, 31, 146n3
Bushell, Allison, 122

Cairns, Alan C., 1, 4, 24, 46, 93-102, 123, 126-28
Calgary Declaration (1997), 68, 90, 91
Calgary School, 42, 43, 45, 148n13

LAW AND
SOCIETY

Janet Mosher and Joan Brockman (eds.)
*Constructing Crime: Contemporary Processes of Criminalization* (2010)

Louis A. Knafla and Haijo Westra (eds.)
*Aboriginal Title and Indigenous Peoples: Canada, Australia, and New Zealand* (2010)

Stephen Clarkson and Stepan Wood
*A Perilous Imbalance: The Globalization of Canadian Law and Governance* (2010)

Amanda Glasbeek
*Feminized Justice: The Toronto Women's Court, 1913-34* (2009)

Kimberley Brooks (ed.)
*Justice Bertha Wilson: One Woman's Difference* (2009)

Wayne V. McIntosh and Cynthia L. Cates
*Multi-Party Litigation: The Strategic Context* (2009)

Renisa Mawani
*Colonial Proximities: Crossracial Encounters and Juridical Truths in British Columbia, 1871-1921* (2009)

James B. Kelly and Christopher P. Manfredi (eds.)
*Contested Constitutionalism: Reflections on the Canadian Charter of Rights and Freedoms* (2009)

Catherine E. Bell and Robert K. Paterson (eds.)
*Protection of First Nations Cultural Heritage: Laws, Policy, and Reform* (2009)

Catherine E. Bell and Val Napoleon (eds.)
*First Nations Cultural Heritage and Law: Case Studies, Voices, and Perspectives* (2008)

Richard J. Moon (ed.)
*Law and Religious Pluralism in Canada* (2008)

Hamar Foster, Benjamin L. Berger, and A.R. Buck (eds.)
*The Grand Experiment: Law and Legal Culture in British Settler Societies* (2008)

Douglas C. Harris
*Landing Native Fisheries: Indian Reserves and Fishing Rights in British Columbia, 1849-1925* (2008)

Peggy J. Blair
*Lament for a First Nation: The Williams Treaties in Southern Ontario* (2008)

Lori G. Beaman
*Defining Harm: Religious Freedom and the Limits of the Law* (2007)

Stephen Tierney (ed.)
*Multiculturalism and the Canadian Constitution* (2007)

Julie Macfarlane
*The New Lawyer: How Settlement Is Transforming the Practice of Law* (2007)

Kimberley White
*Negotiating Responsibility: Law, Murder, and States of Mind* (2007)

Dawn Moore
*Criminal Artefacts: Governing Drugs and Users* (2007)

Hamar Foster, Heather Raven, and Jeremy Webber (eds.)
*Let Right Be Done: Aboriginal Title, the Calder Case, and the Future of Indigenous Rights* (2007)

Dorothy E. Chunn, Susan B. Boyd, and Hester Lessard (eds.)
*Reaction and Resistance: Feminism, Law, and Social Change* (2007)

Margot Young, Susan B. Boyd, Gwen Brodsky, and Shelagh Day (eds.)
*Poverty: Rights, Social Citizenship, and Legal Activism* (2007)

Rosanna L. Langer
*Defining Rights and Wrongs: Bureaucracy, Human Rights, and Public Accountability* (2007)

C.L. Ostberg and Matthew E. Wetstein
*Attitudinal Decision Making in the Supreme Court of Canada* (2007)

Chris Clarkson
*Domestic Reforms: Political Visions and Family Regulation in British Columbia, 1862-1940* (2007)

Jean McKenzie Leiper
*Bar Codes: Women in the Legal Profession* (2006)

Gerald Baier
*Courts and Federalism: Judicial Doctrine in the United States, Australia, and Canada* (2006)

Avigail Eisenberg (ed.)
*Diversity and Equality: The Changing Framework of Freedom in Canada* (2006)

Randy K. Lippert
*Sanctuary, Sovereignty, Sacrifice: Canadian Sanctuary Incidents, Power, and Law* (2005)

James B. Kelly
*Governing with the Charter: Legislative and Judicial Activism and Framers' Intent* (2005)

Dianne Pothier and Richard Devlin (eds.)
*Critical Disability Theory: Essays in Philosophy, Politics, Policy, and Law* (2005)

Susan G. Drummond
*Mapping Marriage Law in Spanish Gitano Communities* (2005)

Louis A. Knafla and Jonathan Swainger (eds.)
*Laws and Societies in the Canadian Prairie West, 1670-1940* (2005)

Ikechi Mgbeoji
*Global Biopiracy: Patents, Plants, and Indigenous Knowledge* (2005)

Florian Sauvageau, David Schneiderman, and David Taras,
with Ruth Klinkhammer and Pierre Trudel
*The Last Word: Media Coverage of the Supreme Court of Canada* (2005)

Gerald Kernerman
*Multicultural Nationalism: Civilizing Difference, Constituting
Community* (2005)

Pamela A. Jordan
*Defending Rights in Russia: Lawyers, the State, and Legal Reform in
the Post-Soviet Era* (2005)

Anna Pratt
*Securing Borders: Detention and Deportation in Canada* (2005)

Kirsten Johnson Kramar
*Unwilling Mothers, Unwanted Babies: Infanticide in Canada* (2005)

W.A. Bogart
*Good Government? Good Citizens? Courts, Politics, and Markets in
a Changing Canada* (2005)

Catherine Dauvergne
*Humanitarianism, Identity, and Nation: Migration Laws in Canada
and Australia* (2005)

Michael Lee Ross
*First Nations Sacred Sites in Canada's Courts* (2005)

Andrew Woolford
*Between Justice and Certainty: Treaty Making in British Columbia* (2005

John McLaren, Andrew Buck, and Nancy Wright (eds.)
*Despotic Dominion: Property Rights in British Settler Societies* (2004)

Georges Campeau
*From UI to EI: Waging War on the Welfare State* (2004)

Alvin J. Esau
*The Courts and the Colonies: The Litigation of Hutterite Church
Disputes* (2004)

Christopher N. Kendall
*Gay Male Pornography: An Issue of Sex Discrimination* (2004)

Roy B. Flemming
*Tournament of Appeals: Granting Judicial Review in Canada* (2004)

Constance Backhouse and Nancy L. Backhouse
*The Heiress vs the Establishment: Mrs. Campbell's Campaign for Legal Justice* (2004)

Christopher P. Manfredi
*Feminist Activism in the Supreme Court: Legal Mobilization and the Women's Legal Education and Action Fund* (2004)

Annalise Acorn
*Compulsory Compassion: A Critique of Restorative Justice* (2004)

Jonathan Swainger and Constance Backhouse (eds.)
*People and Place: Historical Influences on Legal Culture* (2003)

Jim Phillips and Rosemary Gartner
*Murdering Holiness: The Trials of Franz Creffield and George Mitchell* (2003)

David R. Boyd
*Unnatural Law: Rethinking Canadian Environmental Law and Policy* (2003)

Ikechi Mgbeoji
*Collective Insecurity: The Liberian Crisis, Unilateralism, and Global Order* (2003)

Rebecca Johnson
*Taxing Choices: The Intersection of Class, Gender, Parenthood, and the Law* (2002)

John McLaren, Robert Menzies, and Dorothy E. Chunn (eds.)
*Regulating Lives: Historical Essays on the State, Society, the Individual, and the Law* (2002)

Joan Brockman
*Gender in the Legal Profession: Fitting or Breaking the Mould* (2001)

Printed and bound in Canada by Friesens
Set in Stone by Artegraphica Design Co. Ltd.
Copy editor: Lesley Erickson
Proofreader and indexer: Dianne Tiefensee